CONSTITUTIONAL ISSUES

FREEDOM OF THE PRESS

Other Books on Constitutional Law by Bernard Schwartz

CONSTITUTIONAL ISSUES

FREEDOM OF THE PRESS

Bernard Schwartz

A Harold Steinberg Book

Facts On File
New York • Oxford

Freedom of the Press

Facts On File, Inc.
460 Park Avenue South
New York, NY 10016
USA

Facts On File Limited
c/o Roundhouse Publishing Ltd.
P.O. Box 140
Oxford OX2 7SF
United Kingdom

Library of Congress Cataloguing-in-Publication Data
Schwartz, Bernard, 1923-
    Supreme court: freedom of the press by Bernard Schwartz
        p. cm. — (Facts on File handbooks to
        constitutional issues: v. 1)
    Includes bibliographical references and index.
    ISBN 0-8160-2505-3
    1. Freedom of the press—United States. 2. Press law—
    United States. 3. United States. Supreme Court. I. Title. II. Series.
    KF4774.S34 1992   92-9913
    342.73'0853—dc20   CIP
    [347.3.02853]

A British CIP catalogue record for this book is available from the British Library.

Facts On File books are available at special discounts when purchased in bulk quantities for businesses, associations, institutions, or sales promotions. Please call our Special Sales Department in New York at 212/683-2244 (dial 800/322-8755 except in NY, AK or HI) or in Oxford at 865/728399.

Managing Editor: Mark Gabor

Associate Editor: Mary McCarthy Steinberg

Typesetting: DataWorks Corp.

10 9 8 7 6 5 4 3 2 1

This book is printed on acid-free paper.

For Aileen
who set me
on the Fourth Estate track

Contents

Publisher's Preface

According to many political observers, the enduring legacy of the Reagan-Bush presidencies may not be any legislation that Ronald Reagan or George Bush accomplished. The most long-lasting accomplishment may be the fact that between them they have appointed five Justices to the United States Supreme Court (Justices O'Connor, Scalia, Kennedy, Souter, and Thomas, with Justice Rehnquist being appointed as Chief Justice) who will influence the course of constitutional law for the coming decades.

This observation is a reflection of the Supreme Court in the political, social, and economic life of the country — an influence which has never been greater than in the past fifty years. Our entire political structure has been changed by the reapportionment cases that totally altered the manner in which elected representatives are chosen. The Court's decision in *Brown v. Board of Education* ushered in the civil rights revolution.

On other social issues, the changes wrought by the Court have been even greater. Its decisions on abortion affect the life of every American woman. And the entire criminal justice system has been greatly modified by the Supreme Court rulings on such issues as search and seizure, police questioning, and the death penalty.

This is the first book in a series of volumes that will deal with Supreme Court decisions in significant areas of constitutional law. In this volume we examine an area of constitutional law where Supreme Court rulings have affected our lives — freedom of the press. Professor Bernard Schwartz, a leading scholar of the Supreme Court for forty years, examines the basic rules and principles developed through numerous Supreme Court cases that reflect our attachment to the First Amendment guaranty. What is a prior restraint and why is it prohibited by the Constitution? What are the rules on libel and privacy? What can the press report and what can it be prohibited from publishing? What constitutes obscenity?

The materials included in this collection cover not only the basic Supreme Court decisions and the arguments made by lawyers, but unpublished drafts of Supreme Court decisions that show the *process* by which the cases were finally determined. Through this method in this work — and in future volumes dealing with Supreme Court decisions in other areas — we hope to explore the manner in which the Supreme Court affects and changes our society.

Professor Leon Friedman   Harold Steinberg
Hofstra Law School, General Editor   Series Publisher

Introduction

Freedom of the press, says Alexander Hamilton, is the "palladium of liberty." But that is so only because the *ought* of the First Amendment guaranty is transmuted by the Supreme Court into the *is* of positive law. It is judicial enforcement that makes constitutional provisions more than empty words. That is as true of the freedom of the press guaranty as it is of other organic provisions. We have the freest press in the world only because the highest tribunal has given practical effect to the words of the First Amendment.

This book is intended to illuminate the Supreme Court's jurisprudence on freedom of the press. As such, it deals both with the traditional print press known to the Framers and the newer media developed during the present century. It is my hope that it will not only give a concise account of the case law on the subject, but that it will also demonstrate our law's capacity for growth — particularly its adaptation by the Court to changing needs and technological developments that James Madison and his colleagues could not even dimly foresee when they wrote the First Amendment.

It is also my hope that the book will help people to understand how our highest Court operates. My treatment of cases is not limited to the decisions rendered. Emphasis is also placed upon the Justices' decision-making process — their conference discussions, memoranda and correspondence, and draft opinions. These were obtained from various Justices, law clerks, libraries, and others in connection with my research on the Warren and Burger Courts. The conference scenarios are based upon the notes of at least one Justice who was present. The other documents used are identified, except where doing so would violate the confidentiality of a source. I have been given generous access to the papers of the Justices and I also gratefully acknowledge the help given by the Manuscript Division of the Library of Congress.

I should also note that the book is published without footnotes. The hope is that this will make the work less forbidding to the general reader who is often "turned off" by a mass of legal notes. In a law-dominated society, the subject is too important to be left only to the academic specialists. Perhaps they will miss the arcana of copious footnotes whose presence, in my opinion, would limit the appeal of this book.

Bernard Schwartz
Webb Professor of Law, New York University.

Chapman Distinguished Professor of Law,   New York
University of Tulsa   April 1992

1

Pentagon Papers and Prior Restraint

Justice Potter Stewart used to say that the press is "the only organized private business that is given explicit constitutional protection." The press is, of course, more than a business. It is the very fulcrum upon which the First Amendment turns; speech, however free, has little impact if it reaches only those within earshot.

The classic modern case on freedom of the press is *New York Times v. United States* — more popularly known as the *Pentagon Papers Case*. It well illustrates the Supreme Court's attitude toward restraints on expression by the press — particularly prior restraints — and it can serve as the starting point for further discussion of enforcement of the constitutional guaranty by the highest tribunal.

Pentagon Papers Case

In 1971 the Government, for the first time, tried to use the courts to censor news before it was printed. This attempt might well have succeeded if one of the Justices' law clerks had not happened to turn on his radio one late June afternoon.

What was to become one of the most widely publicized Supreme Court cases began without fanfare. On Sunday, June 13, 1971, a low-key headline appeared in the *New York Times*: "Vietnam Archive: Pentagon Study Traces 3 Decades of Growing U.S. Involvement." It was followed by long excerpts culled from a top secret forty-seven-volume history of American involvement in Indochina prepared within the Defense Department.

The study, which was dubbed "The Pentagon Papers," in *Time's* words, "revealed a dismaying degree of miscalculation, bureaucratic arrogance and deception." After a second installment appeared, the Attorney General went to court to suppress further publication. He contended that dissemination would cause "immediate and irreparable harm" to national defense and security.

The lower courts acted with unusual speed. The New York District Court hearing was held on Friday. The district judge who had issued a temporary restraining order against the *Times* on Tuesday lifted the order. Five days later, the court of appeals remanded for further hearing and continued the restraining order pending further decision.

On the day the case was being heard in Manhattan, the *Washington Post* went to press with its own version. Once again, the Justice Department sought an injunction, but the court of appeals in Washington held that the Government was not entitled to any preliminary injunction. It had, however, issued a temporary restraining order pending its decision, and it granted a stay so that the Government could take the case to the Supreme Court. The restraining order was still in force when certiorari (the writ by which Supreme Court review is secured) was sought.

Knowledge of the *Pentagon Papers Case* had, of course, penetrated the Supreme Court's Marble Palace. In most of the Justices' chambers, discussion of the case began the day after the Government filed its initial request for a temporary restraining order. There was substantial speculation about whether the case could be brought to the Supreme Court before the 1970 Term was finished at the end of June 1971. Although virtually everyone outside the Court assumed that the case would ultimately be decided by the Justices, in the Court there was a strong feeling that the best disposition might be a simple denial of certiorari, which meant that the Supreme Court would refuse to hear the case — but that was possible only if both courts of appeals decided completely in favor of the newspapers.

While the case was pending, Justice Hugo L. Black's clerks, returning from dinner at his house, reported that he had said he "never was too fond of injunctions against newspapers." "Even when the national security is involved?" asked his wife. "Well, I never did see how it hurts the national security for someone to tell the American people that their government lied to them," said Black.

The *Times* and *Post* cases were both decided by the lower courts on June 23, 1971. Each of those courts knew what the other was doing; Chief Judges David Bazelon in Washington and Henry Friendly in New York were in regular telephone communication. Late in the morning of June 24, the *Times* filed its application for certiorari and interim relief. It was promptly sent by Justice John M. Harlan to the full Court. The Government's petition for certiorari and interim relief was filed at 7:15 that evening and sent by the Chief Justice to the Justices at their homes.

How the Court Operates

To understand how the Supreme Court dealt with the Pentagon *Papers Case*, one must understand how the Court itself operates. The Justices sit from October to late June or early July, in annual sessions called terms, with each term designated by the year in which it begins. Cases come to the Court from the U.S. courts of appeals and the highest state courts, either by appeals or petitions for writs of certiorari. Technical rules govern whether an appeal or certiorari must be sought. The Justices have virtually unlimited discretion in deciding whether to take an appeal or grant certiorari (or cert, as it is usually called in the Court). Each year the Justices decide to hear only a fraction of the cases presented to them. Thus, in the 1970 Term, when the *Pentagon Papers* certiorari petitions asking the Supreme Court to review the court of appeals decisions were filed, the Court granted review in 214 cases out of 4,212 on its docket. In 1955, Justice Felix Frankfurter had asked another Justice, "Wouldn't you gladly settle for one in ten — such is my proportion — in granting petitions for certiorari?" By the time the *Pentagon Papers Case* arose, the proportion granted had declined to one in twenty.

Following an unwritten rule, when at least four of the nine Justices vote to take a case, certiorari is granted or the appeal is taken. However, if the case elicits fewer than the required four votes, the case in question is over and the last decision of the state court or lower federal court becomes final. In recent years some Justices have urged that changes be made in the Rule of Four, on the ground that it results in the Court agreeing to hear too many cases.

Thus, Justice John Paul Stevens recently proposed that five votes be required to grant certiorari. That would certainly cut down the number of cases taken by the Court. But it would also eliminate important cases which the Court should decide. If a five-vote rule had been in effect during the Warren Court years, at least one of the most important Warren Court decisions, *Baker v. Carr*, which Chief Justice Earl Warren once described as "the most important case of my tenure on the Court," would never have been decided. Only four Justices voted to hear that case.

For those few cases the Supreme Court agrees to take, written briefs will be submitted by the opposing lawyers, and then the attorneys for both sides will appear for oral argument in which they present arguments in favor of affirming or reversing the lower court decision. The arguments are presented publicly in the ornate courtroom. Each side usually has half an hour, and the time limit is strictly observed. Once a lawyer was arguing his case in the last half hour before noon. He was reading to the Justices from his notes and did not notice the red light go on at his lectern, signaling that his time had expired. Finally, he looked up. The bench was empty; the Justices had quietly risen, gathered their black robes, and gone to lunch.

As far as the public is concerned, the postargument decision process in the Court is completely closed. The next time the outside world hears about the case is when the Court is ready to publicly announce its decision; simultaneously, the majority opinion and any dissents or concurrences are distributed. But in that interim period between oral argument and the announcement of the Court's decision, much has gone on. First, the Justices have "conferenced." When Warren E. Burger became Chief Justice, these conferences were held on Fridays. More recently, Wednesday sessions have been held as well. The privacy of the conference is one of the most cherished traditions at the Court. Only the nine Justices may attend. In addition to the conference discussion, ideas are exchanged by the Justices through the circulation of draft opinions and memoranda. Such a memo, sent to all the Justices, is usually titled *Memorandum to the Conference*.

After the vote is taken at the conference, the case is assigned by the Chief Justice, if he is in the majority, either to himself or to one of the Justices for the writing of an opinion of the Court. If the Chief Justice is not in the majority, the senior majority Justice assigns the opinion. Justices who disagree with the majority decision are free to write or join dissenting opinions. If they agree with the result but differ on the reasoning, they can submit concurring opinions. Opinions are usually issued in the name of individual Justices. Sometimes per curiam (literally, "by the court") opinions are issued in the name of the Court as a whole. That, we shall see, is what happened in the *Pentagon Papers Case*, though each of the Justices also wrote an individual opinion explaining the decision from his own point of view.

The last stage is the public announcement of decisions and the opinions filed by the Justices. The custom used to be to have decisions announced on Mondays (a tradition that began in 1857); hence, the press characterization of "decision Mondays." In 1965, this was changed to announcing decisions when they were ready.

When decisions are announced, the Justices normally read only a summary of their opinions, especially when they are long. But some insist on reading every word, no matter how much time it takes. On June 17, 1963, Justice Tom C. Clark was droning through his lengthy Court opinion in the case involving the constitutionality of Bible reading in public schools. Justice William O. Douglas, who could stand it no longer, passed Justice Black a plaintive note: "Is he going to read all of it? He told me he was only going to say a few words — he is on p. 20 now — 58 more to go. Perhaps we need an anti-filibuster rule as badly as some say the Senate does."

Certiorari, Conference, and Arguments

Our discussion of the *Pentagon Papers Case* had reached the point where applications for certiorari had been filed in the Supreme Court on June 24, 1971. The next morning (Friday, June 25), the Justices met in conference to consider the applications. Justices Black, Douglas, William J. Brennan, and Thurgood Marshall were prepared to deny certiorari and vacate the temporary restraining orders issued by the lower courts. The Chief Justice and Justices Harlan, Byron R. White, and Harry A. Blackmun wanted the cases set for argument the following week. Harlan had, indeed, circulated a proposed order that would have denied the *Times*'s application "pending further order of this Court." The issue was ultimately resolved in accordance with the view stated by Justice Stewart, who urged the Court to grant certiorari and continue the stays, but to set argument for the following morning. An order to that effect was issued in the early afternoon.

Justice Brennan had gone to the conference determined to note his opposition to continuing the stays. Three Justices joined him on this and the Court's order contained the notation that Justices Black, Douglas, Brennan, and Marshall would vacate all temporary restraining orders and deny certiorari. The Chief Justice had strongly opposed these Justices' action, but they wanted their opposition to continuing the stays on the public record.

The record in the *Post* case had arrived shortly after the order issued; the record in the *Times* case, which included a complete copy of the secret study, arrived with armed guards about 8:00 P.M. Justices Brennan and White stayed to look at the secret papers and did not leave until 10:30. Other members of the Court looked over the *Pentagon Papers* the next day — except for Justice Black, whose absolutist view of the First Amendment (which prohibited *any* interference at all with freedom of expression) made the documents' content immaterial.

As soon as Justice Brennan arrived at the Court the next morning, Saturday, June 26, he drafted a brief per curiam (an opinion delivered in the name of the Court, not that of a Justice) affirming the lower court in the *Post* case and reversing it in the *Times* case. The oral argument took place from 11:00 A.M. to 1:00 P.M.

Like all Supreme Court sittings, the session began when the entrance of the black-robed Justices through the red velour draperies behind the bench was announced. At the sound of the gavel all in the crowded courtroom rose and remained standing while the Court crier intoned the time-honored cry, "Oyez! Oyez! Oyez! All persons having business before the Honorable, the Supreme Court of the United States, are admonished to draw near and give their attention, for the Court is now sitting. God save the United States and this Honorable Court."

The Court Chamber itself is the most impressive room in the Supreme Court building. It measures 82 by 91 feet and has a ceiling 44 feet high. Its 24 columns are of Siena Old Convent marble from Liguria, Italy; its walls are of ivory vein marble from Alicante, Spain; and its floor borders are of Italian and African marble. Above the columns on the east and west walls are carved two marble panels depicting processions of historical lawgivers. Of the eighteen figures on the panels only one is famous as a judge, and he is the one American represented: John Marshall. His symbolic presence strikingly illustrates the Supreme Court's role as primary lawgiver in the American system.

The room is dominated by the Justices' long, raised bench, straight until 1972, when the Chief Justice had it altered to its present "winged," or half-hexagon, shape. Like all the furniture in the room, the bench is mahogany. Behind the bench are four of the massive marble columns. A large clock hangs on a chain between the two center ones. In front of the bench are seated, to the Court's right, the pages and clerk, and, to the Court's left, the marshal. Tables facing the bench are for counsel. Behind the tables is a section for members of the bar and a much larger general section for the public, with separate areas for the press and distinguished visitors.

After the Justices took their seats in their plush black leather chairs, the Chief Justice leaned forward and announced, in his mellow bass, that the Court denied the Government's motion to conduct part of the argument in camera (with the public and press excluded). He then stated, "Mr. Solicitor General, you may proceed."

Oral arguments in the Supreme Court are often dramatic events, participated in by leading attorneys. That was certainly true of the *Pentagon Papers* argument, which had all the drama associated with the landmarks of Supreme Court jurisprudence. Yet it was not the headlined argument on the merits by Solicitor General Erwin

N. Griswold or Professor Alexander M. Bickel that really influenced the decision. Instead the most important event during the argument was an exchange, which went almost unnoticed, between Justice Brennan and Solicitor General Griswold.

The exchange began when the Justice asked whether it was not "correct that the injunctions so far granted against the *Times* and the *Post* haven't stopped other newspapers from publishing materials based on this study or kindred papers?" Griswold replied that it was his understanding that everything published in other papers was based upon materials in the *Times* and *Post*.

Brennan then asked whether other papers did not have copies of the *Pentagon Papers* or access to the study. Griswold answered that he did not know. But then he conceded, "There is a possibility that anybody has it."

Brennan said that, in view of this, "I've always thought that the rule was that equity has to be rather careful not to issue ineffective injunctions. And isn't that a rule to be, a factor to be considered in these cases?" Griswold, however, said, "there is nothing in this record, or known outside the record, which would indicate that this injunction would be useless."

Postargument Conference

Justice Robert H. Jackson once said that the Court's argument begins where that of counsel ends. That was certainly true when the Justices met in conference to discuss the *Pentagon Papers Case* on the merits. The postargument conference itself was held on Saturday, June 26, soon after the conclusion of the oral arguments, after the Justices had had a brief lunch.

The conference room itself was a large rectangular chamber at the rear of the Court building, behind the courtroom. One of the longer walls had two windows facing Second Street. The other, with a door in the middle, was covered with bookshelves containing reports of decisions of the Supreme Court and federal courts of appeals, as well as copies of the *United States Code* and *U.S. Code Annotated*. Along one of the shorter walls was a fireplace, above which hung a Gilbert Stuart portrait of Chief Justice John Marshall in his robes. To the left of the portrait was a forest painting by John F. Carlson. On the opposite wall hung two landscapes by Lily Cushing, a beach scene and another forest scene. Chief Justice Burger told me that he had these paintings hung for Justice Douglas, always noted for his love of the outdoors.

In the center of the conference room ceiling was an ornate crystal chandelier, and at one end of the room stood a table around which the Justices sat, with the Chief Justice at the head and the others ranged in order of seniority, the most senior opposite the Chief, the next at the Chief's right, the next at the Senior Associate's right, and so on. In the ceiling above the chandelier were bright fluorescent lights — one of the improvements installed by Chief Justice Burger.

The *Pentagon Papers* conference began with the usual handshakes exchanged by the Justices. The formal greetings could not, however, mask the underlying tension, both because of the public controversy surrounding the case and the fact that, as soon became apparent, the Justices were sharply divided on the merits.

Chief Justice Burger complained about what he was to call the "unseemly haste" with which "these cases have been conducted" — the "panic basis" on which the courts had acted, as he put it at the conference. On the merits, however, Burger said that he would decide for the Government, as did Justices Harlan and Blackmun. The latter stated that the *Pentagon Papers* contained "dangerous material that would harm this nation." He added, somewhat gratuitously, that he had "nothing but contempt for the *Times*" for publishing the classified study.

On the other side, Justice Black declared that the "President had deluded the public on Vietnam." Black asserted that it would be "the worst blow to the First Amendment to enjoin these publications." Justices Douglas and Brennan also spoke strongly in favor of the newspapers and were supported by Justice Marshall. Less certain in their presentations were Justices Stewart and White. According to White, the publication had caused "much damage" and he indicated that the newspapers had violated the espionage laws. On the other hand, he did point out that prior restraints on the press were "rare."

The Justices had been discussing the case for about an hour and the conference thus far was inconclusive — with a four-three-two lineup prevailing (Black, Douglas, Brennan, and Marshall for the newspapers, the Chief Justice, Harlan, and Blackmun for the government, and Stewart and White in between). At about 2:30, however, one of Justice Black's clerks called the Brennan chambers. He had just heard on his car radio that the Government had obtained a temporary restraining order against the *St. Louis Post-Dispatch*. Since Justice Brennan was the only Justice who had seemed interested in this question at oral argument, he said, he was relaying the information to his office.

This news, sent immediately to the Justices in the conference room, was the catalyst for the final decision. The new restraining order had been issued while the Solicitor General was stating that, as far as he knew, no further orders would be necessary. Griswold clearly did not know what other papers had what materials. In fact, copies of the *Pentagon Papers* had also been given to the *Boston Globe, Chicago Sun-Times, Christian Science Monitor*, and *Los Angeles Times* and they had begun to print them. The likelihood that any injunction would be futile had become very real. A federal judge likened enforcement to "riding herd on a swarm of bees."

When Justices White and Stewart heard about the *Post Dispatch* injunctions, they quickly told the conference that they would vote for the Brennan-drafted per curiam, which now had a six-Justice Court behind it. The opinion was sent to the printer late that afternoon and announced on the afternoon of June 30.

By then Justice Douglas had left for his summer home in Goose Prairie, Washington, but he had left behind his concurring opinion. Justice Black concurred in it after Douglas's draft was revised to meet Black's objections to a section declaring the Vietnam War unconstitutional. Justice Brennan also wrote an opinion, which he sent to Justice Black, who phoned back to say that he did not disagree with "a phrase, a word, or a comma." Despite this, Black said, he would write separately. By then, the opinion floodgates were opened and each Justice issued a separate opinion. Each explained the decision from its author's own point of view.

The Decision

Technically speaking, the *Pentagon Papers* decision is contained in the per curiam opinion which had been drafted by Justice Brennan just before the oral argument in the case. The per curiam denied the injunction against the newspapers. It stated that any prior restraint of the press bears a heavy presumption against validity; the Government thus carried a heavy burden of showing justification for the imposition of such a restraint. In this case, the per curiam concluded, the Government had not met that burden.

The Court divided six-to-three in the *Pentagon Papers Case*. As already indicated, each of the Justices wrote a separate opinion explaining the decision from his own point of view; none of the majority opinions was concurred in by more than two Justices. One can, nevertheless note three broad divisions in the Court: 1) that the First Amendment bars any restraint upon newspaper publication, regardless of the nature of the material published; 2) that the First Amendment bars an injunction against the publication involved in the case, but may not do so where disclosure will result in direct, immediate, and irreparable damage to the nation; 3) that the "pernicious influence" of publication is primarily for the executive branch of government to determine, and the courts should defer to the executive determination on the impact of disclosure on national security.

The *Pentagon Papers* decision marks the most dramatic assertion of the principle that the press may not be subjected to prior restraints. At the same time, it is plain that the decision is not based upon an absolutist view of that principle. In the first place, the newspapers concerned were subject to temporary injunctions that prevented them from publishing the *Pentagon Papers* pending decision by the courts in the matter. Even more important is the indication in the opinions that six of the Justices would have upheld the issuance of an injunction in certain circumstances. As stated in three of the concurring opinions, there is a narrow class of cases in which the First Amendment's ban on prior judicial restraint may be overridden — where "disclosure . . . will surely result in direct, immediate, and irreparable damage to the Nation or its people." The example given is that of publication that will imperil the safety of a troop transport. It is this exception that provides the legal justification for wartime censorship.

It must, however, be emphasized that the question of whether the exception applies is one for judicial resolution. The majority rejected Justice Harlan's dissenting contention that the judiciary may review only to the extent of satisfying itself that the subject matter of the dispute does lie within the foreign-relations power. If the Executive seeks a judicial remedy against the press, it must submit the basis upon which that remedy is sought to full scrutiny by the judiciary.

One may, however, argue that such a result overlooks what Justice Harlan's dissent termed "the 'pernicious influence' of . . . disclosure." At the time of the case, it was perhaps possible to make such an argument, since it was not really known whether the publication would have any adverse impact upon national security. Today, it is easier to reject the argument, since, so far as we know, no damage was done by the newspapers' action. Indeed, we were told in a 1991 *New York Times* article by Erwin Griswold, who had argued the case as Solicitor General, that the copies of the Pentagon Papers turned over to the newspapers did not contain the four volumes which the Government considered "most troublesome." In addition, in the volumes delivered, materials relating directly to security had been blocked out. The result, says Griswold, was that "the newspapers did not print at the time any items about which the Government was concerned." Hence, Griswold concludes, "In hindsight, it is clear to me that no harm was done by publication of the *Pentagon Papers*."

First Amendment and Prior Restraint

Freedom of the press as a constitutional guaranty is primarily American in origin. To be sure, by the time of the American Revolution, that freedom had also come to be recognized in English law. But that was not because the freedom was based upon any constitutional provision. Indeed, freedom of the press is a typical example of the growth of rights in the English system. Control of the press in England was originally exercised through the Star Chamber. Although that tribunal was one of the first victims of the Long Parliament in 1641, its abolition did not mean press freedom. Censorship survived the Civil War and was given statutory foundation by the Licensing Act of 1662. Still, even that law was an important step forward, since the licensing power now depended not on any claim of inherent executive authority, but on statute law. Then, in 1695, the House of Commons refused to renew the Licensing Act. Consequently, the system of compulsory licensing of all publications, rigorously enforced since Tudor times, expired, and the English press has since been legally free from prior restraints. In Macaulay's phrase, the press "was emancipated from the censorship soon after the Revolution; and the government immediately fell under the censorship of the press." Yet this was brought about, not by constitutional declaration, but by the simple fact that Parliament failed to renew a statute.

In this country, the situation was different. The very first American constitution, that adopted in Virginia in June 1776, contained a Declaration of Rights that specifically guaranteed "freedom of the Press [as] one of the greatest bulwarks of liberty." Similar provisions were included in other state constitutions adopted during the Revolutionary period. The original United States Constitution did not, of course, contain any Bill of Rights. The omission was one of the principal grounds of attack upon the new organic instrument by those who opposed ratification. To quiet the opposition, John Marshall tells us, "In almost every convention by which the Constitution was adopted, amendments to guard against the abuse of power were recommended. These amendments demanded security against the apprehended encroachments of the general government." Five of the ratifying conventions in the states included a freedom of the press guaranty in the Bill of Rights recommended by them.

On June 8, 1789, James Madison introduced the amendments that became the Federal Bill of Rights in the House of Representatives. His proposed amendments contained two guarantees for freedom of the press: "the freedom of the press, as one of the great bulworks of liberty, shall be inviolable" and "No State shall violate . . . the freedom of the press." Though Madison said of the latter that he "conceived this to be the most valuable amendment in the whole list," it was eliminated during the Congressional debate. The general guaranty of press freedom became the provision in the First Amendment that, "Congress shall make no law . . . abridging the freedom of . . . the press."

This provision does not, of course, tell us what constitutes an unconstitutional abridgement of freedom of the press. Yet it has always been assumed that, if it does no more, the First Amendment elevates Blackstone's conception that freedom of the press only bars prior restraints to the constitutional plane. As a member of the Supreme Court stated it in 1799, less than a decade after the Bill of Rights was ratified, "The definition of [freedom of the press] is, in my opinion, no where more happily or justly expressed than by the great author of the commentaries on the laws of England."

According to Blackstone, "the liberty of the press consists in laying no previous restraints upon publications, and not in freedom from censure for criminal matter when published. Every freeman has an undoubted right to lay what sentiments he pleases before the public; to forbid this, is to destroy the freedom of the press; but if he publishes what is improper, mischievous or illegal he must take the consequences of his own temerity."

At a minimum, the First Amendment gives the press the Blackstone freedom from prior restraints. Hence, an early state case tells us, the main purpose of such a constitutional provision is to prevent all such previous restraints upon publications as had been practiced by other governments.

The rule against prior restraints is broader than the principle laid down in the *Pentagon Papers Case*. In the words of the Pennsylvania court construing a provision in that state's Bill of Rights before the First Amendment was adopted, it "effectually preclude[s] any attempt to fetter the press by the institution of a licenser." Freedom of the press under the First Amendment must mean a constitutional interdiction against any system of licensing. Everyone has the right, under the First Amendment, to publish a newspaper, periodical, or circular without any license. In this respect, the business of publishing is different from every other business or occupation. Authority to license businesses and occupations is an essential part of the police power. But licensing power does not extend to the business of publishing, however closely related that business may be to public health, safety, morals, and welfare.

Not only the publication, but also the distribution of newspapers and literature may not be subjected to a requirement of prior licensing. As the Court says in *Schneider v. State* (1939),"To require a censorship through license which makes impossible the free and unhampered distribution of pamphlets strikes at the very heart of the constitutional guarantees."

The leading case is *Lovell v. Griffin* (1938), where a municipal ordinance forbade the distribution of any literature without a permit from the city manager. The ordinance was applied to prohibit distribution of religious literature by Jehovah's Witnesses. Such an ordinance, said a unanimous Court, is invalid on its face. Though used in this case against the distribution of religious literature, it could equally be applied to all other printed matter, including newspapers. It amounted to a previous restraint upon publication and distribution of a type wholly inconsistent with the notion of freedom of speech and press. As the Court put it, "Legislation of the type of the ordinance in question would restore the system of license and censorship in its baldest form."

Freedom from prior restraint also gives the press protection against orders that prohibit the publication of particular information or commentary — i.e., the type of order involved in the *Pentagon Papers Case*. Such a prohibition, according to the *Nebraska Press Assn.* case discussed on page 16, is "the most serious and the least tolerable infringement on First Amendment rights."

In its impact upon the press, such a prior restraint can be more inhibiting than even a system of subsequent punishment, since it shuts off communication before it takes place. "A prior restraint . . ." Chief Justice Burger points out in the *Nebraska Press Assn.* opinion, "by definition has an immediate and irreversible sanction. If it can be said that a threat of criminal or civil sanctions after publication 'chills' speech, prior restraint 'freezes' it at least for the time."

"The Minnesota Rag"

To be sure, freedom of the press, like the other freedoms guaranteed by the Bill of Rights, may be abused. As Justice Brennan tells us in his *Nebraska Press Assn.* concurrence, "the press may be arrogant, tyrannical, abusive and sensationalist." Yet the theory of the First Amendment remains, as Judge Murray Gurfein declared in the lower court in the *Pentagon Papers Case*, that "A cantankerous press, an obstinate press, a ubiquitous press must be suffered by those in authority in order to preserve the even greater values of freedom of expression and the right of the people to know."

The protection given by the First Amendment to even publications clearly of the type referred to by Justice Brennan is illustrated by *Near v. Minnesota* (1931), which happens to be the first Supreme Court case enforcing the no-prior-restraint rule. The publication in question was *The Saturday Press* published in Minneapolis. It was an extreme example of the "yellow journalism" that is usually dated from the 1883 acquisition of the *New York World* by Joseph Pulitzer. According to a Supreme Court Justice, the paper's "regular business was the publication of malicious, scandalous, and defamatory articles concerning the principal public officers, leading newspapers of the city, many private persons, and the Jewish race."

The last edition published before the case declared, "There have been too many men in this city and especially those in official life who have been taking orders and suggestions from JEW GANGSTERS, therefore we HAVE Jew Gangsters, practically ruling Minneapolis." It also asserted, "Practically every vendor of vile hooch, every owner of a moonshine still, every snake-faced gangster and embryonic yegg in the Twin Cities is a JEW." Well might Fred W. Friendly refer to the paper as the "Minnesota Rag."

The Saturday Press was enjoined from publishing any future editions under a Minnesota statute providing that publication of "a malicious, scandalous and defamatory newspaper . . . may be enjoined." The statute was ruled unconstitutional. It set up a ready means for officials to suppress the press by barring publication of newspapers offensive to them. All they had to do was find a judge who shared their view that particular press criticism passed legitimate bounds. "This is of the essence of censorship," declared the *Near* opinion.

Chief Justice Charles Evans Hughes, the author of the opinion, realized that it was the first by the high Court striking down a prior restraint. He wanted it to be a ringing reaffirmation of freedom of the press. Observers noted that he delivered the opinion with particular power and dignity. "Chief Justice Hughes threw all his ardor" into his delivery, wrote the *Chicago Tribune*. "In a loud voice into which he injected considerable feeling at times, the head of the judicial branch . . . argued for the liberty of the press to criticize public officials as an outstanding safeguard of the people from the imposition of tyranny."

The liberal members of the Court, particularly Justice Louis D. Brandeis, had objected to the citation by the Chief Justice of three cases which had stricken down state regulatory laws, such as minimum-wage laws, as invalid interferences with freedom of contract. Justice Brandeis was concerned that the citations legitimized the decisions in which the Court had improperly used substantive due process to strike down legislative attempts to deal with economic abuses. Chief Justice Hughes, however, explained in a memorandum to the Justice, "I cited [those] cases to expose the inconsistency of the dissenters," who were strong supporters of the decisions in those cases. In other words, the Chief Justice was showing that it was inconsistent to hold that the Court could strike down laws that infringed upon freedom of contract, but not one which made a comparable infringement upon freedom of the press.

Chief Justice Hughes was also trying to show that freedom of the press had its own immunity from government, just as freedom of contract did under the jurisprudence of the day. "I understand," the Chief Justice wrote in his memo to Justice Brandeis, "that [the *Near* dissenters] will insist that the only question is whether the State regulation was 'reasonable,' and I am pointing out the decisions in which they have held that, as to contract, there are certain indispensable requirements of the liberty guaranteed. So here, the liberty of the press, by its history and connotation, must be deemed to have certain essential attributes."

The essential element, Chief Justice Hughes stressed in his *Near* opinion was freedom from prior restraint. Indeed, the Chief Justice stated, "the chief purpose" of the First Amendment is "to prevent previous restraints upon publication." That *Near* was the first case of its kind itself indicated the near unanimity on the matter. "The fact that for approximately one hundred and fifty years there has been almost an entire absence of attempts to impose previous restraints upon publications relating to the malfeasance of public officers is significant of the deep-seated conviction that such restraints would violate constitutional right."

If anything, said the Hughes opinion, the need for an unrestrained press is even greater than it was when the First Amendment was drafted: "the administration of government has become more complex, the opportunities for malfeasance and corruption have multiplied, crime has grown to most serious proportions, and the danger of its protection by unfaithful officials and of the impairment of the fundamental security of life and property by criminal alliances and official neglect, emphasizes the primary need of a vigilant and courageous press, especially in great cities."

15

Nor does the abuse of press freedom by the "Minnesota Rag" change the result. "The fact," Hughes affirmed, "that the liberty of the press may be abused by miscreant purveyors of scandal does not make any the less necessary the immunity of the press from previous restraint in dealing with official misconduct." Abuse by the press may be an evil, "but the theory of the constitutional guaranty is that even a more serious public evil would be caused by authority to prevent publication."

However strongly *Near* states the rule against prior restraints, it does not state it in absolutist terms: "the protection even as to previous restraint is not absolutely unlimited." But, the Chief Justice emphasizes, whatever limitation there is applies only "in exceptional cases." Three such exceptions are recognized by the Hughes opinion: 1) obscene publications; 2) incitements to acts of violence and the overthrow by force of orderly government; 3) in time of war, "No one would question but that a government might prevent actual obstruction to its recruiting service or the publication of the sailing dates of transports or the number and location of troops." The third exception was to be restated in the concurring opinions of Justices Brennan and Stewart in the *Pentagon Papers Case*.

Gag Orders

The most important cases applying the *Near* rule against prior restraints, aside from the *Pentagon Papers Case* itself, have been those involving so called gag orders - judicial attempts to censor the press by forbidding news media from publishing material that could impair the right to a fair trial. The conflict in these cases between the right of an accused to a fair trial and the right guaranteed by the First Amendment came before the Court in *Nebraska Press Association v. Stuart* (1976). A state judge in a murder trial had prohibited the press from publishing confessions or admissions and facts "strongly implicative" of the accused.

Chief Justice Burger began the conference on the case by noting, "Issuance of prior restraints may in some cases be permissible." But that was not true here. In fact, the Court "decided this case when we decided the *Pentagon Papers Case*."

All the Justices agreed that the lower court decision upholding the gag order should be reversed. But there was disagreement over whether such orders might ever be validly issued. Justice Brennan urged that the First Amendment should be construed to bar all prior restraints. He was supported by Justices Stewart, White, Marshall, and Stevens. The latter asserted that there was "no clear and present danger found here, so [I would] reverse outright."

The others supported the Burger view on prior restraints. Justice Blackmun stated that he "could join an opinion that rated the First Amendment above the Sixth. But [there] should be no prior restraint on what has occurred in open court." Justices Powell and Rehnquist took the same approach. Justice Rehnquist stressed, "[You] can't forbid the press to report what was said at [an] open preliminary hearing." Justice Powell said, "Courts can't impose prior restraints with respect to public hearing or [materials] that the press gets on its own, however shabbily it gets it." On the other hand, Justice Blackmun stressed, "[I] don't want to close the door completely against some restraint."

When the Chief Justice sent around his typewritten draft opinion of the Court he explained, in his covering Memorandum to the Conference, "I have undertaken to express the views of all but those who would regard prior restraint barred in all cases and for whatever reason. My own reexamination of all the relevant cases suggests that, unlike the situation in England, such a showing is very difficult to make under the First Amendment as construed by the Court, but neither is it a total impossibility, as yet; and this case does not call for going that far."

The Burger memo and draft led Justice Brennan to circulate an opinion concurring in the judgment. As stated in the Brennan covering memo, "its approach, in the Chief's words, is 'forever to bar prior restraint against pretrial publicity,' which I thought was the conference consensus."

The Chief Justice then inquired "whether a majority of the Conference is willing in this case 'to forever bar prior restraint on pretrial publicity.'" The majority ultimately agreed with the Burger view that it was not. "In my view," Justice Powell wrote back to the Chief Justice, "it is not necessary to go so far — certainly in the case before us. Nor did I understand that a majority of the Conference voted to hold that never, under any conceivable circumstances, would a court have the power to restrain prejudicial publicity even for the briefest period of time. I have not thought that our previous decisions justify such a sweeping final conclusion."

Justice Powell wrote that he "would simply decide the case before us and say that it is unnecessary to determine there never could be a prior restraint on pretrial publicity." The Burger opinion did not follow this advice. It indicated that prior restraint might sometimes be permissible — though, as Justice Powell had said, "the presumption is against any such restraint and one who asserts a need for it bears a heavy burden indeed."

As the Powell letter noted, the *Nebraska Press* opinion did indicate that, while the barriers to prior restraints were not insuperable, they remained high. The Burger opinion stated specifically that prior restraints came to court with a heavy presumption against their validity, which the order at issue failed to overcome, since there was no finding that measures short of prior restraint would not have protected the accused's rights.

Nebraska Press leaves the outer limits of the prior restraint prohibition unclear. Despite the contrary indication in the Burger opinion, one may question whether a gag order can ever overcome the presumption against prior restraints. Five Justices indicated in separate opinions that they doubted whether such orders would be justifiable. Should the time come for the Court to announce a general rule, it will probably be that stated in Justice Brennan's concurrence: "resort to prior restraints on freedom of the press is a constitutionally impermissible method for enforcing" the right to a fair trial.

Yet even here we cannot be certain. Justice Stevens, in his concurrence, indicated his agreement with the Brennan view. But Stevens also indicated that he might be troubled by certain cases. He gave an example in a Memorandum to the Conference: "Consider, for example, the possibility of surreptitious recording of strategy conferences between the defendant and his lawyer. Perhaps there is a constitutional right to publish even that kind of information, but I hesitate to decide the most extreme cases in the abstract without the benefit of argument." In the end, all the same, Justice Stevens did indicate that, "if ever required to face the issue squarely, [I] may well accept [Justice Brennan's] ultimate conclusion."

Censorship

The Supreme Court has never had to deal with a system of censorship — at least so far as the traditional press has been concerned. It cannot, however, be doubted that press censorship is utterly incompatible with the First Amendment. Under it, as Justice Black stated in his *Pentagon Papers* opinion, "The Government's power to censor the press was abolished so that the press would remain free to censor the Government."

Though freedom from prior restraint through censorship is as much a part of freedom of the press as immunity from licensing, the general principle may give way in certain circumstances. Under the exception to the rule against prior restraints stated in *Near* and *Pentagon Papers*, a system of censorship over the press may be imposed in time of war. Though there are no cases involving the validity of wartime censorship, the war power is broad enough to include such emergency restraint upon the press.

In addition, other governmental powers may be used to establish what amounts to a system of indirect censorship. Thus, newspapers and periodicals are entitled to be sent as second-class mail, with extremely low rates charged for their carriage. The Postmaster General is given authority to deny or revoke second-class mail rates on specified grounds. That power, if abused, may, in Justice Brandeis' words in the *Milwaukee Leader* case (to be discussed shortly), enable the Postmaster General to "become the universal censor of publications." That is true because, as Justice Oliver Wendell Holmes noted in his *Leader* opinion, "To refuse the second class rate to a newspaper is to make its circulation impossible."

During World War I the Postmaster General revoked the second-class mail status of the Socialist *Milwaukee Leader* because of its publication of articles opposing the war. When the publisher objected, the Postmaster General replied, "The instant you print anything calculated to dishearten the boys in the army or to make them think this is not a just or righteous war — that instant you will be suppressed."

Three years after the war ended, the Supreme Court sustained the Postmaster General's action. The second-class mail permit was only a privilege which could be denied to those who counseled obstruction of the war. According to the Court "The Constitution was adopted to preserve our Government, not to serve as a protecting screen for those who while claiming its privileges seek to destroy it."

The Court gave several examples of the *Leader* articles which justified the revocation: articles denouncing the war and the draft as capitalistic and arbitrary, calling the President an autocrat and Congress "rubber stamp," and denouncing the Food Control Law as "Kaiserizing America." It is ironic that only a week earlier, the Court itself had ruled that the same Food Control Law was unconstitutional.

The *Milwaukee Leader* decision has not been expressly overruled. But it is plainly inconsistent with the whole thrust of First Amendment Law during the past half century. At the least, we may doubt, with Justice Holmes in his dissent, "that Congress ever intended to give such a practically despotic power to any one man." If it did grant such an authority, the Court today would deal differently with the matter than it did in the *Leader* case. Indeed, according to a more recent case, "grave constitutional questions are immediately raised once it is said that the use of the mails is a privilege which may be extended or withheld on any grounds whatsoever."

Under such a "privilege" view, which was, of course, the one that was followed in the *Leader* case, "the second-class rate could be granted on condition that certain economic or political ideas not be disseminated." That would mean "a radical departure from our traditions and . . . clothe the Postmaster General with the power to supervise the tastes of the reading public of the country."

The quoted statements were made in *Hannegan v. Esquire* (1946), where the Postmaster General again revoked a second-class mailing permit — this time from *Esquire* magazine. His action was based on his opinion that *Esquire* contained writings and pictures which, though not obscene, were "indecent, vulgar, and risqué." According to him, the special rate afforded to magazines possessing the privilege was only for those which contributed to "the public good and the public welfare." This was asserting in himself a power to determine whether a particular publication conformed to his norm as to what was "good" or "bad." To uphold the withdrawal order would therefore, said the Court, be to grant the Postmaster General a power of censorship: "Such a power is so abhorrent to our traditions that a purpose to grant it should not be easily inferred." The clear implication is that, despite the *Leader* case, such a power would be unconstitutional. Even limited to the second-class mail permit, "a requirement that literature or art conform to some norm prescribed by an official smacks of an ideology foreign to our system."

Without any doubt, the prohibition of prior restraint by censorship applies with full force to the conventional press of newspapers, books, and periodicals, as well as to the newer medium of broadcasting. But the Supreme Court has refused to hold that it applies as fully to motion pictures.

Joseph Burstyn, Inc. v. Wilson (1952), held motion pictures to be within the protection that the First Amendment secures to freedom of the press. In so holding the Court squarely overruled a 1915 case, decided in the infancy of the motion picture industry, which refused to hold movies within the constitutional guaranty, on the ground that moving pictures were "a business, pure and simple, originated and conducted for profit." The *Burstyn* opinion rightly pointed out that this was irrelevant to the First Amendment issue, since books, newspapers, and magazines are also published and sold for profit: "It cannot be doubted that motion pictures are a significant medium for the communication of ideas. They may affect public attitudes and behavior in a variety of ways, ranging from direct espousal of a political or social doctrine to the subtle shaping of thought which characterizes all artistic expression. The importance of motion pictures as an organ of public opinion is not lessened by the fact that they are designed to entertain as well as to inform." As organs of public opinion, they fall within the First Amendment's aegis.

It may be thought from this that motion pictures are now no more subject to censorship restraints than are printed materials. In *Times Film Corp. v. Chicago* (1961), however, the Court expressly refused to rule that the ambit of First Amendment freedom "includes complete and absolute freedom to exhibit, at least once, any and every kind of motion picture." On the contrary, the Court held that "motion pictures were not 'necessarily subject to the precise rules governing any other particular method of expression. Each method . . . tends to present its own peculiar problems.'" Under such an approach, a broadside attack upon all motion picture censorship must fail: "Certainly petitioner's broadside attack does not warrant, nor could it justify . . . our saying that the State is stripped of all constitutional power to prevent, in the most effective fashion, the utterance of this class of speech."

As recently as 1975, the Court indicated its agreement with this holding. At the same time, the Court has limited the film censorship power in two important respects. In the first place, laws providing for film censorship cannot, any more than laws regulating other expression, vest uncontrolled discretion in government officials. As the Supreme Court told us in 1975, "the risks of freewheeling censorship are formidable." In *Burstyn*, where a movie had been banned under a law permitting officials to deny a license to exhibit films on the ground that they were "sacrilegious," the statute was condemned as vesting unbridled discretion in the censor. The term "sacrilegious" is so broad and ill-defined that it furnishes no standard to control the censor's discretion.

In addition, there is the limitation imposed by *Freedman v. Maryland* (1965). The Court there struck down a state system for licensing of motion pictures, saying that such a system avoids constitutional infirmity only if it operates under procedural safeguards designed to obviate the dangers of censorship. As explained in a more recent case, *Freedman* holds that prior restraint censorship runs afoul of the First Amendment if it lacks the following safeguards: 1) the burden of initiating judicial proceedings, and of proving that the material is unprotected, must rest on the censor;

2) any restraint prior to judicial review can be imposed only for a specified brief period and only to preserve the status quo; 3) a prompt final judicial determination must be assured.

One may, however, wonder whether a censorship system so alien to the spirit of the First Amendment should be saved by a few procedural band-aids. One can only share the sentiment expressed by Justice Douglas in his *Freedman* dissent: "I do not believe any form of censorship — no matter how speedy or prolonged it may be — is permissible."

If, under *Burstyn*, the motion picture is now within the ambit of First Amendment protection, should it not also be wholly free from previous restraints? In Blackstone's classic words, "To subject the press to the restrictive power of a licenser, as was formerly done. . . is to subject all freedom of sentiment to the prejudices of one man, and make him the arbitrary and infallible judge of all controverted points in learning, religion and government." Today, few will controvert this, as far as the conventional press is concerned. But if the motion picture now has First Amendment protection similar to that enjoyed by the newspaper or the magazine, it should also be the beneficiary of full freedom from previous restraints. In this nation, everyone protected by freedom of the press, no matter what medium of expression may be used, should be freed from the censor.

Prior Restraint Exceptions

Vital though it is, the rule against prior restraints is not an absolute prohibition. Here, as in other areas of First Amendment law, as Justice Blackmun put it in his *Pentagon Papers* opinion, absolutism has never commanded a majority of the Supreme Court. In both *Near v. Minnesota* and the *Pentagon Papers Case*, the Justices indicated that the rule against prior restraint may be overridden where, in Justice Stewart's *Pentagon Papers* words, "disclosure . . . will surely result in direct, immediate, and repairable damage to the Nation or its people." The example given in both cases is publication that will imperil a troop transport. The Supreme Court has not yet had to deal with a case involving this narrow exception. However, it did come up in a striking case in a lower federal court.

During the *Pentagon Papers* argument in the lower court, Professor Alexander Bickel was asked to give an example of a justified prior restraint. He referred to a situation where the "hydrogen bomb turns up." Just such a situation arose in 1979 when the *Progressive* magazine was going to publish an article on how the H-bomb works.

The Government sought an injunction against the publication and a preliminary restraining order was granted by the district court. It was argued that the projected article merely contained data already in the public domain and readily available to any diligent seeker. The court, however, found "concepts within the article that it does not find in the public realm — concepts that are vital to the operation of the hydrogen bomb." As such, "the article could possibly provide sufficient information to allow a . . . nation to move faster in developing a hydrogen weapon. It could provide a ticket to bypass blind alleys."

Since the case, we have learned that the *Progressive* article contained nothing more than the *Encyclopedia Americana* article by Edward Teller, the father of the H-bomb. However, Judge Robert Warren, who decided the case, felt at the time that he could not challenge the Government's assertion, backed by the affidavit of Hans A. Bethe, a preeminent physicist, that "the design and operational concepts" described in the article should not be revealed. Judge Warren concluded that he simply could not take the risk of deciding that the Government was wrong in its assertion that publication would mean a substantial increase in the risk of thermonuclear proliferation: "A mistake in ruling against *The Progressive* will seriously infringe cherished First Amendment rights. . . . A mistake in ruling against the United States could pave the way for thermonuclear annihilation for us all. In that event our right to life is extinguished and the right to publish becomes moot." After all, as Judge Warren stated from the bench, "I want to think a long, hard time before I'd give a hydrogen bomb to Idi Amin."

The *Progressive* case never reached the Supreme Court. While an appeal was pending in the Seventh Circuit Court of Appeals, a similar article on how an H-bomb worked was published in a Wisconsin newspaper. The government then requested that the *Progressive* case be dismissed. The *Progressive* H-bomb article was then published — and, so far as we know, to no one's detriment.

If the case had reached it, how would the Supreme Court have decided it? In his *Pentagon Papers* opinion, Justice Brennan gave another illustration, in addition to the *Near* troopship example, of the exception to the rule against prior restraint, saying, "the power of presently available armaments would justify even in peacetime the suppression of information that would set in motion a nuclear holocaust." Even one as devoted to the rule against prior restraints as Justice Brennan would hesitate before finding that the *Progressive* article would definitely "not cause the happening of an event of that nature."

At the time of the case, the court could not know that the

article would not harm national security. Confronted by the Government evidence and experts such as Dr. Bethe, the Supreme Court would probably have agreed with the district court that *Progressive* "publication of the technical information on the hydrogen bomb contained in the article is analogous to publication of troop movements or locations in time of war and falls within the extremely narrow exception to the rule against prior restraint."

In such a case, one must conclude, as the *Progressive* editor did in discussing his case, "who would not gladly permit a trivial and temporary incursion against the Bill of Rights when the alternative might be military defeat or even a nuclear holocaust? That was precisely the logic Judge Warren articulated in the *Progressive* case when he stated, 'you can't speak freely when you're dead.' "

In his opinion in the *Nebraska Press Association* case, Justice Brennan stated that the troopship type of case is "the sole possible exception to the prohibition against prior restraints." That this statement is not completely accurate is shown by *Snepp v. United States* (1980). Snepp had worked for the CIA. After he left the agency, he published a book based on his experiences as a CIA agent about CIA activities in South Vietnam. As an express condition of his employment, Snepp had executed an agreement promising that he would "not . . . publish . . . any information or material relating to the Agency, its activities or intelligence activities generally, either during or after the term of [his] employment . . . without specific prior approval by the Agency." The Government brought suit to enforce Snepp's agreement not to publish any information without prepublication clearance. The Supreme Court found that Snepp had willfully breached his secrecy agreement by publishing his book without submitting it for prepublication review.

The Court held that Snepp should be enjoined from future breaches of his agreement and that a constructive trust should be imposed on Snepp's profits from his book. As the per curiam opinion put it, "If the agent publishes unreviewed material in violation of his fiduciary and contractual obligation, the trust remedy simply requires him to disgorge the benefits of his faithlessness. Since the remedy is swift and sure, it is tailored to deter those who would place sensitive information at risk."

The element of deterrence is, however, just the point so far as prior restraint is concerned. The *Snepp* decision makes for a type of prior restraint that is now permitted in our law. As Justice Stevens points out in his dissent, "The mere fact that the Agency has the authority to review the text of a critical book in search of classified information before it is published is bound to have an inhibiting effect on the author's writing." According to Justice Stevens, the right to delay publication pending review by the agency "is itself a form of prior restraint that would not be tolerated in other contexts." However, even Justice Stevens concedes that this was not the ordinary case. "In view of the national interest in maintaining an effective intelligence service," the Stevens dissent concedes, "I am not prepared to say that the restraint is necessarily intolerable in this context."

We can thus conclude that the rule against prior restraint may give way where the individual concerned has agreed to prepublication clearance, at least where there is a national interest justifying the clearance, as in the intelligence service context. In that context, the individual may by contract voluntarily limit his own right to publish free of prior restraints. In other contexts such a limitation might not be enforced where the employee has not used confidential information. In the intelligence agency context, on the other hand, enforcement is proper since, as the Court puts it in *Snepp*, "a former intelligence agent's publication of unreviewed material relating to intelligence activities can be detrimental to vital national interests even if the published information is unclassified."

There may also be other exceptions to the rule against prior restraints not mentioned in *Near v. Minnesota* or the *Pentagon Papers Case*. In *Seattle Times Co. v. Rhinehart*, the head of a religious sect sued the *Times*, which had published articles about the sect, for libel. During pretrial discovery, the *Times* sought certain financial information and donor and membership lists. The trial court ordered disclosure, but also issued a protective order prohibiting the paper from publishing or otherwise using the information except in connection with the libel case. The *Times* claimed that the prohibition was a prior restraint that violated the First Amendment.

The Supreme Court rejected the claim, saying, "A litigant has no First Amendment right of access to information made available only for purposes of trying his suit." On the contrary, rules authorizing discovery are only a matter of legislative grace. Hence, restraints placed on discovered information are not a restriction on a traditionally public source of information. The protective order issued by the trial court furthers a substantial governmental interest unrelated to the suppression of expression. Liberal pretrial discovery has a significant potential for abuse. Litigants can obtain information that if publicly released could be damaging to reputation and privacy. The prevention of such abuse is sufficient justification for the authorization of protective orders.

Judicial limitations on a party's ability to disseminate information secured by pretrial discovery do not violate freedom of the press even if the party restrained is a newspaper. It is true that the protective order operates as a prior restraint. Yet, if it were not imposed, as a recent book by Lucas Powe puts it, "discovery could operate as a state-sanctioned illegal search and seizure — which would discourage civil litigation against the press."

Another type of prior restraint was at issue in *Pittsburgh Press Co. v. Pittsburgh Commission on Human Rights* (1973). The commission had found that the newspaper had violated an ordinance prohibiting sex-designated employment advertisements and issued an order directing the paper to cease the violation and to publish the advertisements with no reference to sex. The paper claimed that the order violated its First Amendment rights, since it interfered with editorial judgment as to the makeup of the help-wanted section of the paper. The commission's response was based upon the argument that the speech at issue was commercial speech unprotected by the First Amendment.

At the time of the case, the governing rule was that "commercial speech," such as an advertisement, was not at all protected by the First Amendment. Whatever restrictions may otherwise be imposed on governmental power over expression, affirmed *Valentine v. Chrestenson* (1942), then the leading case, "the Constitution imposes no such restraint on government as respects purely commercial advertising."

Chief Justice Burger began his conference presentation in *Pittsburgh Press* by asserting that there was "no evidence the Press practice clearly aids discrimination. . . . I have trouble distinguishing a paid ad from the rest of the newspaper." He stated that the paper's "makeup, layout, etc." were beyond state control "and a statute that conflicts with it runs afoul of the First Amendment."

Justice Stewart also favored a reversal. "I never thought," he said, "*Valentine* meant the government could tell a newspaper what it could print or how it must print it. And this ordinance does just this and it's verboten under the First Amendment." Justice Blackmun agreed, saying, "This is an intrusion into newspaper policy and close to a prior restraint." The others were for affirmance. Justice Marshall dealt succinctly with the freedom of the press argument, saying, "Editorial privilege ends where want ads begin." Justice Powell, who was to write the opinion, made the most complete statement in favor of the ordinance: "I start from the premise that I'm not absolutist about freedom of the press. A newspaper ad as to availability of marijuana would not be protected. . . . This ordinance is not directed against the press; it's against employers and is simply an implementation of a state policy rested on the police power." Justices Brennan and White also voted for affirmance.

The *Pittsburgh Press* decision followed the conference view and affirmed the commission's action. The decision rested on two main grounds: 1) the advertisements were commercial speech not protected by the First Amendment; 2) the rule discussed in Chapter 4 that the press is not normally immune from regulatory laws. Since the commission's "order does not endanger . . . protected speech," it was not subject to the prior restraint rule.

The first prop of the decision has, however, been removed by more recent cases overruling *Valentine* and bringing commercial speech within the reach of the First Amendment. With commercial speech now protected speech, would the Court decide *Pittsburgh Press* the same way? It is probable that the Court would so decide, since the rule it relied on (i.e., subjecting the press to general regulatory laws) would still serve as its basis of decision.

One wonders, nevertheless, whether the rule was not misapplied in *Pittsburgh Press*. Certainly, if the newspaper had refused to hire or otherwise discriminated against women or minorities, no one would claim that the First Amendment is violated by an order to cease and desist from such unlawful discrimination. But that was not the order approved in *Pittsburgh Press*. In Justice Stewart's words in his dissent, "what the Court approves today is wholly different. It approves a government order dictating to a publisher in advance how he must arrange the layout of pages in his newspaper."

Pittsburgh Press was the first case to permit a government agency to dictate to a newspaper publisher the layout and makeup of the newspaper's pages. Certainly, the goal of the Pittsburgh ordinance was laudable. But, as the Stewart dissent asks, should that alone justify permitting government "to lay its heavy editorial hand on any newspaper?"

2

Access to News

Chief Justice Earl Warren was disturbed when he spoke to his law clerk in April 1965 about a recently argued case that involved television in the courtroom. Warren told his clerk that televising criminal trials "turns the clock backwards and converts the court-room into a public spectacle." The Chief Justice denied that the freedom of the press guaranty gave the news media any special right of access to the courtroom. On the contrary, he said, "The press is entitled to be present at trials not because it is the press, but because it is a part of the public."

This meant that the press had only the same right as members of the public to be present at a trial. Warren summarized the law on the matter for his clerk: "Like any other segment of the public it has the right within the limits of the courtroom's facilities to be present, to speak publicly of what transpires, and to communicate courtroom events to the other members of the public. But there is no specific right of the news media to be present at trials, there is merely the right of the public to be present."

Warren's statement brings into sharp focus the crucial current issue so far as freedom of the press is concerned. No one doubts that the press is entitled to the full freedom of expression guaranteed by the First Amendment. As discussed in the previous chapter, the press has the broadest right to publish whatever information it may possess, free from any governmental restraint or penalty. Yet that is only the same as the right possessed by all of us to speak and write freely. The press, however, is more than a private individual exercising his right of free expression. The press is an institution — indeed, the only private institution given specific constitutional protection. The institutional role of the press is to give effect to the people's right to know — to inform the public and in particular to serve as a check on government by exposing misdeeds and other actions contrary to the public interest.

It has been urged that the informing function of the press means that the First Amendment must guarantee more than the right to publish free from governmental restraints. In Justice

Stevens' words in the *Houchins* case (which will be discussed shortly), "It is not sufficient . . . that the channels of communication be free of governmental restraints. Without some protection for the acquisition of information about the operation of public institutions . . . by the public at large, the process of self-governance contemplated by the Framers would be stripped of its substance." The right to publish may be empty if the press does not have access to government information. Does the Constitution confer upon the press a judicially enforceable right of access to files, trials, and prisons?

In answering this question, the Supreme Court has followed the view expressed by Chief Justice Warren to his law clerk: The press has only the same right of access as the general public. There is no constitutional right of access for the press as such. Where members of the public have such a right, the press does also. But where proceedings or files may be closed to the public, the press has no right of access to them. To repeat Warren's words to his clerk, the "right of the news media . . . is merely the right of the public."

Access to Public Institutions

In 1991, KQED, which operates television and radio stations in the San Francisco area, brought an action to require the warden of San Quentin prison to allow the televising of a convicted murderer's scheduled execution. Just before the case was to go to trial, the warden broadened his ban from one on television cameras to one barring the press altogether. The federal court held that the prohibition of cameras was reasonable, but the outright ban was too broad. The press had, by long standing practice, been allowed to attend executions in the state and must be permitted to do so in the future. On the other hand, cameras and recorders — anything, indeed, but pads, pencils, and sketchbooks — may be excluded.

The ruling allowing the press in but keeping cameras out was not appealed. Apparently that was what the defendant warden wanted, for he had testified that he would permit the press back in if he were allowed to ban cameras. In fact, the court noted, the outright ban "appears to be something that the warden has never taken seriously." If he had done so and appealed the decision, he probably would have won under the Supreme Court jurisprudence on the matter.

The Supreme Court did not deal with the right of access to news until *Estes v. Texas* (1965) — the case on television in the courtroom about which Chief Justice Warren spoke to his law clerk.

The original draft opinions in *Estes* rejected the notion of a press right of access. Both the draft opinion of the Court by Justice Stewart and the draft dissent of Justice Clark expressly denied that the First Amendment grants news media such a privilege. Had this remained in the final *Estes* opinions, it might have foreclosed fresh consideration in later cases. Instead, the final Clark opinion of the Court in *Estes* said that the press was "entitled to the same rights as the general public" — i.e., the view stated by Warren to his clerk.

The rule stated by *Estes* and Warren turned out to be the basis of the decision in *Houchins v. KQED* (1978), another case brought by KQED to secure television access to a prison, which was ultimately decided by the highest Court. Houchins was the sheriff of Alameda County, just across the Bay from San Francisco. KQED reported the suicide of a prisoner in the Greystone portion of the county jail and requested permission to inspect and take pictures in Greystone. After permission was refused, KQED filed suit, arguing that Houchins violated the First Amendment by refusing to provide any effective means by which the public could be informed of conditions at Greystone or the prisoners' grievances.

Houchins then announced regular monthly tours for twenty-five persons to parts of the jail. But Greystone was not included and cameras, tape recorders, and interviews with inmates were forbidden. The lower court enjoined Houchins from denying KQED and other responsible news media access to the jail, including Greystone, and from preventing their using photographic or sound equipment or from conducting inmate interviews.

At the conference on the case, the Justices were closely divided. The case for reversal was stated bluntly by Justice White: "I don't see any right of access for anyone or why, if [they] let the public in [they] must let the press in with their cameras." On the other side, Justice Stevens asked, "Can a policy denying all access be constitutional? I think not." Stevens emphasized the public interest "as to how prisons are run."

Of particular interest, in view of his position as the "swing vote," was the ambivalent statement of Justice Stewart: "The First Amendment does not give [the press] access superior to that of the general public. Moreover, there is no such thing as a constitutional right to know." Nevertheless, the Justice concluded, "Basically, I think the injunction here does not exceed [the permitted] bounds." Stewart also noted, "If the sheriff had not allowed public tours, he did not have to allow the press in."

The conference, with Justices Marshall and Blackmun not participating, divided four (Justices Brennan, Stewart, Powell, and

Stevens) to three (the Chief Justice and Justices White and Rehnquist) in favor of affirmance. The opinion was assigned to Justice Stevens who circulated a draft opinion essentially similar to the dissent ultimately issued by him. It contained a broad recognition of a constitutional right of access to information on the part of the press — a right that "is not for the private benefit of those who might qualify as representatives of the 'press' but to insure that the citizens are fully informed regarding matters of public interest and importance."

Under the Stevens draft, "information gathering is entitled to some measure of constitutional protection," and had it come down as the *Houchins* opinion of the Court, it would have established a First Amendment right of access to news. The Stevens draft was, however, not able to retain its majority. Justice Stewart, whose vote had helped to make up the bare majority for affirmance, wrote to Stevens, "Try as I may I cannot bring myself to agree that a county sheriff is constitutionally required to open up a jail that he runs to the press and the public. . . . it would be permissible in this case to issue an injunction assuring press access equivalent to existing public access, but not the much broader injunction actually issued by the District Court." This was essentially the view taken in Justice Stewart's *Houchins* concurrence.

Chief Justice Burger prepared a draft dissent which he explained in a Memorandum to the Conference: "I have devoted a substantial amount of time on a dissent in this case with some emphasis on systems of citizen oversight procedures which exist in many states. . . . This approach, rather than pushy TV people interested directly in the sensational, is the way to a solution. . . . I agree with Potter's view that media have a right of access but not beyond that of the public generally."

But the Burger draft was not to be a dissent. Its holding for reversal received a majority when Justice Stewart concurred in the judgment for reversal. The Chief Justice then sent a "Dear Potter" letter that pointed out that any press right of access could hardly be limited to the news media: "there are literally dozens of people . . . who tour prisons. . . . Many of them write books, articles, or give lectures or a combination. I'm sure you will agree they have the same rights as a TV reporter doing a 'documentary.' Can they have greater First Amendment rights than these others whose form and certainty of communications is not so fixed?"

"I do not believe," the Burger letter declared, "First Amendment rights can be circumscribed by the scope of the audience. If so, the early pamphleteers who could afford only 100 sheets were 'suspect.' " On the contrary, the Chief Justice noted, "a team of TV cameramen (camera-persons!) will tend to produce far more disruption than the serious student or judge, lawyer, or penologist who wants to exercise First Amendment rights with a somewhat different objective."

A later memo summarized the Burger approach in the case: "As a legislator I would vote for a reasonably orderly access to prisons, etc., by media, because it would be useful. But that is not the issue. The question is whether special access rights are constitutionally compelled." He answered in the negative.

The Burger opinion was joined by Justices White and Rehnquist. This made it the plurality opinion of a seven-Justice Court, as Justice Stewart's concurrence enabled the decision for reversal to come down as the Court decision. Justice Stevens' affirmation of a First Amendment right of access became the dissenting view.

When he joined the *Houchins* opinion, Justice White sent a "Dear Chief" letter in which he explained that he had joined the new majority because of the broad implications of the result reached in the original Stevens draft opinion. "If the First Amendment," Justice White wrote, "requires a government to turn over information about its prisons on the demand of the press or to open its files and properties not only to routine inspections but for filming and public display, it would be difficult to contain such an unprecedented principle. I would suppose there are many government operations that are as important for the public to know about as prisons, or more so; yet I cannot believe that the press has a constitutional right to be at every administrator's elbow and to read all of his mail."

It is not for the courts, the White letter urged, to impose a duty on "governments to submit themselves to daily or periodic auditing by the press." What the final *Houchins* decision did, as White saw it, was to "resist taking over what is essentially a legislative task and by reinterpreting the First Amendment assigning to ourselves and other courts the duty of determining whether the state and Federal Governments are making adequate disclosures to the press."

Access to Court Proceedings

Houchins illustrates the general rule that the press has no constitutional right of access to news. Instead, the Supreme Court has taken the position stated by Chief Justice Warren to his clerk. The right to publish does not carry with it the right to gather information. As the Court summed it up in another case, "The

Constitution does not . . . require government to accord the press special access to information not shared by members of the public generally."

The Supreme Court has, however, confirmed a press right of access in one important area — to court proceedings. But it did so hesitantly. Indeed, its first decision on the matter ruled against the press claim — although the first draft opinion would have given a broad right of access. But a Justice changed his vote six weeks later and that opinion became the dissent.

The difficult constitutional cases are not those in which the courts are asked to protect a given right but those in which conflicting rights — each by itself deserving of judicial protection — are at issue. The courts must then balance the rights in light of the social and other values involved and define the precise course and texture of the interface between the competing rights. Just such a conflict between rights was presented in *Gannett Co. v. DePasquale* (1979). On the one hand, criminal defendants asserted their right to a fair trial, which could require exclusion of the public and press from a pretrial hearing at which would be aired evidence and issues not permitted at the trial itself. On the other hand, a reporter claimed that the press and the public had a right of access to judicial proceedings even where the accused, the prosecutor, and the trial judge all had agreed to closure.

Gannett arose out of a murder prosecution in New York. Defendants moved to suppress certain evidence. At the pretrial hearing on the motion, defendants requested that the public and the press be excluded from the hearing, arguing that the unabated buildup of adverse publicity had jeopardized their ability to receive a fair trial. The district attorney did not oppose the motion, and it was granted by the trial judge. A newspaper challenged the exclusion order, but it was upheld by the highest New York court.

The claims of the press in *Gannett* rested on both the Sixth Amendment guaranty of a public trial and the First Amendment guaranty of freedom of the press. During the postargument conference on the case Chief Justice Burger indicated that neither amendment supported a reversal. In his view, the Sixth Amendment public trial right did not apply "because the motion to suppress [is] not part of the trial." And, as for the "First Amendment argument, there isn't any for me."

Justice Stewart, who ultimately wrote the *Gannett* opinion, also spoke in favor of the exclusion order. He agreed with the Chief Justice on the First Amendment: "I don't think the First Amendment claim is valid, since the press has no greater rights than the public." On the Sixth Amendment issue, Stewart reached the same result as the Chief Justice, but he refused to follow the Burger approach, saying, "I can't agree it's not part of the trial."

Justice Stewart, nevertheless, reached the same result because, he said, "the right to a public trial is explicitly given to the accused; but there is a public interest and who but the accused can trigger that?" Stewart answered this query, "I'm inclined to hold that only the prosecutor can speak for the public where a motion for closure is made by the defendant."

Justices Rehnquist and Stevens also were in favor of exclusion. "The Sixth Amendment," said Justice Rehnquist, "means for me only protection for the rights of the accused . . . the Framers didn't give the public a right to access." Justice Stevens relied on what he called "a critical difference between seeing a live hearing and reading a transcript of it. If the public has a right of access to the live performance, we'll be holding that the electronic media must be allowed."

The other five Justices spoke in favor of reversal. They were led by Justice Brennan, who wanted to establish a constitutional right of access for the press and the public. Justices White and Marshall took the same approach, saying that the suppression hearing was part of the trial. "The public," Justice Marshall declared, "has a right because, if the accused is done dirt, the public interest is hurt. The public is entitled to know what happens when it happens."

Of particular interest were the statements of Justice Blackmun, who wrote the first *Gannett* draft, and Justice Powell, who was ultimately the swing vote in the case. Justice Blackmun said that he agreed that the Sixth Amendment provided for the "public character of trial. . . . I think the public directly and the press indirectly have an interest in preventing the abuse of public business. I'd take the Sixth Amendment approach." Justice Powell, who was to change his mind on this point, agreed. As he put it, "This is Sixth [Amendment] and not First." Powell also agreed that this "suppression hearing is part of a criminal trial." In his view, "the trial judge didn't do enough when he heard the accused and the prosecutor agreed to closure." The judge should also have allowed the press to be heard.

In a letter to Justice Blackmun, Justice Powell wrote that, at the *Gannett* conference, "I do not think a majority of the Court agreed as to exactly how the competing interests in this case should be resolved." On the other hand, the tally sheet of a Justice present at the conference indicates that a bare majority (Justices Brennan, White, Marshall, Blackmun, and Powell) favored reversal.

The opinion was assigned to Justice Blackmun, who circulated a draft of the Court that was a broadside rejection of the decision below. In his final *Gannett* dissent, Blackmun began by stating that he could not "join the Court's phrasing of the 'question presented.' " How he saw that question was indicated by the first sentence of the Blackmun draft opinion of the Court. "This case presents the issue whether, and to what extent, the First, Sixth, and Fourteenth Amendments of the Constitution restrict a State, in a criminal prosecution, from excluding the public and the press from a pretrial suppression-of-evidence hearing, when the request to exclude is made by the defendant himself."

Justice Blackmun's draft was virtually the same as his *Gannett* dissent, with the omission of the statement of facts (which was used by Justice Stewart in the opinion of the Court ultimately issued) and those changes made to convert the draft from a majority opinion to a dissent (e.g., changing "we" in the draft opinion of the Court to "I"). The Blackmun draft implied a broad right of public and press access to all criminal proceedings from the Sixth Amendment's public trial guaranty: "The public trial guarantee . . . insures that not only judges but all participants in the criminal justice system are subjected to public scrutiny as they conduct the public's business of prosecuting crime."

Had the Blackmun draft opinion come down as the final *Gannett* opinion, it would have completely resolved the issue of access to criminal proceedings in favor of a wide right on the part of the public and the press. Such a broad holding would have made the *Richmond Newspapers* decision (which will be discussed shortly) unnecessary. It would also have answered the question left unanswered by *Richmond Newspapers* — does the press have a right of access to pretrial proceedings as well as to criminal trials? — with a strong affirmative.

But the Blackmun draft was not able to secure the five votes needed to make it into a Court opinion. The day after it was circulated, Justice Stewart sent a "Dear Harry" note: "I shall in due course circulate a dissenting opinion."

The same day, Justice Blackmun received a letter from Justice Stevens indicating that, "Although I agree with a good deal of what you say in your opinion," he would not change his conference vote. "I probably will adhere to my view that the public interest in open proceedings can be adequately vindicated by the combined efforts of the two adversaries and the trial judge, coupled with a right of access to a transcript promptly after the risk of prejudice has passed." Justice Stevens saw dangers to defendants in the Blackmun holding. "I am fearful that your holding will tolerate prejudice that may not be serious enough to violate the defendant's constitutional rights but will nevertheless enhance his risk of conviction."

The promised Stewart draft dissent was an abbreviated version of his opinion of the Court in *Gannett* with changes made in the latter to convert the draft dissent into the Court opinion (this time changing "I" in the draft to the "we" of the opinion of the Court). Justice Stewart stressed that the Sixth Amendment public trial guaranty is one created for the benefit of the defendant alone and was personal to the accused. Even if the contrary were the case, the tentative decision was wrong; the public trial guaranty applies only to trials, not pretrial proceedings. Nor does the First Amendment compel a different result, since it gives the press no right superior to that of the public. "If the public had no enforceable right to attend the pretrial proceeding in this case, it necessarily follows that the petitioners had no such right under the First and Fourteenth Amendments."

Justice Stevens also circulated a brief draft dissent, which asserted, "I do not believe the Court has the authority to create this novel remedy for a random selection of bystanders." The Stevens draft was, however, withdrawn by its author several weeks later.

The general expectation in the Court was that the Blackmun draft would come down as the *Gannett* opinion. Then, a month and a half after the drafts were circulated, Justice Powell wrote to Justice Blackmun: "I was inclined to view this case as presenting primarily a First Amendment rather than a Sixth Amendment issue. . . . I had become persuaded that my views as to the Sixth Amendment coincide substantially with those expressed by Potter. . . . I therefore will join his opinion." Justice Powell also had written a draft, originally as a dissent, which would be issued as a concurring opinion, "in which I address the First Amendment issue. I am sorry to end up being the 'swing vote.' At Conference I voted to reverse. But upon a more careful examination of the facts, I have concluded that the trial court substantially did what in my view the First Amendment requires."

The case was now assigned by the Chief Justice to Justice Stewart, whose revised version of his draft dissent was issued as the *Gannett* opinion of the Court. The most substantial change was pointed out in Stewart's covering memorandum. "You will note that I have unabashedly plagiarized Harry Blackmun's statement of facts in Part I and discussion of mootness in Part II. I offer two excuses: 1) the pressure of time, and 2) more importantly, I could not have said it better."

When Justice Blackmun learned that he had lost his *Gannett* majority, he wrote a "Dear Bill, Byron, and Thurgood" letter: "You were kind enough to join me when I attempted an opinion for the Court. Please feel free to unhook, if you wish, in my conversion of that opinion to a concurrence in part and a dissent in part." As it turned out, none of the Blackmun supporters wanted "to unhook," and all four joined the *Gannett* dissent that he issued.

As finally decided, *Gannett* held that the press did not have a Sixth Amendment right of access to the preliminary hearing on the motion to suppress. The *Gannett* decision did not, however, finally resolve the issue of access to criminal proceedings. The next year, in 1980, the Justices were again presented with the issue in *Richmond Newspapers v. Virginia.* Once again, the trial court had closed a criminal proceeding to the public and the press and refused to grant a newspaper's motion to vacate the closure order. This time it was the trial itself that was closed. The closure order was upheld by the highest state court.

According to Chief Justice Burger at the postargument conference, the fact that the case involved the trial and not a pretrial proceeding differentiated this case from *Gannett.* Hence, he began his presentation, "*Gannett* didn't decide this case." The Chief Justice noted that open trials were always the practice in our system. "The assumption has been that trials must be public. They were taken for granted from 1787 to 1791" — that is, from the drafting of the Constitution to the ratification of the Bill of Rights. "There's a common thread for public trials." But that still left the question: "What's the constitutional handle?"

The Chief Justice's answer was different from that given by the other Justices. "I'm not persuaded," Burger said, "it's in the First Amendment either as an access right or an associational right." Then the Chief Justice indicated the constitutional approach he would favor, "I would rely on the fact it was part of judicial procedure before adoption of the Bill of Rights. The Ninth Amendment is as good a handle as any."

Had the Burger suggestion of reliance on the Ninth Amendment ("The enumeration in the Constitution, of certain rights, shall not be construed to deny or disparage others retained by the people") been followed, *Richmond Newspapers* might have become a leading case in the revival of what used to be termed "the forgotten amendment." But the Chief Justice's suggestion was not supported by the others and the Burger *Richmond Newspapers* opinion does not discuss the Ninth Amendment beyond a brief reference in a footnote.

Justice Rehnquist, who alone spoke for affirmance, asserted, "There are tensions between *Gannett* and this case." The others (with the exception of Justice Powell, who did not participate) all agreed with the Chief Justice that *Gannett* did not apply and that the lower court decision in *Richmond Newspapers* should be reversed. At the argument, Professor Lawrence Tribe, speaking for the newspaper, had relied on the Sixth as well as the First Amendment, despite the categorical *Gannett* restriction of the public trial guaranty's scope. Justice White alone said that the Court "might get some mileage out of the Sixth." The others who spoke on the matter agreed with Justice Stewart when he said, "Tribe's Sixth Amendment argument is not appealing."

Instead, the others relied upon the First Amendment to support the right of access. Once again, their view was best expressed by Justice Stewart, who pointed out, "The Sixth was resolved against public trials in *Gannett*. The press has no right superior to the public of access to institutions like prisons which are traditionally closed." On the other hand, Justice Stewart recognized, "trials have been open traditionally subject to time, place, and manner regulations." The Justice concluded that the First Amendment furnished the basis for a reversal. "I agree there is a First Amendment right, subject to the overriding interest in a fair trial."

The ultimate conference conclusion was, as stated by Justice Stevens, that "the First Amendment protected some right of access. . . . I'd be prepared to hold that, in the absence of any rational basis for denying access, the benefits of openness argue for it."

The *Richmond Newspapers* draft opinion of the Court was circulated by Chief Justice Burger. He realized by then that none of the others supported his conference reliance on the Ninth Amendment. Therefore, he wrote in his covering memorandum, "I have refrained from relying on the Ninth Amendment but the discussion of its genesis gives at least 'lateral support' to the central theme." The discussion referred to was relegated to a footnote in the Burger opinion. Even so, Justice White wrote to the Chief Justice "that as I see it, your invocation of the Ninth Amendment is unnecessary, and in any event, it may be that I shall disassociate myself from that portion of the opinion." There were also animadversions against the Burger reference to the Ninth Amendment in the opinions issued by Justices Blackmun and Rehnquist.

The White letter also repeated the Justice's preference for the Sixth Amendment approach, "Although I thought, and still do, that the Sixth Amendment is the preferable approach to the issue of public access to both pretrial and trial proceedings, particularly the latter, it does not appear that the Conference is prepared to proceed on this basis." Because of this, Justice White went on, "I join your opinion based on the First Amendment and would expect to stay hitched if three or more Justices in addition to myself join your opinion. If there is a Court only for the judgment, I may leave you and say my own piece."

As it turned out, the Burger opinion could attract only two others (Justices White and Stevens). Except for Justice Rehnquist, who dissented, the others issued separate opinions concurring in the judgment. This included Justice White, who wrote a short concurrence pointing out that the *Richmond Newspapers* case would have been unnecessary, had *Gannett* ruled that the Sixth Amendment gave the public and the press a right of access to criminal proceedings — that is, the approach taken in Justice Blackmun's draft *Gannett* opinion of the Court. That approach would also have answered the question still left open by *Richmond Newspapers* — whether the First Amendment right of access recognized by the decision there is limited to trials or extends to pretrial proceedings, such as that closed in *Gannett.*

The opinions in *Richmond Newspapers* — both the plurality opinion of the Chief Justice and the concurring opinions of Justices Stevens, Brennan, Stewart, and Blackmun — followed the Stewart conference approach. The Court squarely held that access to court proceedings is protected by the First Amendment. This is a more satisfactory basis for decision than the Sixth Amendment route followed in the Blackmun *Gannett* draft.

We can end our discussion of *Richmond Newspapers* with a human-interest touch. In his *Richmond Newspapers* concurrence, Justice Brennan stated that the First Amendment plays a structural role in securing and fostering our system of self-government. "Implicit in this structural role is . . . the antecedent assumption that valuable public debate — as well as other civil behavior — must be informed." In a recirculation of his opinion, Justice Brennan added a new footnote 3, "This idea has been foreshadowed in Mr. Justice Powell's dissent in [another case]" and quoted a paragraph from the Powell opinion.

Justice Powell was so pleased by this that he sent a written note to Brennan:

June 6th

Dear Bill,

Thank you so much for your new Note 3 in Richmond Newspapers. You are a scholar and a gentleman — and a generous one!

Lewis

Even after *Richmond Newspapers*, many assumed that the case held only that the First Amendment guaranteed access to trials, not to the *Gannett* type of pretrial proceedings. A case decided during the last Burger term — *Press-Enterprise Co. v. Superior Court* (1986) — dealt specifically with a closed preliminary hearing in a California murder case. A newspaper sued to have the transcript of the proceedings released. The state court held that there was no First Amendment right of access to preliminary hearings.

At the *Press-Enterprise* conference, Justice Brennan delivered the strongest statement in favor of reversal, saying "that there is a First Amendment right of public access to judicial proceedings" because "at its core, the First Amendment protects public debate about how government operates. The ultimate reason for protecting such speech is to facilitate the process of self-governance. . . . the right to speak necessarily includes a corollary right to obtain the information necessary to speak; in other words, a 'right to know.' "

Justice Brennan asserted that a right of access would not mean the "parade of horribles" urged by the state. It would not mean access to grand jury proceedings or police interrogations, which "must be private to work effectively. In fact, a First Amendment right of access is appropriate for only a very few government functions. Other than judicial proceedings, the only candidates I can think of are legislative debates and perhaps administrative hearings."

The Brennan conference conclusion was, "it is clear that there is a right of public access to preliminary hearings." That was true, in the Justice's view, because "The same considerations that led to the results in our earlier cases apply here with equal force. Historically, preliminary hearings have been open to the public in the same way and for the same reasons as trials. . . . the preliminary hearing serves exactly the same sort of 'public show' purposes as the trial."

The crucial Brennan point was that "the preliminary hearing is really a part of the 'trial' for purposes of the right of public access. It is part of the state's official proceedings for dealing with criminals, part of the public show that — like the trial — reveals how we treat criminals. Consequently, the importance of public access in fulfilling the purposes of preliminary hearings and the public's need to be able to attend such hearings are the same as for the trial."

The *Press-Enterprise* decision held that the First Amendment right of access to criminal proceedings applied to the preliminary hearing in the California criminal case. The same is presumably true of other pretrial proceedings, such as that in *Gannett*. But Chief Justice Burger's *Press-Enterprise* opinion was not as forthright as one would have wished. The opinion stressed that the right of access applied to California, where there had been a tradition of public accessibility. There may be an implication that the same result might not be reached in a case from another state. Thus the question raised by *Richmond Newspapers* may not have been unqualifiedly answered in favor of a First Amendment right of access.

Television in the Courtroom

There is no doubt about how Earl Warren felt about television in the courtroom. After Fred W. Friendly had been appointed President of CBS News, he met the Chief Justice at a 1964 cocktail party. Warren wished Friendly well in his new job. In thanking the Chief Justice, Friendly said he hoped he would still head CBS News when they had television cameras on the moon and on the floor of the Supreme Court. Warren responded with a smile, "Good luck! You will have more luck with the former than the latter."

Later that year, the Chief Justice turned down a CBS request to televise the Supreme Court arguments. Warren wrote that "the Court has had an inflexible rule to the effect that it will not permit photographs or broadcasting from the courtroom when it is in session." The Chief Justice was sure that the Court "has no intention of changing that rule."

Chief Justice Warren believed even more strongly that television had no legitimate place in a criminal trial. To allow televising of criminal proceedings, he declared in an unissued draft dissent in *Estes v. Texas* (1965), means "allowing the courtroom to become a public spectacle and source of entertainment."

Estes itself was the first Supreme Court case involving the television-in-the-courtroom issue. At that time, only two states (Texas and Colorado) allowed television cameras in the courtroom, and both the federal rules and the American Bar Association Canons of Judicial Ethics excluded them. The *Estes* trial was notorious and received national attention. Defendant moved to exclude television and other cameras. A two-day hearing on the motion was itself televised. Twelve cameramen jostled for position in the courtroom. Their activities, even Justice Stewart's dissent concedes, "led to considerable disruption of the hearings." For the trial itself, a booth was constructed at the rear of the courtroom, to televise the proceedings. The Texas courts rejected defendant's claim that the televised hearing and trial had deprived him of due process.

To Chief Justice Warren, the *Estes* issue was not difficult.

The very idea of televised trials was repulsive to him. If they are permitted, he told his law clerk, "we turn back the clock and make everyone in the courtroom an actor before untold millions of people. We are asked again to make the determination of guilt or innocence a public spectacle and a source of entertainment for the idle and curious."

The Chief Justice recalled for his clerk how "The American people were shocked and horrified when Premier Castro tried certain defendants in a stadium." The same thing could happen here, Warren warned his clerk, "[I]f our courts must be opened to the pervasive influence of the television camera in order to accommodate the wishes of the news media, it is but a short step to holding court in a municipal auditorium, to accommodate them even more. As public interest increases in a particular trial, perhaps it will be moved from the courtroom to the municipal auditorium and from the auditorium to the baseball stadium."

The presence of the television camera, the Chief Justice asserted in his remarks to his clerk, meant that all in the courtroom would act differently. "To the extent that television has such an inevitable impact, it deprives the courtroom of the dignity and objectivity that is so essential for determining the guilt or innocence of persons whose life and liberty hinge on the outcome of the trial." Feeling the way he did, it is hardly surprising that Chief Justice Warren led the case against televised trials at the *Estes* conference.

"I think," he declared, "this violates due process. To stage a trial this way violates the decorum of the courtroom, and TV is not entitled to special treatment." Warren rejected any First Amendment claim the other way, saying he could "see no violation of [freedom of] speech or press. They may be in the courtroom, like the press, only as part of the public. The way this is set up bears on the question of fair trial." The Chief Justice went far toward excluding television in all circumstances. "Here," he noted, "there was objection. But even with the consent of the accused and his lawyers, I'd be against it."

Warren was supported by Justices Douglas, Harlan, and Goldberg. "The constitutional standard," Douglas pointed out, "is a fair trial. Trial in a mob scene is not a fair trial." Here, Douglas referred to the 1936 case of *Brown v. Mississippi*, where the Court had reversed convictions because of mob violence. He said, "that was a judgment not hinged to any particular specific." Douglas seconded the Chief Justice in his objection to televised trials. "A trial," he observed, "is not a spectacle, whether he objected or not. This is the modern farce — putting the courtroom into a modern theatrical production."

Justice Harlan said that the case "comes down to the concept of what is the right to a public trial. It doesn't mean for me that the public has the right to a public performance. This goes more deeply into the judicial process than just the right of the defendant." Justice Goldberg asserted that "the shambles deprived defendant of a fair trial. In the present state of the art, this was an obtrusive intervention of the outside into this trial."

Justices Clark, Stewart, and White opposed a flat ban on television in the courtroom. Clark stressed that the trial judge's finding that no prejudice had been shown was not clearly erroneous. The Justice had tried to avoid the constitutional issue by moving to dismiss the case as one in which certiorari had been improvidently granted. In a later memorandum, Clark noted, "not mustering any other votes for this disposition I then voted to affirm on the narrow basis of the facts, *i.e.*, the pretrial televising of September 23-24 indicated no prejudice; the trial on the merits in October was telecast piecemeal — only picture, for the most part, without sound; the jury was sequestered and no prejudice was shown."

Justice Brennan was not as certain in his presentation. "What," he asked, "is the concept of a fair trial? Is there a court concept independent of the individual?" He pointed out that "technology may bring this into line within the courtroom." He then referred to the trial "as theatre or spectacle that's been part of our heritage," as well as to a "legislative inquisition," and asked about them, in light of this case. The Justice stressed that "this was no sham. The jury was sequestered. There's no suggestion that the witnesses, the judge, or others were affected in a way to hurt." Brennan conceded that, in such a case, "the totality [of circumstances] might knock it down," but said that was not the case here.

Justice Black, who had spoken after Chief Justice Warren, indicated even greater doubt. As a starting point, he said, "I'm against television in courts. But this is a new thing that's working itself out." Black conceded that the case presented difficulties for his normal constitutional approach. "For me," he affirmed, "the test is, 'what is in the Constitution on which I can grasp as a handle?' On lawyers, confrontation, etc., I have no problem. I can't do this on how bad it is short of the *Brown* [*v. Mississippi*] test." Justice Black concluded that "the case for me comes down to only a slight advance over what we've had before." He also noted that, "some day the technology may improve so as not to disturb the actual trial." But, even with the disturbance involved in Estes' trial, Black ultimately came down on the side of affirmance. The *Estes* conference vote was for affirmance by a bare majority consisting of Justices Black, Clark,

Stewart, Brennan, and White.

The senior member of the conference majority, Justice Black, assigned the case to Justice Stewart. He circulated a draft opinion of the Court that would have affirmed the decision below holding that the televising of the *Estes* trial did not involve any constitutional violation. If the draft had come down as the *Estes* opinion, it would have adopted the reasoning of the ultimate Stewart dissent as that of the Court and substantially changed the legal picture with regard to TV in the courtroom.

The Stewart draft rejected the claim that the introduction of cameras into a criminal trial, over defendant's objection, violates the Fourteenth Amendment. "On the record of the case," the draft stated, "we cannot say that any violation of the Constitution occurred." It pointed (much as Stewart's final dissent does) to the facts, saying that, while the situation during the pretrial hearing was plainly disruptive, there was nothing to indicate that the conduct of anyone in the courtroom during the trial was influenced by the television.

This meant, according to Justice Stewart, that the Court was "presented with virtually an abstract question. We are asked to pronounce that the United States Constitution prohibits all television cameras and all still cameras from every courtroom in every State whenever a criminal trial is in progress.... We are asked to hold that the Constitution absolutely bars television and cameras from every criminal courtroom, even if they have no impact upon any witness, and no influence upon the conduct of the judge." This, the Stewart draft concluded, the Court could not do and the judgment below was affirmed.

Justice Stewart's draft made an important point not contained in his *Estes* dissent. The draft stated that a majority of the Court believed that the demands of TV and other photographers to set up their equipment in a courtroom and portray or broadcast a trial "are not protected by any valid First Amendment claim."

In his *Estes* dissent, not only did Justice Stewart delete this rejection of the First Amendment claim, but he also included an intimation that the First Amendment did support the right of the press to be in the courtroom. The Stewart dissent declares, "The idea of imposing upon any medium of communications the burden of justifying its presence is contrary to where I had always thought the presumption must lie in the area of First Amendment freedoms." This First Amendment presumption was rejected in the *Estes* opinion of the Court ultimately delivered by Justice Clark. It was, however, the basis for the more recent decision in *Richmond Newspapers v. Virginia*. One may wonder what effect the original rejection of the

First Amendment claim in the Stewart *Estes* draft would have had on the recent law, culminating in *Richmond Newspapers*, if the Stewart draft had been issued as the final *Estes* opinion of the Court.

If nothing more had occurred in the Court's deliberative process, the Stewart draft would have become the *Estes* opinion of the Court. That would have drastically changed the law on the subject. The Court's imprimatur might well have led to the widespread televising of trials two decades before that practice was to become common. That was not to happen, however, as the bare majority for affirmance in *Estes* did not hold. The crucial shift was by Justice Clark. That the Chief Justice himself played a key part in the Clark switch cannot be doubted. As seen, Warren felt strongly about the baneful effect of television on court proceedings, and this was just the sort of thing he would talk over with Clark on their morning walks part of the way to the Court building.

Almost two months after he had voted for affirmance at the *Estes* conference, Justice Clark circulated a *Memorandum to the Conference* telling of his change in position. "After circulation of the opinions and dissents, along with my interim study," Clark informed the Justices, "I became disturbed at what could result from our approval of the emasculation by TV of the trial of a case. My doubts increased as I envisioned use of the unfortunate format followed here in other trials which would not only jeopardize the fairness of them but would broadcast a bad image to the public of the judicial process."

"It appears to me," the Clark memo stated, "that the perils to a fair trial far outweigh the benefits that might accrue in the televising of the proceedings." Clark then enumerated the factors that made him conclude "simply that such an operation, at least in its present state, presents too many hazards to a fair trial." Clark's list is the most complete statement by a Supreme Court Justice of the undesirable elements that would be introduced by televising of trials and, for that reason, deserves quotation in full:

> 1. The quality of the testimony would be impaired because of the confusion of the witness caused by the knowledge of being televised; accuracy would be jeopardized; memories would fail because of stage fright; self-consciousness would be uppermost because of the knowledge that millions were watching every expression and gesture; and witnesses would evade appearance in order to avoid the attendant embarrassment and torture.
> 2. The intermittent selection by the telecaster of the parts of testimony to be telecast would not portray a fair image of the trial; a distorted picture of the case would result and our present problem in newspaper reporting would be compounded. The entire proceeding could not be telecast from a

profitable commercial standpoint; telecasting is expensive, particularly outside of the studio and video tape together with the clipping of it to show only the most publicly appealing parts of the trial would result.

3. The accused is placed in a helplessly precarious position. He unwillingly, despite his constitutional protections, becomes a victim of the continual glare of the close range lens of the camera revealing his most intimate and personal sensibilities. Such a psychological torture is reminiscent of the third degree. In addition, the accused must risk being mugged, lip read and otherwise overheard when in consultation over his defense with his lawyer at the counsel table.

4. The camera is an all powerful weapon. It may leave, intentionally or not, a distorted impression of the facts with consequent prejudgment of the witness that may be most damaging to the defense.

5. Many states do not sequester the juries in all felony cases and the additional hazard of jury misconduct in viewing the telecast would be present.

6. Witnesses placed under the rule would be able to view the telecast and contrary to the rule would be advantaged by the testimony of previous witnesses.

7. In case of a new trial or reversal being granted it would be impossible to secure a jury that had not witnessed the previous trial thus placing the fairness of the second trial in jeopardy.

8. Telecasting will lead inevitably to discrimination because the media will televise only the horrendous trials. As a result only the most sordid crimes will be telecast or possibly those that appeal to the prurient interest. This will but accumulate a wrongful store of public information as to the courts.

9. The judge and the jury's attention — as well as that of the lawyers — will be distracted from the serious work of the trial. In this case the court was interrupted time and time again on account of the presence of the television and radio media.

10. Commercials would degrade the judicial process, making the court a 'prop' for some product of the sponsor and forcing the parties to become its actors and raise attendant connotations of some connection between the trial participants and the sponsor.

Justice Clark then circulated an opinion embodying his changed view. It was intended as a potential opinion of the Court and, with important changes, was used as the ultimate *Estes* opinion. The Clark draft contains strong language rejecting the claim that the First Amendment gives the press any right to attend trials. The Sixth Amendment, the draft notes, guarantees the accused a public trial. "The Constitution says nothing of any comparable right to the public or to the news media." The draft then refers specifically to the assertion that the First Amendment gives the press, including television, a right of access to the courtroom. According to Justice Clark, "This is a misconception of the right of the press. . . . it is clear beyond question that no language in the First Amendment grants any of the news media such a privilege."

Had this categoric language not been deleted from the final *Estes* opinion of the Court (which stated only that the press was "entitled to the same rights as the general public"), the subsequent law on the press and the First Amendment might have been different — particularly if Justice Stewart had left in the rejection of the press's First Amendment right contained in his original *Estes* draft opinion of the Court. Instead, Justice Stewart inserted a paragraph on the First Amendment right of the press toward the end of his *Estes* dissent. This was put in to answer the refusal in Justice Clark's draft to recognize a constitutional right of the press to be present in the courtroom.

The major difference between the Clark draft and the Clark opinion of the Court in *Estes* was the draft's specific rejection of the state's contention "that the televising of portions of a criminal trial does not constitute *per se* a denial of due process." Toward the end of the draft, there is the flat statement "The facts in this case demonstrate clearly the necessity for the adoption of a *per se* rule" — a statement substantially watered down (with the per se language eliminated) in the final opinion. The draft contains other passages that support the statement of a per se rule, such as the following: "The introduction of television into petitioner's trial constituted a violation of due process regardless of whether there was a showing of isolatable prejudice" (omitted from the *Estes* opinion); "Such untoward circumstances are inherently bad and prejudice to the accused must be presumed" (changed in the final opinion to, "Such untoward circumstances as were found in those cases [four cited Supreme Court decisions] are inherently bad and prejudice to the accused must be presumed"); "In light of the inherent hazards to a fair trial that are presented by television in the courtroom I would hold that its use violated petitioner's right to due process" (the draft's concluding sentence, absent in the published opinion).

One interested in what John Greenleaf Whittier called the "might have been" in Supreme Court jurisprudence has ample cause for speculation in *Estes v. Texas*. If Justice Stewart's original draft opinion of the Court had been the final *Estes* opinion, the law on television in the courtroom would have evolved differently. Instead of the relatively slow development of televised court proceedings that has occurred, *Estes* might have opened the broadcast floodgates. By now, the TV camera might be as common in every courtroom as it is in other areas of American life.

On the other hand, had Justice Clark's draft come down as the *Estes* opinion of the Court, television in the courtroom might have been constitutionally doomed. The Clark draft announced a per se rule, under which TV by its very nature became constitutionally incompatible with the proper conduct of criminal trials. Regardless of the circumstances of the particular case, and any improvements that might be made in TV coverage, any televised trial would, under the Clark draft's rule, automatically violate due process.

After Justice Clark sent around his *Estes* draft, Justice Stewart revised his draft opinion of the Court and circulated it as a dissent. The Stewart draft dissent was intended as an answer to the Clark draft opinion. As such, it began, "If, as I apprehend, the Court today holds that any television of a state criminal trial constitutes a *per se* violation of the Fourteenth Amendment, I cannot agree."

The Stewart draft led Justice Clark to delete the per se references from his final *Estes* opinion, and Justice Stewart in turn removed the sentence just quoted from his *Estes* dissent. The *Estes* opinion of the Court, as it was finally issued, could be characterized in the Stewart dissent as a "decision that the circumstances of this trial led to a denial of the petitioner's Fourteenth Amendment rights."

Justice Harlan issued a concurrence which also stressed that the *Estes* holding was only "that what was done in this case infringed the fundamental right to a fair trial assured by the Due Process Clause." On the other hand, Harlan stressed "that the day may come when television will have become so commonplace an affair in the daily life of the average person as to dissipate all reasonable likelihood that its use in courtrooms may disparage the judicial process. If and when that day arrives the constitutional judgment called for now would of course be subject to re-examination."

Justice Brennan also issued a separate short *Estes* opinion emphasizing that, because of Justice Harlan's concurrence, only four members of the majority held that televised trials would be invalid, regardless of the circumstances. Brennan also joined a White concurrence asserting that the Clark opinion of the Court prevented a flexible approach to use of cameras in the courtroom. In effect, Brennan was having it both ways, joining with White to condemn the majority's inflexible approach and then denying that a majority had really voted for it.

It was, nevertheless, the Brennan approach that the Court followed in *Chandler v. Florida* (1981), which upheld a Florida rule permitting television coverage of criminal trials, notwithstanding the objections of the accused. All the Justices agreed at the conference that the Florida rule did not violate due process, but there was disagreement over whether a holding to that effect could be made without overruling *Estes*. Chief Justice Burger pointed out that "this is like *Estes* in some respects. No prejudice is shown in either case and both were notorious cases." The basic question was: "Should the states be left to experiment? I think so, in general." On the other hand, "Anything that endangers a fair trial is suspect and must be justified on some ground." Burger concluded his presentation by stating that he agreed with Justice Harlan. According to Burger, Harlan's *Estes* concurrence had denied that the decision there categorically prohibited any televised trials.

As Justice Stewart saw it, *Chandler* was "indistinguishable from *Estes* which I'd overrule and affirm." Justice White was less categorical, saying, "I think [we] have to chop up *Estes* some to affirm, but I'd do that." Justice Marshall, on the other hand, stated, "I'd leave *Estes* alone"; and Justice Blackmun said, "I don't think this is *Estes*."

Justice Powell indicated that he was troubled by televised trials and that there was "a substantial per se argument that ought to exclude TV from the courtroom." At the same time, "*Estes* can be read as you want. I'd leave it on the books and follow John Harlan's notion that TV is part of everyday life, like it or not."

In his *Estes* dissent, we saw, Justice Stewart had deleted the statement that "the Court today holds that any television of a state criminal trial constitutes a *per se* violation of the Fourteenth Amendment." In *Chandler*, however, Stewart asserted "that *Estes* announced a *per se* rule." He said that a decision for the Florida rule would require the overruling of *Estes* and "I would now flatly overrule it." The majority agreed with the Chief Justice and Justice Powell, and their position was stated by Justice Blackmun, who wrote to Burger, "I share your reading of *Estes*."

The *Chandler* opinion of the Court was based upon a laborious effort to distinguish *Estes*, rather than overrule it. The *Chandler* opinion relies on Harlan's *Estes* concurrence to show that the statement of a per se rule in the Clark opinion of the Court received the support of only a plurality of four Justices. Yet the final Clark *Estes* opinion, as we saw, did not announce a per se rule. And Justice Harlan, in his *Estes* concurrence, did no more than stress what should have been obvious once Justice Clark deleted the per se references from his draft — namely, that the *Estes* decision held that the televised trial deprived defendant of due process under the "facts in this case." Despite the contrary assumption in the *Chandler* opinion, the Harlan *Estes* concurrence was not issued to demonstrate Harlan's refusal to subscribe to a per se rule, since the *Estes* opinion of the Court stated no such rule. Instead, Harlan was only stressing that, in an area of such rapid technological change, the decision was based upon "television as we find it in this trial."

In these circumstances, whether the Burger or Stewart view on *Estes* was correct may be irrelevant. As Justice Blackmun said in a "Dear Chief" letter, "I am not really sure that the ultimate disposition of *Estes v. Texas* by way of overruling it or not overruling it, is very important. Whether overruled or not, *Estes* now certainly fades into the background."

In practice, *Chandler* has served as a virtual green light for television in the courtroom. In the decade since *Chandler*, cameras have proliferated in courts throughout the nation. Such a result would, of course, have dismayed Chief Justice Warren and probably most of the Justices who sat with him.

Chief Justice Burger may have written the *Chandler* opinion. Yet he himself was far from approving television in every case. "For me," he wrote to Justice Stewart, "there *may be* a risk of due process and equal protection violations in putting a few out of thousands of trials on TV or in a 'Yankee Stadium' setting." Indeed, when a network asked permission to carry live coverage of the arguments in what promised to be a landmark case, Chief Justice Burger replied with a one-sentence letter: "It is not possible to arrange for any broadcast of any Supreme Court proceeding." Handwritten at the bottom was a postscript: "When you get the Cabinet meetings on the air, call me!"

The other *Chandler* Justices were also troubled at the notion of TV in every courtroom. Justice Powell wrote in a letter of the "enduring concern . . . that the presence of the camera may impair the fairness of a trial, but not leave evidence of specific prejudice." Powell suggested that the *Chandler* opinion should be "clear as to the protection that the Constitution affords a defendant who objects to his trial being televised . . . . I am inclined to think it desirable that we make explicit that the defendant who makes a timely motion to exclude the cameras, and alleges specific harms that he fears will occur, is entitled as a matter of right to a hearing."

There was a general uneasiness at what Justice Blackmun called "the risk of adverse psychological impact on various trial participants." In criminal trials, Blackmun wrote in a letter to Chief Justice Burger, "any type of media coverage is capable of creating an impression of guilt or innocence. Assuming *arguendo* that more people are likely to watch the news than read about it, the incremental risk of juror prejudice seems to me a difference in degree rather than kind."

Press Privileges

The general principle, we shall see in Chapter 4, is that the press is not exempt from laws that reach equally other persons and businesses. Only where a governmental act impinges upon the operation of the press in an unequal manner does it run afoul of the First Amendment.

The press has, however, urged that the First Amendment gives it privileges which are not available to other persons. A corollary of the right to publish, it is claimed, is the right to gather news. Informants are necessary to the news gathering process. Many of them would be unwilling to provide information if their confidentiality could not be assured. Nondisclosure is necessary for most investigative news gathering. Hence, Justice Stewart argued in the *Branzburg* case (discussed in the next paragraph), "The right to gather news implies, in turn, a right to a confidential relationship between a reporter and his source." Forcing reporters to reveal their sources would violate the so-called reporter's privilege which, the press has claimed, is implicit in the First Amendment.

The reporter's privilege was, however, put to the constitutional test and found wanting in *Branzburg v. Hayes* (1972). It arose out of three cases in which reporters had refused to reveal their sources for stories involving alleged criminal activities. In the lead case, Branzburg, a *Louisville Courier-Journal* reporter, had written articles describing his interviews with drug dealers in Kentucky. He refused to testify about those he had interviewed before grand juries investigating drug use and sales. He made the argument already summarized: To gather news, he had to protect his sources; otherwise, the sources would not furnish information, to the detriment of the free flow of information protected by the First Amendment.

At the *Branzburg* conference, Chief Justice Burger declared, "I reject categorically the suggestion that this is a specific constitutional right." He didn't "think anyone except the President of the U.S." was immune from a grand jury subpoena. "They must appear."

Justice White, who wrote the opinion, agreed. "Presently, I don't think I'd establish any privilege at all. . . . I would not in any event allow a privilege to the extent of keeping confidential what [he] has seen as [an] actual crime."

Justices Blackmun, Powell, and Rehnquist agreed with the Burger-White view. "It would be unwise," said Justice Powell, "to give the press any constitutional privilege and we're writing on a clean slate, so we don't have to give constitutional status to newsmen. I'd leave it to the legislatures to create one."

The other four favored the claimed privilege, though Justice Marshall did state, "I think the press exaggerates the importance of [confidentiality]." The dissenters asserted the view that, as Justice Stewart expressed it, "The First Amendment requires some kind of qualified privilege for confidences to reporters." Justice Douglas based his vote for the reporters on a different theory. "The Ninth Amendment," he said, "stated the proper constitutional rule. It's in the realm of items of association, belief, etc."

The *Branzburg* decision, reflecting the conference division, ruled against the reporter's privilege by a bare majority. The White opinion of the Court stated the issue narrowly: "The sole issue before us is the obligation of reporters to respond to grand jury subpoenas as other citizens do and to answer questions relevant to an investigation into the commission of crime." The Court held that reporters have the same obligation as other citizens to respond to grand jury subpoenas. The public interest in the investigation of crimes outweighs whatever interest there may be in protecting sources.

Nor was the Court convinced that the failure to recognize the privilege would unduly chill the First Amendment right to gather news. According to Justice White's opinion, "this is not the lesson history teaches us. From the beginning of our country the press has operated without constitutional protection for press informants, and the press has flourished." The lack of privilege has thus not been a serious obstacle to the gathering of news based upon confidential sources.

In addition, there is the point made by Chief Justice Burger in his already quoted letter to Justice Stewart in the *Houchins* case: If a reporter's privilege is recognized, who would be entitled to claim it? "Sooner or later," states the *Branzburg* opinion, "it would be necessary to define those categories of newsmen who qualified for the privilege, a questionable procedure in light of the traditional doctrine that liberty of the press is the right of the lonely pamphleteer who uses carbon paper or a mimeograph just as much as of the large metropolitan publisher who utilizes the latest photocomposition methods." After all, as Justice Rehnquist asked during the conference on another case, "Why, should only *Time* and the *New York Times* have First Amendment protection?"

The *Branzburg* approach was applied in *Zurcher v. Stanford Daily* (1978) to a search warrant based upon probable cause to search a newspaper office for evidence of crimes committed by other persons. It was argued that whatever might be true of third-party searches generally, where the third party was a newspaper, there were additional factors derived from the First Amendment that justified a nearly per se rule forbidding the search warrant. The Court rejected the argument. Warrants may be subjected to restraints under the Fourth Amendment. But there are no additional limitations where the press is concerned. Like other persons, the press is subject to properly issued warrants. With a warrant, indeed, any business may be searched, even, as in *Zurcher*, for evidence of third-party criminality.

Thus, in refusing to accept the newspaper's *Zurcher* claim, the Court treated the case as a virtual *Branzburg* reprise. The Fourth Amendment's warrant requirements must, of course, be complied with in every search case. Yet, "As we see it, no more than this is required where the warrant requested is for the seizure of criminal evidence reasonably believed to be on the premises occupied by a newspaper."

Whether or not we agree with the result in the cases discussed in this chapter, we must conclude that they do make for a consistent corpus on the subject, governed by the principle stated by Chief Justice Warren when he was discussing the *Estes* case with his law clerk — that whatever right the press has of access to news it possesses "not because it is the press, but because it is part of the public." Under a case like *Houchins*, the press does not possess a constitutional right of access to information not available to the public generally; under *Branzburg* and *Zurcher* it does not have any immunity from grand jury subpoenas or search warrants not possessed by other citizens.

3

Sedition, Incitement, and Contempt

In its early years, freedom of the press under the First Amendment was interpreted as a restatement of the already-quoted rule in Blackstone: "The liberty of the press . . . consists in laying no previous restraints upon publications and not freedom from censure for criminal matter when published. Every freeman has an undoubted right to lay what sentiments he pleases before the public; to forbid this, is to destroy the freedom of the press; but if he publishes what is improper, mischievous or illegal, he must take the consequence of his own temerity."

At the very beginning, Justice Iredell stated that freedom of the press as defined in the First Amendment was "no where more happily or justly expressed than by" Blackstone. Even so ardent a disciple of liberty as Thomas Paine took the same position. In an 1806 article, *Liberty of the Press*, Paine wrote, "the term . . . refers to the fact of printing free from prior restraint, and not at all to the matter printed. . . . he becomes answerable afterwards for the atrocities he may utter."

It is, however, all but self-evident that freedom of the press would be without real substance if it meant only freedom from the licensor and the censor. "It would," as Madison asserted, "seem a mockery to say that no laws should be passed preventing publications from being made, but laws might be passed for punishing them in case they should be made." A law inflicting penalties may have the same chilling effect as one authorizing a prior restraint. As a Congressman put it during the debate on the 1798 Sedition Act, because of fear of punishment printers "would not only refrain from publishing anything of the least questionable nature, but they would be afraid of publishing the truth, as, though true, it might not always be in their power to establish the truth to the satisfaction of a court of justice."

During the same debate, Albert Gallatin asserted, "It appeared to him preposterous to say, that to punish a certain act was not an abridgement of the liberty of doing that act." For Gallatin, the

First Amendment prohibition against abridgement of freedom of the press "must necessarily mean . . . that no punishment should by law be inflicted upon it."

During this century, the Supreme Court came to agree with the Gallatin view. In the 1907 *Patterson* case (to be discussed later in this chapter) Justice Oliver Wendell Holmes had stated categorically that the purpose of the First Amendment and similar state constitutional provisions "is to prevent all such *previous restraints* upon publications . . . and they do not prevent the subsequent punishment of such as may be deemed contrary to the public welfare." Nor, in the Holmes interpretation of what he saw as the governing rule, did it matter whether what the press published was true or false. According to his typically aphoristic statement, "The preliminary freedom extends as well to the false as to the true; the subsequent punishment may extend as well to the true as to the false."

Justice Holmes soon came to see that his early view on the matter was inconsistent with the true meaning of the First Amendment. In a 1922 letter, Holmes confessed, "in the earlier Paterson [sic] case, if that was the name of it, I had taken Blackstone . . . as unrefuted, wrongly. I simply was ignorant." By then Holmes had come to recognize that the First Amendment is more than a mere restatement of the English law against only prior restraints as summarized in Blackstone. Instead, as Holmes pithily summarized it in a 1919 First Amendment opinion, "the prohibition of laws abridging the freedom of speech [and press] is not confined to previous restraints."

Sedition Law

It may well be that, as Justice Black said in his James Madison lecture, "It was the desire to give the people of America greater protection against the powerful Federal Government than the English had had against their government that caused the Framers to put these freedoms of expression beyond the reach of this Government." In the beginning, however, the First Amendment was not interpreted that way — but only, we have stressed, as the elevation of the Blackstone definition of freedom of the press to the constitutional plane. That is the only way we can explain the passage by Congress of the Sedition Act of 1798 and its vigorous enforcement by the federal courts. To the jurists of the day, even such a law posed no First Amendment problem, since it did not impose any prior restraints upon speech or the press.

The Sedition Act, the Supreme Court told us in 1964, "first crystallized a national awareness of the central meaning of the First Amendment." It was passed by a Congress confronted with the threat of war with France and badly frightened by the seeming spread of the Revolutionary doctrines then emanating from France — facts that have a familiar sound two centuries later. The Sedition Act criminally punished those publishing false, scandalous, or defamatory writings with an intent to discredit the Government, the President, or the Congress or to excite the hatred of the people against them or to stir up sedition, to excite resistance to law, or to aid any hostile designs of any foreign nation against the United States.

In the year or two after its adoption, the Sedition Act was vigorously enforced by the Federalist Party then in power. The lengths to which such enforcement went are well shown by cases like the following: A Vermont Congressman, who accused the President of "unbounded thirst for ridiculous pomp, foolish adulation, and a selfish avarice," was punished by a thousand dollar fine and four months in jail. When President Adams visited Newark, New Jersey, an artillery company fired a salute. One of the observers casually remarked that "he wished the wadding from the cannon had been lodged in the President's backside." For this "seditious" remark he was fined one hundred dollars.

Among the most striking cases were those in which the Sedition Act was applied directly to the press. Two editors who had criticized the President and Administration — one had written in his paper that Adams was "in the infancy of political mistake" and had "interfered . . . to influence the decision of a court of justice" — were sentenced to imprisonment and fines.

Perhaps the best known press case was the trial of James T. Callender, a prominent journalist who had written *The Prospect Before Us* with Jefferson's encouragement. The pamphlet was a bitter attack upon President Adams, charging that his "reign . . . has been one continued tempest of malignant passions," that "he was a professed aristocrat," "faithful to the British interest," "whose hands are reeking with the blood." The judicial approach in such a case is shown by the statement of Justice Samuel Chase, who presided at the trial: "The indictment charges the defendant with publishing a false, scandalous and malicious writing against the President, and the law provides against the publication of false, scandalous and malicious writing against the President. The offences stated in the indictment correspond with those expressed in the law." The only question for the jury was thus whether Callender had published the pamphlet. Since there was no doubt about that, he was convicted and sentenced to nine months imprisonment and a two hundred dollar fine.

The Sedition Act was bitterly resented by most Americans as an unwarranted invasion of freedom of expression. Its constitutionality was strongly assailed by Jefferson, who pardoned all persons imprisoned under it when he became President in 1800. Congress eventually ordered all fines to be repaid, and the law itself was permitted to expire in 1801, though, in the words of Justice Story, "It has continued, down to this very day, to be a theme of reproach."

The Sedition Act itself was never tested in the Supreme Court. However, in the 1964 case of *New York Times Co. v. Sullivan* (to be discussed in detail in Chapter 6), the Court went out of its way to state specifically that the law of sedition must now be considered inconsistent with the First Amendment: "For good reason, 'no court of last resort in this country has ever held, or even suggested, that prosecutions for libel on government have any place in the American system of jurisprudence.'"

For the first time (over a century and a half after that ill-fated law itself was enacted), the Supreme Court ruled squarely on the constitutionality of the 1798 Sedition Act: "Although the Sedition Act was never tested in this Court, the attack upon its validity has carried the day in the court of history . . . . the Act, because of the restraint it imposed upon criticism of government and public officials, was inconsistent with the First Amendment."

Under *New York Times Co. v. Sullivan*, it can be stated categorically that prosecutions for libel on government are out of place in our constitutional system. That is true whether the particular libel is on government as such or on the official conduct of the governors, i.e., the individuals who, for the time being, make up the government. One may go further and say that, where prosecutions for seditious libel are concerned, the possible existence of malice (which, we shall see in Chapter 6, is the one exception to the rule of civil immunity for statements defaming public officials laid down in *New York Times*) should be irrelevant. The very notion of defamation of government is utterly inconsistent with the First Amendment. To attach criminal consequences to any such defamation is to permit the common law of seditious libel to continue in our system.

Criminal Libel

To one who agrees with Justice Holmes in his disagreement in his *Abrams* dissent (which will be discussed later) "with the argument . . . that the First Amendment left the common law as to seditious libel in force," *Garrison v. Louisiana* (1964) is a troubling case.

Garrison was the New Orleans District Attorney. During a dispute with the criminal court judges, he issued a statement disparaging their judicial conduct. As a result, he was convicted of criminal defamation. The conviction was based upon his attribution of a large backlog of pending cases to the inefficiency, laziness, and excessive vacations of the judges and his accusation that the judges had hampered his efforts to enforce the vice laws. "This raises interesting questions," Garrison asserted, "about the racketeer influences on our eight vacation-minded judges." The state court rejected the claim that the Louisiana Criminal Defamation Law violated Garrison's freedom of expression.

The Supreme Court majority voted to reverse, and the opinion was assigned to Justice Brennan. His sixteen-page draft opinion held that criminal libel prosecutions such as that against Garrison violated the First Amendment: "criminal statutes punishing speech which merely censures government or government officials cannot survive the constitutional test. . . . Our Constitution flatly bars criminal prosecutions based on the mere criticism of public men for their public conduct."

The Brennan draft's broadside approach was unable to secure a majority. Justices Black and Douglas concurred in the reversal on their usual absolutist ground, rejecting any libel suit, criminal as well as civil, against a public official. Justice Clark circulated a dissent, joined by Justice Harlan, as did Justice White. As summarized in a June 1964 letter from Harlan to Clark, White's draft opinion, "although upholding Louisiana's right to enforce its criminal libel laws, argues that this case be remanded because the conviction was not based on a finding that the false defamatory statements were made with 'reckless disregard' of their accuracy. According to that view, it is constitutionally permissible to punish reckless defamation but impermissible to punish defamation when . . . it is prompted by 'actual malice,' defined as 'hatred, ill will or a wanton desire to injure.' "

The separate Black, Douglas, Clark-Harlan, and White opinions meant that there were only four (Chief Justice Warren, and Justices Stewart, Goldberg, and of course, Brennan) for the position taken in Justice Brennan's draft opinion. Late in the term, Justice Stewart indicated that he was wavering. In these circumstances, the case was set for reargument.

At the conference after the reargument, Chief Justice Warren urged a difference approach. He said that the Court should "use the *Times* standard," and noted that "no actual malice was shown here." Warren also said that the Louisiana statute was "void on its face, since he's liable whether it's true or false if he's guilty of actual malice." He also thought that "these remarks are not defamatory" and could not be the "subject of a prosecution."

Justices Clark, Harlan, Brennan, and Stewart agreed that the Warren standard (actually that of *New York Times Co. v. Sullivan*, which holds that no libel liability occurs without proof that the published statement was known to be false, or made with reckless disregard for the truth — to be discussed in Chapter 6) should be applied. Justice Brennan expanded on Warren's presentation. He said that the conviction could be reversed under the *Times* standard, provided that the peculiar history of criminal libel did not require a different treatment. Justice Brennan concluded that it did not and said that the statute was unconstitutional on its face because it did not meet the *Times* standard by requiring proof that Garrison knew his statement was false or made with reckless disregard for the truth.

Justices Black and Douglas persisted in the view expressed in their draft concurrences of the prior term. Justice Douglas asserted, "we have to go on the ground [that] the statute's void on its face. This is seditious libel. It's out of step with the *Times Case*, since it preserves the cause of action for libel." Justice Goldberg said, "I agree with Bill Douglas," but indicated he would join an opinion along the lines indicated by Justice Brennan.

Justice Brennan then circulated a new draft that held that the *Times* approach applied to criminal, as well as civil, libels. It found the Louisiana statute invalid because, contrary to the *Times* standard, it directed punishment for true statements made with malice and also punished false statements without requiring malice as defined in the *Times* case. The draft indicated that Garrison could not be retried under the statute because under the "vagueness" doctrine the statute was totally unavailable in the area of public libels.

Justices Clark, Harlan, Stewart, and White objected to the latter approach. Because of this and because of the fact that the political situation in Louisiana now made it extremely unlikely that Garrison would be retried, Brennan omitted the portion of the draft that related to a possible retrial. In a memorandum to Justices Clark, Harlan, Stewart, and White, Justice Brennan noted, "from what each of you has said to me . . . your difficulties with my *Garrison v. Louisiana* lie principally with my conclusion that Garrison may not be retried." Brennan wrote, "I have therefore revised my latest circulation as shown on the attached copy to propose that I delete the [offending] material."

Justice Brennan also explained the disposition at the revised opinion's end: "I suggest the simple word 'Reversed' so as to leave it to the State to figure out, without instruction from us, whether or not to try Garrison again. I have sufficient confidence in the correctness of my view that I could not join in anything which said affirmatively that the State is at liberty to retry him."

When Justice Brennan delivered his *Garrison* opinion of the Court, there were no dissents. Only Justices Black, Douglas, and Goldberg issued separate concurrences asserting the view that the First Amendment bars all libel proceedings, criminal or civil, based on criticisms of official conduct.

It is unfortunate that the original Brennan *Garrison* draft could not command a majority. As issued, the *Garrison* opinion of the Court holds only that "the *New York Times* rule also limits state power to impose criminal sanctions for criticism of the official conduct of public officials." That means that there may be no criminal punishment for criticisms of official conduct where such criticisms are truthful, even though truth was no defense at common law in a seditious libel prosecution. The state statute directing punishment for true statements made with "actual malice" was thus invalid; the First Amendment absolutely prohibits punishment of truthful criticism.

The state statute, under which Garrison's conviction had been secured was also ruled invalid as interpreted to cover false statements against public officials. The statute punishes false statements without regard to the *New York Times* standard, which prohibits punishment for false statements, "unless made with knowledge of their falsity or in reckless disregard of whether they are true or false."

There is a troubling implication here that the Constitution permits prosecutions for seditious libels where they are published with malice. Such an exception of malice for the otherwise proscribed offense of seditious libel is unjustified. The critic of government in our system should remain wholly free from the threat of criminal sanctions while he confines his acts to verbal or printed criticism alone. The very notion of criminal prosecution for any criticisms of government strikes at the heart of our system; no matter how we disguise it, the mere possibility of punishment for such criticisms results in what Justice Brandeis once termed "silence coerced by law — the argument of force in its worst form." The Supreme Court itself must ultimately hold, if it is to give true effect to the underlying rationale of the First Amendment, that, in Justice Black's words, "under our Constitution there is absolutely no place in this country for the old, discredited English Star Chamber law of seditious criminal libel."

It should, however, be pointed out that in the field of criminal libel, as in so many other fields, the law in the books and the law in action are two entirely different things. While criminal libel may not have been ruled invalid by *Garrison* and though it still exists as an offense throughout the country, it is fair to say that prosecutions have become increasingly rare. Statistics on the matter tell us, in fact, that the crime has become almost obsolete, at least insofar as the number of cases prosecuted in this century are concerned. Even in New York City, the very center of opinion and communications in the nation, there have been no criminal libel prosecutions in recent years. The situation in this respect has recently been confirmed by *People v. Ryan*, a 1991 Colorado case that strikes down a criminal libel law that reaches libelous statements about public officials.

World War I Sedition Laws

More than a century passed after the Sedition Act of 1798 before the Congress again attempted to place comparable statutory restrictions upon freedom of expression. After this country's entry into the First World War, Congress, in the so-called Espionage and Sedition Acts, rendered criminal such activities as willfully making or conveying false statements with intent to interfere with the success of the American war effort or to promote the success of its enemies, willfully obstructing the recruitment of military personnel or attempting to cause the disloyalty of such personnel, saying or doing anything with intent to obstruct the sale of government bonds, uttering or writing any disloyal, profane, scurrilous, or abusive language to cause contempt, scorn, contumely, or disrepute in regard to the form of government of the United States, the flag, or the uniform of the army or navy, or urging the curtailment of production of anything necessary in the prosecution of the war.

These laws of 1917 and 1918 constituted the first important legislative restrictions of the right of free expression since the 1798 Sedition Act. It may well be, as former Attorney General Francis Biddle once conceded, that, "On its face, the Espionage Act of 1917, under which most of the war cases were tried, does not seem objectionable. *Willfully* false reports with *intent* to interfere with the operation of the war, *willful* attempts to cause insubordination or disloyalty, *willful* obstruction to recruitment or enlistment were punishable." Nevertheless, what was made punishable under it and the Act of 1918 was not only action interfering with the war effort but also speech or writing made with that end in view. Emphasis in the laws was as much upon exhortation as upon action. In this respect, they constituted a legislative attempt to punish incitements to action deemed harmful to the war effort.

Many of the cases enforcing the Espionage Acts appear all but ludicrous today. About two thousand prosecutions were brought under the 1917 law alone, and many of them now seem as ridiculous as the standing of a tanner in the pillory during Queen Anne's reign because of his remark that Charles I had been rightly served in having his head cut off. The cases under the Espionage Acts were summarized in Zechariah Chafee's *Free Speech in the United States*: "It became criminal to advocate heavier taxation instead of bond issues, to state that conscription was unconstitutional though the Supreme Court had not yet held it valid, to say that the sinking of merchant vessels was legal, to say that a referendum should have preceded our declaration of war, to say that war was contrary to the teachings of Christ. Men have been punished for criticizing the Red Cross and the YMCA, while under the Minnesota Espionage Act it has been held a crime to discourage women from knitting by the remark, 'No soldier ever sees these socks.' "

The reductio ad absurdum of the Espionage Act jurisprudence was the conviction of a film producer for presenting a motion picture, titled *The Spirit of '76,* about the American Revolution, because one scene depicted British soldiers shooting and bayoneting women and children and carrying away young girls, on the ground that it incited hatred and enmity toward an ally of the United States, "Particularly [among] the American military and naval forces."

In the *Milwaukee Leader* case, discussed in Chapter 1, the Supreme Court indicated that the *Leader* had violated the Espionage Act by its publication of articles that were plainly "in violation of the Espionage Law." More than that, the *Leader* opinion declared that such an application of the Espionage Act to the press did not violate the First Amendment: "Freedom of the press may protect criticism and agitation for modification or repeal of laws, but it does not extend to protection of him who counsels and encourages the violation of the law as it exists." The law punishing such "sedition" was ruled consistent with the press guaranty, since, in the Court's already-quoted words, "The Constitution was adopted to preserve our government, not to serve as a protecting screen for those who while claiming its privileges, seek to destroy it."

Clear and Present Danger

In its *New York Times Co. v. Sullivan* opinion, the Court stated that there is now "a broad consensus" that a sedition law such as those discussed, "because of the restraint it imposed upon criticism of government and public officials, was inconsistent with the First Amendment." That consensus has developed since articulation of the so-called Clear and Present Danger Test just after World War I by Justice Holmes.

Holmes himself is, of course, one of the seminal figures in modern American Law. His conception of the First Amendment drastically changed the Court's approach to freedom of speech and of the press. The Holmes concept of freedom of expression is a direct descendant of John Milton and John Stuart Mill. It found its fullest expression in the Justice's dissent in the 1919 case of *Abrams v. United States*, which Max Lerner termed "the greatest utterance on intellectual freedom by an American." Milton's *Areopagitica* argues for "a free and open encounter" in which "[Truth] and Falsehood grapple." The *Abrams* dissent sets forth the foundation of the First Amendment as "free trade in ideas," which through competition for their acceptance by the people would provide the best test of truth. Or as Holmes put it in a letter, "I am for aeration of all effervescing convictions — there is no way so quick for letting them get flat."

Like Milton and Mill, Holmes stressed the ability of truth to win out in the intellectual marketplace. For this to happen, the indispensable sine qua non is the free interchange of ideas. As the crucial passage of the *Abrams* dissent puts it, "when men have realized that time has upset many fighting faiths, they may come to believe even more than they believe the very foundations of their own conduct that the ultimate good desired is better reached by free trade in ideas — that the best test of truth is the power of the thought to get itself accepted in the competition of the market."

Those who govern, Holmes is saying, too often seek to "express [their] wishes in law and sweep away all opposition," including "opposition by speech." They forget that time may also upset their "fighting faiths" and that, in the long run, "truth is the only ground upon which their wishes safely can be carried out." That is the case because government is an experimental process. The Constitution itself, wrote Holmes in *Abrams*, "is an experiment, as all life is an experiment." To make the experiment successful, room must be found for new ideas which will challenge the old, for the "ultimate good desired is better reached by free trade in ideas."

The *Abrams* case itself arose when, early one morning in

1918, the air above passersby at the corner of Houston and Crosby Streets in New York City was filled with leaflets thrown from a loft window. Written in lurid language, they contained a bitter attack against the sending of American soldiers to Siberia, urging a workers' general strike in support of the Russian Revolution and as a "reply to the barbaric intervention" by the United States. Six factory workers who had printed and distributed the leaflets were arrested and were convicted under the Espionage Act of 1917 for the publishing of language which incited resistance to the American war effort by encouraging "curtailment to cripple or hinder the United States in the prosecution of the war." The Supreme Court affirmed the convictions, holding that, even though the defendants' primary intent had been to aid the Russian Revolution, their plan of action had necessarily involved obstruction of the American war effort against Germany.

As already noted, the Holmes *Abrams* dissent set forth his conception of the "free trade in ideas" as the foundation of the right of expression. The Holmes conception did not, however mean that the Justice was an adherent of an absolutist interpretation of the First Amendment. Despite Holmes's deep faith in the free interchange of ideas, Justice Felix Frankfurter tells us, "he did not erect even freedom of speech into a dogma of absolute validity nor enforce it to doctrinaire limits."

The Supreme Court, too, has rejected the absolutist view of freedom of expression. According to a 1976 case, "the prohibition on encroachment of First Amendment protection is not an absolute. Restraints are permitted for appropriate reason." It has been steeled from the beginning that the Constitution does not provide for an unfettered right of expression. Holmes's famous example in *Schenck v. United States* (1919) of the man falsely shouting "fire!" in a theater is simply the most obvious instance of speech that can be controlled.

But the fire-in-a-theater example was a far cry from the facts presented in the *Abrams* case. There, the Holmes dissent argued that the "silly" leaflets thrown by obscure individuals from a loft window presented no danger of resistance to the American war effort. Not enough, he said, "can be squeezed form these poor and puny anonymities to turn the color of legal litmus paper."

According to Holmes, "Only the emergency that makes it immediately dangerous to leave the correction of evil counsels to time warrants making any exception to the sweeping command, 'Congress shall make no law . . . abridging the freedom of speech.' " But when does such an "emergency" arise? Holmes himself had provided the answer a few months earlier in the *Schenck* case: When "the words used are used in such circumstances and are of such a nature as to create a clear and present danger that they will bring about the substantive evils that Congress has a right to prevent."

Under this Clear and Present Danger Test, expression may be restricted only if there is a real threat — a danger, both clear and present, that the expression will lead to an evil that the legislature has the power to prevent. In the *Abrams* case, the legislature had the right to pass a law to prevent curtailment of war production; but, said Holmes, there was no danger, clear and present, or even remote, that the leaflets would have had any effect on production.

According to a 1946 opinion by Justice Frankfurter, the Clear and Present Danger Test, as stated by Holmes, "served to indicate the importance of freedom of speech to a free society but also to emphasize that its exercise must be compatible with the preservation of other freedoms essential to a democracy and guaranteed by our Constitution. When those other attributes of a democracy are threatened by speech, the Constitution does not deny power to the [government] to curb it." As characterized by Justice Brandeis in a 1920 case, the Holmes test "is a rule of reason. Correctly applied, it will preserve the right of free speech both from suppression by tyrannous, well-meaning majorities and from abuse by irresponsible, fanatical minorities."

Although even the Clear and Present Danger Test has been criticized by some as too restrictive, it represents a real step forward in favor of free expression. The Holmes test is above all a test of degree. "Clear and present" danger is a standard, not a mathematical absolute. "It is a question of proximity and degree," said Holmes, after the passage stating the test quoted above. As such, its application will vary from case to case and will depend upon the particular circumstances presented.

Speech that would be innocuous if addressed to an audience of divines might produce an entirely different result in quarters where a light breath would be enough to kindle a flame. This was seen acutely by John Stuart Mill a century ago. In his essay *On Liberty*, he said: "An opinion that corn-dealers are starvers of the poor, or that private property is robbery, ought to be unmolested when simply circulated through the press, but may justly incur punishment when delivered orally to an excited mob assembled before the house of a corn-dealer, or when handed about among the same mob in the form of a placard."

That the Holmes test is sound can be seen from the analogy of the law of criminal attempts. Just as a criminal attempt must come sufficiently near completion to be of public concern, so there must be an actual danger that inciting speech will bring about an unlawful act before it can be restrained. In both cases, the question of how near to the unlawful act itself the attempt or speech must come is a question of degree to be determined upon the special facts of each case.

Thus, to use Professor Chafee's example, if I gather sticks and buy some gasoline to start a fire in a house miles away and do nothing more, I cannot be punished for attempting to commit arson. However, if I put the sticks against the house and pour on some gasoline and am caught before striking a match, I am guilty of a criminal attempt. The fire is the main thing, but when no fire has occurred, it is a question of the nearness of my behavior to the outbreak of a fire. So under the Constitution, lawless acts are the main thing. Speech is not punishable as such, but only because of its connection with lawless acts. But more than a remote connection is necessary, just as with the attempted fire. The fire must be close to the house; the speech must be close to the lawless acts. So long as the speech is remote from action, it is protected by the Constitution. But if the speech will result in action that government can prohibit, then the speech itself can constitutionally be reached by governmental power, provided there is a clear and present danger that the action will result from the speech.

Imminent Incitement and the Press

The Clear and Present Danger Test was further refined in *Brandenburg v. Ohio* (1969). Defendant had organized a Klu Klux Klan "rally" at a farm in Ohio. A film showed twelve hooded figures at the event. Defendant made a speech urging a march on Congress and the taking of "revengeance" for the Government's suppression of "the white caucasian race." He was convicted of violating a state law making it a crime to "advocate . . . the duty, necessity, or propriety of crime, sabotage, violence, or unlawful methods of terrorism." The Supreme Court reversed, holding that advocacy even of violence was protected by the First Amendment as long as the advocacy did not incite people to imminent action

The key under *Brandenburg* is not *incite* but *imminent*. The Court stated the test for speech which advocates violence or other unlawful conduct: "the constitutional guarantees of free speech and free press do not permit a State to forbid or proscribe advocacy of the use of force, except where such advocacy is directed to inciting or producing imminent lawless action and is likely to incite or produce such action."

Two things appear clear under the *Brandenburg* modification of the Clear and Present Danger Test. The first is that *Brandenburg* is even more protective of freedom of expression than the Holmes test. Rare will be the speech that not only incites to imminent lawless action, but is likely to succeed in accomplishing that result. Under *Brandenburg*, it is much more difficult for the state to show the required nexus between given expression and imminent lawless action.

The second thing to be noted about *Brandenburg* is the point made by Anthony Lewis in *Make No Law*, his recent book on *New York Times Co. v. Sullivan*: "Altogether *Brandenburg v. Ohio* gave the greatest protection to . . . subversive speech that it has ever had in the United States, and almost certainly greater than such speech has in any other country."

In particular, it is most unlikely that any publication by the press can come within the *Brandenburg* test. No matter how fiery the advocacy in a newspaper, magazine, book, or pamphlet, it is hard to see how it can meet the *Brandenburg* requirement that imminent lawless action is likely to result. We can refer again to the Mill corn-dealer example. No matter how extreme a newspaper statement on corn dealers as starvers of the poor may be, it can scarcely have the impact of the same statement by a rabble-rouser to a mob before a corn dealer's house. Only the latter incites to imminent lawless action that is likely to be produced by the agitator's arousing. Even the most extreme advocacy in the press is now shielded by *Brandenburg*, since print alone is hardly likely to succeed in producing imminent violence or other lawless action.

Contempt by Publication

Justice Holmes is, of course, now considered the very paradigm of the First Amendment judge. In his first Supreme Court case on the subject, however, Holmes was anything but the judicial protector of the freedom of expression. In *Patterson v. Colorado* (1907), a publisher had been convicted of contempt because of his paper's severe criticism of a state supreme court decision, which charged the judges with being the tools of the Amendment.

Patterson involved so-called "contempt by publication" — another area of the law where there is a conflict between freedom of the press and proper administration of justice. In *Patterson*, Justice Holmes came down on the side of the latter interest by his decision upholding the contempt conviction. In more recent years, however, the conflict has been resolved by the Court in a manner which emphasizes the First Amendment freedom — even if, to some degree, at the expense of some interference by the press with untrammeled administration of justice in pending cases.

The leading case on contempt by publication is *Bridges v. California* (1941). There, according to a 1962 opinion, "this Court . . . for the first time had occasion to review a State's exercise of the contempt power utilized to punish the publisher of an out-of-court statement." The publisher had been cited for contempt for the publication of certain editorials, particularly one which dealt with the pending sentencing of two convicted defendants, which asserted that the judge would "make a serious mistake" if he granted probation.

As stated by Justice Frankfurter in his dissent, the *Bridges* editorial constituted an "attempt to overawe a judge in a matter immediately pending before him." According to the majority, nevertheless, such an editorial may not constitute the basis of a contempt citation. That is true because contempt by publication must be judged in the light of the Clear and Present Danger Test: "we cannot start with the assumption that publications of the kind here involved actually do threaten to change the nature of legal trials, and that to preserve judicial impartiality, it is necessary for judges to have a contempt power by which they can close all channels of public expression to all matters which touch upon pending cases. We must therefore turn to the particular utterances there in question and the circumstances of their publication to determine to what extent the substantive evil of unfair administration of justice was a likely consequence, and whether the degree of likelihood was sufficient to justify summary punishment."

As explained in *Craig v. Harney* (1947), *Bridges v. California* means that the First Amendment forbids "the punishment by contempt for comment of pending cases in absence of a showing that the utterances created a 'clear and present danger' to the administration of justice." And the test is strictly applied in the post-*Bridges* cases. As the Court put it in 1962, "to warrant a sanction '[t]he fires which [the expression] kindles must constitute an imminent, not merely a likely threat to the administration of justice. The danger must not be remote or even probable; it must immediately imperil.' "

In its most recent reference to the subject (in *Nebraska Press Association v. Stuart*, discussed in Chapter 1), the Court stated that *Bridges* and subsequent cases have limited sharply the circumstances in which the courts may exact punishment for contempt by publication. One may go further and ask whether such contempt still has a place in our system. In applying *Bridges* we must assume, in the words of the *Craig* case, that "Judges are supposed to be men of fortitude, able to thrive in a hardy climate." It is difficult to see how published words can really interfere with the conduct of cases by such men. That being the case, we may wonder whether any published matter can present the required danger to the administration of justice. At any rate, in every case involving contempt by publication since *Bridges*, the Court has ruled that contempt sanctions may not be imposed.

4

Broadcast Media and
General Legislation

The Framers of the First Amendment were, of course, familiar only with the printed press — newspapers, books, periodicals, pamphlets, and leaflets. There is no doubt that they intended the constitutional guaranty to be fully applicable to the traditional press which they knew. During the present century, however, the Age of Gutenberg has given way to the Age of McLuhan. The linear press has been supplemented by the electronic media which now constitute a primary source of news dissemination. Are the broadcast media protected by the First Amendment? If they are, does that mean that they are protected to the same extent as the traditional print media? The Supreme Court began to answer these questions soon after the radio had become established as a significant medium of news dissemination.

Licensing and Fairness

If the First Amendment means anything so far as the traditional press is concerned, it means (as we saw in Chapter 1) a constitutional prohibition against any system of licensing. Everyone has the right to publish and distribute a newspaper, periodical, book, or circular without any license. Nor is the editorial judgment of the traditional press subject to any governmental control. It is for the editor, not the censor, to determine what should or should not be printed in any publication.

First Amendment protection in this respect for the printed press is illustrated by *Miami Herald Publishing Co. v. Tornillo* (1974). At issue there was a state law granting a political candidate a right to equal space in a newspaper to reply to criticism and attacks. In effect, the law provided for the converse of censorship — forcing the press to print copy. Such a law, as the *Miami Herald* opinion stated, "operates as a command in the same sense as a statute or regulation forbidding [a newspaper] to publish specified matter." In both cases, government seeks to determine the content of the newspaper.

The advocates of the *Miami Herald* law relied on the relative scarcity of media outlets to which members of the public (even those running for office) may have access. At the conference, Justice Stewart pointed out that this claim did not have a technological basis, as it did in radio and television. "The spectrum of frequencies," he stated, "is not limited as claimed in [broadcasting]." But Stewart noted, "the monopoly of newspapers ironically is doing just that."

Despite this, the basic principle remains that stated in a 1978 Stewart opinion: "If the constitutional protection of a free press means anything, it means that government cannot take it upon itself to decide what a newspaper may and may not publish. Though government may deny access to information and punish its theft, government may not prohibit or punish the publication of that information once it falls into the hands of the press." Hence, the *Miami Herald* decision unanimously struck down the right-to-reply law. The First Amendment, said the Court, prohibits "compulsion exerted by government on a newspaper to print that which it would not otherwise print." Government may not intrude into the function of editors.

Under *Miami Herald*, the First Amendment erects a complete barrier between government and the print media. The same is not necessarily true where the broadcast media are concerned. The starting point here, it is true, is the inclusion of broadcasting within the "press" protected by the First Amendment. "We have no doubt," said the Court in 1948, "that . . . radio [is] included in the press whose freedom is guaranteed by the First Amendment." Application of this general principle is illustrated by *Cox Broadcasting Co. v. Cohn* (1975). At issue there was a statute making it a misdemeanor to publish the name or identity of a rape victim. Such a law would plainly be invalid as applied to the traditional press; the First Amendment categorically prohibits government from punishing a newspaper for publishing or not publishing particular news. In *Cox*, however, the statute had been violated, not by a newspaper, but by a television station. A television reporter had learned the name of a rape victim from the indictment and had revealed it in a broadcast.

At the *Cox* conference, the Justices treated the case exactly as they would have if a newspaper had been involved. As such, all at the conference agreed that the statute was invalid. "I think," said Justice Stewart, "that on its face it's unconstitutional. . . . Here we have a truthful report of a public proceeding." Even Justice Rehnquist, who ultimately dissented on other grounds, stated the same view. "On the merits," he told the conference, "I agree that you can't constitutionally [prohibit] the right of a newspaper truthfully to report a public proceeding."

The Court was thus unanimous on the statute's invalidity. As Justice Blackmun put it, "You can't bridle the press constitutionally this way." The Justice recognized that there were dangers of abusive exercise of press power, but he concluded, "As a practical matter, we have to rely on the self-restraint of the press in these cases."

The *Cox* decision followed the conference and ruled that the First Amendment was violated by a statute prohibiting publication of the rape victim's name. Freedom of the press, said the Court, "command[s] nothing less than that the States may not impose sanctions on the publication of truthful information." Under the First Amendment, government has no power to suppress publication of the news. Under *Cox* the same result may not be accomplished by penalizing publication, which has the same effect as censorship. In Justice Douglas' *Cox* words, "there is no power in government to suppress or penalize the publication of 'news of the day.'" That principle applies to both the traditional press and the newer electronic media.

There are, however, differences between the printed press and the newer media which make for differences in the extent of First Amendment protections available. The crucial difference stems from the technological nature of broadcasting. The mass media of radio and television are such, by their physical characteristics, as to make impossible the literal application of the Blackstone theory of freedom of the press. Every person can distribute handbills or even (if he has the financial means) publish a newspaper or magazine without any governmental permission. But the same is not true of the broadcast media with their inherent physical limitation of frequencies for radio and TV stations. Frequencies are scarce and must be portioned out among applicants. Government allocation and regulation of broadcast frequencies are thus essential.

In its 1969 *Red Lion* decision the Court stated that there can be no First Amendment right to broadcast comparable to the right to speak, write, or publish. In broadcasting, government cannot sit by and allow all who choose to use the media. In the words of the 1943 *National Broadcasting Co.* case, "Unlike other modes of expression, radio inherently is not available to all. That is its unique characteristic, and that is why, unlike other modes of expression, it is subject to governmental regulation."

Owing to their physical characteristics, radio and television must be both rationed and regulated by the government. Otherwise, there would be chaos. These practical considerations have led Congress to authorize, and the Court to approve, a scheme of selective licensing by the Federal Communications Commission. The right of free speech does not, in the *NBC* case's phrase, include the right to use the facilities of radio or television without a license.

As we saw in Chapter 1, if the First Amendment means anything so far as the traditional press is concerned, it means a ban against any system of licensing. Yet even that categorical prohibition gives way in the case of the broadcast media, where physical scarcity makes government allocation and regulation essential. The Court has upheld the exercise of broad regulatory power by the FCC. It has held that the Commission may limit the number of stations which may be owned by one person and may even prohibit ownership of stations by newspapers in the same community. In the latter case, the opinion stated, "we see nothing in the First Amendment to prevent the Commission from allocating licenses so as to promote the 'public interest' in diversification of the mass communications media."

In its *Red Lion* decision, the Court went further and held, in effect, that the *Miami Herald* limitation on government power over the press did not apply to the broadcast media. *Miami Herald*, we saw, struck down the right-of-reply law on the ground that government might not command a newspaper to publish specified matter. *Red Lion*, on the other hand, upheld the so-called fairness doctrine of the Federal Communications Commission, which required broadcasters to provide reply time to personal attacks or political editorials. Acting under its doctrine, the FCC had ordered a radio station, which had broadcast a vigorous personal attack against an author, to provide reply time without requiring the author to pay for it. The Court justified the decision as one for "enforced sharing of a scarce resource." Government may prevent such a resource from being made available only to the highest bidders to communicate only those views with which the broadcasters agree. The alternative is "private censorship operating in a medium not open to all."

As the Court summarized it in the *Pacifica* case to be discussed next, "although the First Amendment protects newspaper publishers from being required to print the replies of those whom they criticize . . . it affords no such protection to broadcasters; on the contrary, they must give free time to the victims of their criticism."

Hence, what *Miami Herald* held that government might not require of newspapers *Red Lion* ruled it might demand of broadcasters. "Because of the scarcity of radio frequencies," said the Court, "the Government is permitted to put restraints on licenses in favor of others whose views should be expressed on this unique medium."

Obscenity versus Indecency

Obscene speech, we shall see in the next Chapter, is not protected by the First Amendment. That is the case even where the obscene speech is published by the press — whether in the traditional print media or transmitted by the broadcast media. The converse of this principle is, however, also true: if speech is not obscene, its publication is entitled to First Amendment protection, no matter how "offensive" or "indecent" it may be to most people. *FCC v. Pacifica Foundation* (1978) indicates, however, that this converse proposition may apply only to the traditional press, not to the newer media.

As stated by the Court, the issue in *Pacifica Foundation* was "whether the Federal Communications Commission has any power to regulate a radio broadcast that is indecent but not obscene." The broadcast in question was a twelve-minute monologue by George Carlin, a satiric humorist, entitled "Filthy Words." The monologue consisted of a comedy routine that was almost entirely devoted to the use of seven four-letter words depicting sexual or excretory organs and activities. After receiving a complaint from a man who had heard the broadcast while driving in his car with his young son, the FCC issued a declaratory order finding that the seven four-letter words contained in the Carlin monologue did depict sexual or excretory organs and activities in a patently offensive manner, judged by contemporary community standards for the broadcast medium, and accordingly, were indecent. The Commission found a power to regulate indecent broadcasting in a statute which forbids the use of "any obscene, indecent, or profane language by means of radio communication," Pacifica argued that the monologue was not obscene under the *Roth-Miller* test (to be discussed in the next Chapter), requiring appeal to prurient interest in sex, patent offensiveness, and lack of redeeming social value. Hence, it was entitled to First Amendment protection. The court of appeals accepted this argument, with a strong dissent by Judge Harold Leventhal, who stressed the widespread access of radio to children and the overriding need to protect them from this type of broadcast.

The Supreme Court conference was closely divided. The case for affirmance was stated by Justices Brennan, Stewart, White, and Marshall. Justice White, who had delivered the *Red Lion* opinion, asserted that its reasoning did not justify treating broadcasters differently in this case. As he saw it, *Red Lion's* limited spectrum rationale supported only the fairness doctrine and did not extend to restricting this broadcast. Justices Brennan and Marshall stressed that this was censorship in violation of the First Amendment. Justice Stewart pointed out that, in other statutory provisions, "indecent" had been construed to mean "obscene"; since "there is no claim that this broadcast was 'obscene,' I'd affirm on this ground."

Chief Justice Burger and Justices Blackmun, Powell, and Rehnquist essentially agreed with Judge Leventhal's opinion below and supported the view that "indecent" was not equivalent to "obscene" in the statute. Justice Stevens was somewhat ambivalent, saying, "I've flip flopped on this case and may do so again." Ultimately, however, Stevens came down in favor of reversal. "This is TV and radio," he said, "and [there is] greater latitude than in newspapers. So even if protected in newspapers . . . anything that goes into the living room under TV and radio may be regulated in the public interest. So constitutionally I would sanction this bar."

The final *Pacifica* vote was the same as that at the conference. Chief Justice Burger followed the technique of assigning the case to Justice Stevens as the most lukewarm member of the majority — what Burger called, in a 1978 letter to Justice Brennan, "the old English rule-of-thumb as the 'least persuaded,' hence likely to write narrowly." The Stevens *Pacifica* opinion of the Court was, however, a broad confirmation of the inferior First Amendment position of the broadcast media. "[O]f all forms of communications," the Stevens opinion declared, "it is broadcasting that has received the most limited First Amendment protection."

In *Pacifica* itself, the Court gave two reasons for treating the broadcast media differently: "first, the broadcast media have established a uniquely pervasive presence in the lives of all Americans. Patently offensive, indecent material presented over the airwaves confronts the citizen, not only in public, but also in the privacy of the home, where the individual's right to be left alone plainly outweighs the First Amendment rights of an intruder . . . . Second, broadcasting is uniquely accessible to children, even those too young to read. The ease with which children may obtain access to broadcast material . . . amply justify special treatment of indecent broadcasting."

Ultimately the Court's *Pacifica* decision, like the FCC order in the case, rests upon an approach analogous to that in the law of nuisance, where according to a famous 1926 statement by Justice Sutherland, a "nuisance may be merely a right thing in the wrong place — like a pig in the parlor instead of the barnyard." In *Pacifica*, said the Stevens opinion, "We simply hold that when the Commission finds that a pig has entered the parlor the exercise of its regulatory power does not depend on proof that the pig is obscene."

Access to Airwaves

The *Red Lion* decision was, as seen, based on scarcity — "the lack of available frequencies for all who wished to use them." But it also relied upon "the purpose of the First Amendment to preserve an uninhibited marketplace of ideas . . . rather than to countenance monopolization of that market, whether it be by the Government itself or a private licensee." The crucial factor, said *Red Lion*, was "the right of the public to receive suitable access to social, political, esthetic, moral and other ideas and experiences." The implication is that there may be a right of individual access to the airwaves to ensure that the public right to receive diverse materials is vindicated.

When the issue was squarely presented, however, the Court refused to recognize such a constitutional right of access to the broadcast media. In *Columbia Broadcasting System v. Democratic National Committee* (1973), CBS had refused to sell time to the Democratic National Committee for political advertising and to an organization for anti-Vietnam War announcements. It was claimed that the First Amendment barred a broadcaster from following a general policy of refusing to sell time for comment on controversial public issues. The lower court upheld the claim.

Chief Justice Burger began the *Democratic National Committee* conference by stating the issue: "Whether TV may have a policy not to sell advertising time to responsible advertisers with controversial messages to deliver." The Chief Justice stated that "the FCC relies on the fairness doctrine as sufficient." Judge McGowan, in his court of appeals dissent, had relied on that doctrine and urged that it imposed the only relevant obligation on broadcasters. Burger told the conference, "I think Judge McGowan was correct below."

Justice White agreed with the Chief Justice. Referring to the claim that the Communications Act required access, he declared, "The statutory argument is absurd." On the constitutional argument, White said, "The Constitution doesn't require FCC regulation. Even though *Red Lion* said TV must act as a spokesman for other voices, this doesn't go that far." Justices Stewart, Blackmun, Powell, and Rehnquist agreed with the Burger-White approach.

The *Democratic National Committee* decision followed the conference consensus that there is no constitutional right of individual access to the airwaves. Broadcasters, said the Court, are given journalistic freedom except where the public interest outweighs their right to exercise editorial judgment, including the decision of who is to command the use of broadcast facilities. This means that, unless Congress or the FCC mandate particular individual access, the matter of access is for the broadcaster's editorial judgment. There is no constitutionally commanded right of access which requires the broadcaster to accept any particular program or advertising.

The emphasis in the *Democratic National Committee* opinion was on the primary responsibility over broadcasting vested in Congress and the regulatory agency established by it. This indicates that a different result may be demanded where Congress requires broadcasters to grant access to their facilities. Such a Congressional provision was at issue in *Columbia Broadcasting System v. Federal Communications Commission* (1981). The statutory provision there authorized the FCC to revoke a broadcast license because of the broadcaster's "failure to allow reasonable access to or to permit purchase of reasonable amounts of time by a legally qualified candidate for federal elective office." The broadcast networks challenged the statute on First Amendment grounds, claiming that it unduly circumscribed their editorial discretion. The networks had sought review of an FCC decision that they had violated the statute by refusing to sell time to the Carter-Mondale Presidential Committee for December 1979, which they felt was too early for the 1980 campaign.

In effect, the statute provided an affirmative right of access to the broadcast media for individual candidates for federal office. And it was a new right created by Congress. As Justice White put it at the conference, "Congress intended to change the law. The old law never allowed a candidate to do this."

The conference vote was five to four to reverse the decision below affirming the FCC order. Chief Justice Burger said that he had only a "skeptical confidence in the FCC." The issue was, "Could the networks' judgment as to when the campaign was in full swing be reviewed [by the FCC]? . . . I'd be inclined to sustain the networks' judgment unless clearly wrong. Even if the networks made the wrong decision, in my view, to avoid censorship I'd give them the benefit of the doubt."

The view of the conference majority was best stated by Justice White, who delivered the dissent. "I think the FCC put too tight a grip on the broadcasters — particularly on the threshold issue of when the campaign began. My standard would be something like, if reasonable men could differ, the networks' decision should be sustained." Justices Powell, Rehnquist, and Stevens agreed with White. As Powell put it, "The Commission went beyond its authority in saying it decided when the campaign commenced."

Justices Brennan, Stewart, Marshall, and Blackmun spoke for affirmance. Their opinion was that Congress could change the law to provide for the right of access and, in Blackmun's words, "I'd let the Commission decide when the campaign begins." Justice Marshall's statement was pithy: "The networks are the biggest censors of all. I don't mind the FCC censoring the censors."

Chief Justice Burger and Justice Powell changed their conference votes and the final decision in *CBS v. FCC* was to uphold the statute and the FCC order. The result is consistent with our discussion of the subject. As stated by the Chief Justice at the conference, "TV has large, but not as much as the print media, discretion in editing." Congress and the regulatory agency may impinge upon that discretion in a manner not permissible for the traditional press. They may, we saw, impose upon broadcasters the kind of fairness requirement ruled unconstitutional for newspapers in *Miami Herald*. *CBS V. FCC* carries this one step further and holds that Congress may even create a right of access though none is otherwise demanded by the First Amendment. In such a case, the *CBS* opinion affirmed, "the statutory right of access . . . properly balances the First Amendment rights of federal candidates, the public, and broadcasters."

But there are limits to the Congressional power in this respect: Congress may not restrict broadcasters in a manner that limits the public's access to ideas. The Court held that that limit had been exceeded in *Federal Communications Commission v. League of Women Voters* (1984). A federal statute prohibited any noncommercial broadcast station that received federally funded grants to "engage in editorializing." The lower court ruled that the statute violated the First Amendment. The court rejected the contention that the prohibition served a compelling government interest in ensuring that publicly funded broadcasters do not become propaganda organs for the Government.

The Chief Justice, who passed at the conference, said that "whether public broadcasting is as different as the Solicitor General argues, and thus regulable this way, is troublesome." Burger did, however, indicate what his ultimate vote would be when he pointed out that the "strongest argument [to support the law] is the spending-power one."

Justices White, Rehnquist, and Stevens, who with the Chief Justice were to be the dissenters in the case, spoke in favor of the law. Justice Rehnquist noted that "this is an act of Congress specifically

prohibiting what's at issue here and [is] entitled to deference."
Rehnquist also stressed that public spending was involved. "I'd tell
people, you get the money on conditions and, if you want it, you must
comply with the conditions." The Justice also made two other points:
1) "The Government has control over broadcasting beyond that over
the press"; and 2) there was "very little restriction on speech anyway."
Justice White also made the latter point, saying that, under the law,
there were "no programming limits and no restrictions on any news."

On the other side, Justice Blackmun conceded that "limitations on broadcast speech have been upheld on the scarcity ground.
But this prohibition is at the core of the First Amendment." Justice
O'Connor, who provided the fifth vote for affirmance, agreed. "A
complete ban goes to the heart of the First Amendment. I don't think
the government interest here is compelling."

Justice Powell, who also spoke in favor of affirmance, stated,
"This is regulation of speech content with a negligible state interest."
Justice Stevens answered Powell much as he was to do in a dissent.
"True," said Stevens, "it's content regulation, but it's neutral — no
bias at all." In addition, Stevens pointed out that publicly funded
stations "give the impression it's the official view because of funding."

The *League of Women Voters* decision struck down the law
prohibiting editorializing by public broadcasters. The broadcast
industry may operate under restraints not imposed upon the traditional press. According to the opinion of the Court, however, the
restrictions permitted are intended to secure the public's First
Amendment interest in receiving a balanced presentation of views,
including those of broadcasters themselves. Preserving the free
expression of editorial opinion is an essential part of the First
Amendment scheme. The interests served by the ban on editorializing are not substantial enough to justify the abridgement of important journalistic freedoms.

The Press and General Legislation

We saw that the FCC may limit the number of stations that
may be owned by broadcasters. It will, however, be said that this is
but an illustration of the application to a business of the antitrust
laws and other laws preventing concentration of economic power. It
is, of course, true as a general proposition that the press is subject to
general legislation applicable to businesses, including laws intended
to further competition. The press is not exempt from general burdens
imposed upon other businesses. Since newspapers and the other

media are businesses, they must expect to share the normal burden imposed by law upon other businesses.

This principle has been applied in numerous cases. An example is *Associated Press v. National Labor Relations Board* (1937), where the press was held subject to the Wagner Act's prohibition against discharge of an employee because of his membership in a union. "The publisher of a newspaper," said the Court, "has no special immunity from the application of general laws. He has no special privilege to invade the rights and liberties of others. He must answer for libel. He may be punished for contempt of court. He is subject to the anti-trust laws. Like others he must pay equitable and nondiscriminatory taxes on his business."

A recent illustration of the subjection of the press to general laws is contained in *Cohen v. Cowles Media Co.* (1991). The Court there held that a newspaper could be held liable in damages for breach of its promise of confidentiality to a person who had furnished it with adverse information about a political candidate. The paper contended that such a result infringed upon its First Amendment right to publish any news in its possession. The Court rejected this claim, saying that the paper's liability was based upon ordinary principles of contract law, since the press can be liable for breach of contract just as anyone else can be. The case, said the opinion of Justice White, is "controlled by the equally well-established line of decisions holding that generally applicable laws do not offend the First Amendment simply because their enforcement against the press has incidental effects on its ability to gather and report the news."

Though the First Amendment does not shield the press from general laws such as the National Labor Relations Act, applicable to all businesses, it does protect the press from discriminatory laws which single out the press for unequal treatment. The tax cases can be used to show this. Of course, the publisher is subject to ordinary forms of taxation in the same manner as other persons. The same is not true, however, where the tax impinges exclusively upon the press. The leading case is *Grosjean v. American Press Co.* (1936). The Louisiana tax there, on gross receipts from advertising, was imposed upon newspapers with a circulations over 20,000. Such a tax imposed upon newspapers is comparable in its impact to the strict control upon all publications which existed in England prior to 1695. In dealing with the tax, indeed, the *Grosjean* Court compared it to the pre-Revolutionary English taxes upon the press, the main purpose of which was "to suppress the publication of comments and criticisms objectionable to the Crown." According to *Grosjean*, "the revolution really began when, in 1765, that government sent stamps for newspaper duties to the American colonies."

In light of this background, it is scarcely surprising that the *Grosjean* tax was stricken down. Such a tax, said the Court, "is bad because, in the light of its history and of its present setting, it is seen to be a deliberate and calculated device in the guise of a tax to limit the circulation of information to which the public is entitled in virtue of the constitutional guaranties. A free press stands as one of the great interpreters between the government and the people. To allow it to be fettered is to fetter ourselves."

The *Grosjean* holding was applied in *Minneapolis Star Tribune Co. v. Minnesota Commissioner of Revenue* (1983). Minnesota imposed a tax on the cost of the ink and paper used in producing newspapers, exempting the first $100, and the highest state court held that it did not violate freedom of the press.

There was an interesting discussion of *Grosjean* at the *Minneapolis Star* conference. As we saw, *Grosjean* held that the Louisiana tax at issue was an abridgement of the freedom of the press. But the Court also emphasized that the tax was intended to penalize the state's large newspapers, which had strongly opposed Senator Huey Long. In *Minneapolis Star*, there was no such invidious motive, but the Minnesota tax did single out newspapers.

Chief Justice Burger began the *Minneapolis Star* conference pointing out that "a nondiscriminatory sales tax would be O.K. But this is a tax limited to newspapers." Burger came out for reversal, though he did say, "I reject the argument that the Stamp Tax history supports the newspaper." Burger also noted that he was "not sure that *Grosjean* is the complete answer. There Huey Long's vendetta was influential. I see no motive here to interfere with press freedom."

As stated in a 1991 opinion by Justice O'Connor, "*Minneapolis Star* resolved any doubts about whether direct evidence of improper censorial motive is required in order to invalidate a differential tax on First Amendment grounds." The *Minneapolis Star* conference foreshadowed the opinion in indicating that the absence of improper motive was irrelevant. Instead, the key was the fact that the tax was imposed upon the press alone. The First Amendment, Justice Blackman told the conference, is a "prohibition [against] putting special burdens on the press and that's what this tax is." Justice White said, "This singles out publications which turn out to be newspapers, and only a few of them." Or as Justice Powell put it, "This singles out newspapers for special and discriminatory treatment."

Justice Rehnquist alone spoke in support of the tax: "If a sales tax is O.K., I can't see why this tax isn't all right." Rehnquist also was not persuaded by the singling-out argument. The tax, he stated, "applies only to newspapers because [they] can't collect a sales tax as easily.

With only Justice Rehnquist dissenting, the *Minneapolis Star* decision struck down the tax. The First Amendment does not permit a state to tailor a tax so that it singles out the press. As Justice O'Connor explained it in her 1991 opinion, "the threat of exclusive taxation of the press could operate as effectively as a censor to check critical comment."

5

Obscenity

After Justice Felix Frankfurter had sent him Alfred North Whitehead's *Symbolism*, Justice Stanley Reed wrote, "I liked his phrase about the 'many problematic futures which will never dawn.' I am not so sure he is correct, however, in our work. They seem to dawn sooner or later."

During the years when Earl Warren was Chief Justice, the Supreme Court was confronted with problems entirely different from those presented to prior Courts. Among the problems that "dawned" in the Warren Court was that of the relation of obscenity to the First Amendment. Thus, referring to the question "whether obscenity is utterance within the area of protected speech and press," the opinion of the Court in *Roth v. United States* (1957), a case involving the federal statute prohibiting the mailing of obscene materials, states, "this is the first time the question has been squarely presented to this Court."

During the *Roth* decision process, Chief Justice Warren wrote a short memorandum on a legal-size yellow pad summarizing his approach to obscenity. "The known history and meaning of the term 'obscenity,' " Warren stated, "at the time of the adoption of our Bill of Rights, together with the uninterrupted action of all but one of the States as they came into the Union, convinces me that it was considered by the American people then as now to be an abuse of freedom of expression rather than a protected right."

The Chief Justice recognized the First Amendment implications in banning obscene publications. Still, he had no doubt that obscenity had to remain beyond the constitutional pale. "Essential as it is," the Warren *Roth* memo concluded, "that the term be not expanded so as to abridge free expression either in the discussion of public affairs, the freedom of the press or in the arts and sciences, we should not deprive the States of the right to protect their people from this form of depravity."

Earl Warren is, of course, now considered the very paradigm

of the liberal judge who actively enforces the Bill of Rights guarantees. Where obscenity was concerned, however, Warren's commitment to First Amendment values could not overcome his personal abhorrence of pornography and what he called smut-peddlers.

The day after *Roth* was argued, Justice Frankfurter wrote to Warren, "I don't know whether you were as much in need of a whiff of fresh air after the obscenity arguments as I was." To Warren, more than "fresh air" was necessary to deal with material so foreign to his scale of values. If there was one matter on which his law clerks disagreed with the Chief Justice, it was what they deemed his puritanism in obscenity cases. Once, when they were pressing Warren on his views about pornography, his answer was, "You boys don't have any daughters yet." Warren found the sexual material that had become so widely available "unspeakable." *Newsweek* quoted him telling a colleague, when he was shown a pornographic work, "If anyone showed that book to my daughters, I'd have strangled him with my own hands."

Some observers have depicted the glee with which the Justices have viewed exhibits in obscenity cases. Chief Justice Warren's attitude was entirely different. "Do we have to read all of them to determine if they have social importance?" asked Warren plaintively as the argument began in a 1965 obscenity case. "I'm sure this Court doesn't want to read all the prurient material in the country."

It was not until a 1966 case, indeed, that Warren could bring himself to read obscenity exhibits. Then, to put it mildly, he was shocked. "Do you realize what's in there?" he asked his clerk. "This stuff is terrible." The Chief Justice would never personally view the films in obscenity cases. He would either send his clerks or rely on the report of one of the Justices. "It's all garbage," Warren used to tell his colleagues. "How can you know if you don't look at it?" asked one of the Justices. "I *know* what that stuff is!" came back the firm answer.

For most of the Justices, however, "movie day" (when films were shown that were exhibits in obscenity cases) was an event not to be missed. Yet, if the Justices were eager to view the allegedly pornographic films, more "elevating" fare failed to bring in the judicial customers. After arranging a private 1967 screening of *The Last Frontier*, a Department of the Interior film, Justice Douglas circulated a memorandum: "You may be interested to know that one Justice appeared, no law clerks, no one from the Clerk's Office, no one from the Library, no one from the Marshal's office except Mrs. Allen and Mr. Kippitt, four from the labor force, and four secretaries. There was a total of 12 from the entire building."

Obscenity Defined: Roth Case

The law on obscenity starts in 1663 with a case involving the Restoration wit and minor dramatist Sir Charles Sedley, who (in the corrupt law French of the period) "monstre son nude corps in un balcony in Covent Garden al grand multitude de people & la fist tiel choses" — notably, "making water on the persons below." The law, according to the Court of King's Bench decision in the case, "is custos morum of all the King's subjects and it is now high time to punish such profane actions."

For more than two centuries after this decision, it was never doubted that the law possesses the authority to proceed against obscenity, though more recently it has done so more on the basis of legislative prohibitions than under the common-law power of the courts. Nor, until our own day, had it seriously been urged that governmental restrictions upon obscenity infringed upon the rights of expression secured by the First Amendment. To such an assertion, there would have been the simple answer that the organic guaranty was not intended to abrogate the protection of public morals as a legitimate end for exertion of the police power. Or, to put it another way, obscene speech is not the kind of speech protected by the Constitution.

The principle just stated was, in fact, the basis of the Supreme Court's 1957 decision in *Roth v. United States*. The opinion there starts by stating: "the dispositive question is whether obscenity is utterance within the area of protected speech and press. Although this is the first time the question has been squarely presented to this Court, either under the First Amendment or under the Fourteenth Amendment, expressions found in numerous opinions indicate that this Court has always assumed that obscenity is not protected by the freedoms of speech and press."

At issue in *Roth* was the constitutionality of the federal criminal obscenity statute. It prohibited mailing material that was "obscene, lewd, lascivious, or filthy." Roth, who had been convicted for violating the statute, contended that it was contrary to the First Amendment.

At the *Roth* conference, Chief Justice Warren indicated that he would vote to affirm Roth's conviction. "To reverse on the First Amendment," he said, "would go too far. The Federal Government must have a right to protect itself. The states and the Federal Government both have it." Warren further expressed the opinion that the statute was not too vague. In his view "obscenity" and "filth" were sufficient terms.

Justices Black and Douglas, of course, had no difficulty in such a case. Their absolutist view of the First Amendment, as they wrote in the dissent they filed in *Roth*, prohibited placing "any form of expression beyond the pale of the absolute prohibition of the First Amendment." They repeated this simple view at the *Roth* conference. Justice Frankfurter supported Warren and voted for affirmance. Obscenity, he said, is an adequate phrase. "The Fourteenth Amendment is similarly vague and it's O.K. I don't propose to define it. We can't rest on a formula such as 'clear and present danger.'" Justices Burton, Clark, and Whittaker also spoke in favor of affirmance. Justice Harlan indicated doubt on whether the Federal Government could act, saying that the states had "a wider field" here, since obscenity was a local problem.

Aside from Chief Justice Warren, the most important contribution to the *Roth* conference was made by Justice Brennan. Speaking in favor of affirmance, he argued that the question of obscenity was a judicial question. The Court should restate it in terms of criminal law. "The test should be the 'dominant theme' test" and it was the place of the judge to apply it "before it goes to the jury."

What Justice Brennan meant was made clear when the Chief Justice assigned him the *Roth* opinion. In addition to laying down the important principle "that obscenity is not within the area of constitutionally protected speech or press," the Brennan opinion also gave effect to his conference statement on the need to restate the test of obscenity.

Before the *Roth* opinion addressed itself to the problem, courts in this country had, in the main, applied the rule laid down in the leading English case, *Regina v. Hicklin* (1868). The test of obscenity was stated by Lord Chief Justice Cockburn there to be "this, whether the tendency of the matter charged as obscenity is to deprave and corrupt those whose minds are open to such immoral influences, and into whose hands a publication of this sort may fall." In addition, Lord Cockburn emphasized that obscenity could be determined from isolated passages deemed objectionable, rather than from the nature of the given work as a whole.

Though American courts tended to adopt the *Hicklin* standard, by the time of the *Roth* case it had been subjected to increasing criticism — particularly in a noted 1913 opinion by Judge Learned Hand, who questioned whether "truth and beauty are [not] too precious to society at large to be mutilated in the interests of those most likely to pervert them to base uses." The *Roth* Court based its test of obscenity upon rejection of the two aspects of the *Hicklin* rule summarized in the preceding paragraph: the judging of obscenity by 1) the effect of isolated passages upon 2) the most susceptible persons. Since the *Roth* definition, no constitutionally valid test of obscenity may include these objectionable elements as they had been stated in the *Hicklin* case.

Instead, Justice Brennan's *Roth* opinion articulated the following as the basic test to determine whether particular material is obscene: "whether to the average person, applying contemporary community standards, the dominant theme of the material taken as a whole appeals to prurient interest."

Under this test, first of all, whether particular material is obscene must be determined with reference to "the average person." If, to such average person, the material would not be obscene within the other elements of the *Roth* test, it may not be condemned merely because it might have a different effect upon "those whose minds are open to . . . immoral influences." In effect, what *Roth* is doing here is to adopt a statement from the celebrated 1933 opinion of Judge John Woolsey in the case on the alleged obscenity of James Joyce's *Ulysses*, "It is only with the normal person that the law is concerned."

It is also clear from *Roth* that obscenity may no longer be judged on the basis of particular passages taken in isolation from an allegedly obscene work. Hence, the practice followed some years ago of marking offending passages in red and basing the decision solely upon them would no longer be valid. The result is now that once stated in a state case, where certain marked paragraphs in Gautier's *Mademoiselle de Maupin* were claimed to make the work obscene: "No work may be judged from a selection of such paragraphs alone. Printed by themselves they might, as a matter of law, come within the prohibition of the statute. So might a similar selection from Aristophanes or Chaucer or Boccaccio or even from the Bible. The book, however, must be considered broadly as a whole."

In addition, under *Roth*, the test of obscenity must be based upon "applying contemporary community standards." This means that the law of obscenity is one which varies with changing moral standards. The purpose of this aspect of *Roth* is to meet the objection stated by Judge Learned Hand to the pre-*Roth* rule when he declared, in his 1913 opinion, "that the rule as laid down, however consonant it may be with mid-Victorian morals, does not seem to me to answer to the understanding and morality of the present time." Such an objection can no longer validly be raised. The *Roth* test enables the definition of obscenity to adjust to alterations in contemporary mores; without a doubt, many of the cases applying the *Roth* test, would have been decided altogether differently under Victorian moral standards. "Can it be doubted," asked Justice Frankfurter in a 1959 opinion, "that there is a great difference in what is to be deemed obscene in 1959 compared with what was deemed obscene in 1859?"

This brings us to the principal element in the *Roth* definition of obscenity: whether "the dominant theme of the material taken as a whole *appeals to prurient interest.*" In the end, it has been well said, this is all that matters. The "appeal to prurient interest" is the essence of what makes particular material obscene; unless this aspect of the *Roth* test is met, the other aspects of the test become irrelevant.

Referring to the test of obscenity as enunciated in *Roth*, a state court has remarked, "we have doubts if the 'average person' whether he be judge or juror, would be able to apply the phrase 'appeals to prurient interest' without conjecture or resort to a dictionary." That may well be true. But the Supreme Court in *Roth* also told us (though only in general terms) what it means by the requirement that obscene material "appeals to prurient interest."

According to the *Roth* opinion, "Obscene material is material which deals with sex in a manner appealing to prurient interest." The Court refined this statement by appending the following footnote: "i.e., material having a tendency to excite lustful thoughts."

Having thus indicated that the contrary may be the case, the *Roth* opinion goes on to assure us that "sex and obscenity are not synonymous . . . . The portrayal of sex, e.g., in art, literature and scientific works, is not itself sufficient reason to deny material the constitutional protection of freedom of speech and press." Sex itself, says the Court, "a great and mysterious motive force in human life, has indisputably been a subject of absorbing interest to mankind through the ages," and it is a legitimate subject of public interest and concern. "It is therefore," *Roth* concludes, "vital that the standards for judging obscenity safeguard the protection of freedom of speech and press for material which does not treat sex in a manner appealing to prurient interest."

Need to Refine

Soon after the case was decided, Chief Justice Warren told his son that while he was not wholly satisfied with *Roth*, "It's the best we could do with what we had." Later, in a 1964 case, he declared, "For all the sound and fury that the Roth test has generated, it has not been proved unsound."

Despite this, one who analyzes the *Roth* test must conclude that, in important respects, it is too broad. In *Roth* itself, as seen, the Court was careful to state that sex and obscenity are not synonymous. This means that the treatment of sex in literature is entitled to constitutional protection if it is not obscene. But it also means, in accordance with the definition laid down in *Roth*, that such treatment is not entitled to First Amendment protection if it "deals with sex in a manner appealing to prurient interest" — which, we saw, the Court defined as "having a tendency to excite lustful thoughts."

Slight reflection will demonstrate that the *Roth* Court could not have intended its statement of the relationship between sex and obscenity to be taken in all its literal broadness. So taken, the *Roth* definition would plainly brand as obscene much in the contemporary scene that the law manifestly does not place beyond the reach of the right of free expression.

Referring to the test of tendency to produce lustful thoughts, a federal judge declares: "That cannot suffice: Notoriously, perfumes sometimes act as aphrodisiacs, yet no one will suggest that therefore Congress may constitutionally legislate punishment for mailing perfumes. It may be that among the stimuli to irregular sexual conduct, by normal men and women, may be almost anything — the odor of carnations or cheese, the sight of a cane or a candle or a shoe, the touch of silk or a gunnysack. For all anyone now knows, stimuli of that sort may be far more provocative of such misconduct than reading obscene books or seeing obscene pictures."

Many persons, we are told, see a phallic symbol in the radiator ornamentation of automobiles; is such ornamentation, which may thus "have a tendency to excite lustful thoughts" in one sensitive to symbols, consequently obscene?

Leaving such fanciful illustrations aside, can it be denied that, in the sex-oriented society, the individual is met on all sides by sex symbols which do fall within the broadside *Roth* definition and yet are not considered to come within the legitimate scope of obscenity laws? As Justice Douglas tells us in a 1966 opinion, "The advertisements of our best magazines are chock-full of thighs, ankles, calves, bosoms, eyes, and hair, to draw the potential buyer's attention to lotions, tires, food, liquor, clothing, autos, and even insurance policies." From women's fashions to pin-up pictures, from rock music to brassiere advertisements — all can be considered as "having a tendency to excite lustful thoughts." In fact, with regard to most such materials, that is their primary *raison d'etre*; if they did not stir sexual impulses, there would be little reason for them.

Then, too, it cannot be doubted that the wholesale aspect of the *Roth* definition now under discussion would bring many of the classics of world literature within the law's proscription of obscenity. Henry Miller may have gone too far when he asked, "what is it that enables the classics to live at all . . . ? What preserves them against the ravages of time if it be not the salt that is in them?" At the same time, if we are candid, we must concede that, from Boccaccio to Byron, many of the classics of literature have been based upon what Balzac once termed "a pithy frankness" in sexual matters, which may easily violate the broad construction of the *Roth* definition. In Justice Harlan's words in a 1962 opinion, "one would not have to travel far even among the acknowledged masterpieces . . . to find works whose 'dominant theme' might, not beyond reason, be claimed to appeal to the 'prurient interest' of the reader."

A test of obscenity like that laid down in *Roth*, if applied in its literal broadness, cannot, as Judge Jerome Frank put it in 1956, be reconciled "with the immunity of such 'classics' as e.g., Aristophanes' *Lysistrata*, Chaucer's *Canterbury Tales*, Rabelais' *Gargantua and Pantagruel*, Shakespeare's *Venus and Adonis*, Fielding's *Tom Jones*, or Balzac's *Droll Stories*. For such 'obscene' writings, just because of their greater artistry and charm, will presumably have far greater influence on readers than dull inartistic writings."

Despite the implication in the *Roth* opinion to the contrary, the constitutional definition of obscenity cannot include all materials which, in their dominant theme and taken as a whole, appeal to "prurient interest," in the sense of "having a tendency to excite to lustful thoughts." Instead, one must reject the view that *Roth* made "prurient interest" appeal the sole test of obscenity. The Court, in Justice Harlan's 1962 words, could not have intended "any such quixotic and deadening purpose as would bar . . . all material . . . which stimulates impure desires relating to sex."

The *Roth* test was narrowed in another important respect in *Manual Enterprises, Inc. v. Day* (1962). The Post Office had barred three magazines from the mails on the ground that they were obscene and nonmailable under the so-called Comstock Act. The magazines consisted largely of photographs of nude or near-nude male models. The publishers brought suit for injunctive relief which was denied by the lower court.

To Chief Justice Warren, with his personal abhorrence of pornography and smut peddlers, the case was a simple one. At the conference on the case, the Chief Justice opened the discussion with a short statement for affirmance. As he saw it, "Congress has power to regulate the mail and to exclude obscenity. This is not censorship because they can distribute some other way, by express, truck, etc."

Warren then asked, "Is this obscenity?" He felt it was. "On the showing made and the admissions, these appeal to prurient interest" — i.e., under the *Roth* test. Warren also thought that "the procedure is as expeditious as a thing of this kind can be."

Justice Clark agreed with Warren. The others were hopelessly split, with Justices Black and Douglas rejecting any Post Office power to exclude from the mails and Justices Harlan and Stewart upholding the power to exclude obscene matter, but doubting that the magazines were obscene. Justice Brennan stated still another view. He voted to reverse on the ground that there was no statutory authorization for the administrative proceeding and, even if there was, the Post Office procedure ran afoul of the limitations imposed where prior restraint — preventing publication or distribution — is employed.

The case was assigned to Justice Harlan, whose opinion concluded that the magazines were not obscene under a test requiring "patent offensiveness" as well as the "prurient interest" appeal demanded by *Roth*.

After he had received the Harlan draft adding the "patent offensiveness" requirement to the *Roth* test, Justice Brennan wrote to Justice Harlan that he had "some difficulty with the element 'patent offensiveness.' I have the reaction that this element would only serve to limit obscenity to 'hard core' pornography . . . . And I have trouble defining 'hard core,' although no trouble at all recognizing it when I see it" — which anticipated Justice Stewart's famous 1964 statement that, though he could not define hard-core pornography, "I know it when I see it." Brennan wondered "whether the introduction of the element of 'patent offensiveness' would really be an improvement upon the *Roth* test, or only result in still further confusing an already confused subject."

Despite the Brennan objection, the "patent offensiveness" requirement has been adopted by the Court as a needed limitation upon the *Roth* test. According to the Harlan opinion, to hold that the determination of obscenity "does not require any determination as to the patent offensiveness . . . of the material itself might well put the American public in jeopardy of being denied access to many worthwhile works in literature, science, or art." It is, wrote Harlan, only "material whose indecency is self-demonstrating" — i.e., meets the test of patent offensiveness, as well as that of prurient-interest appeal — that must be deemed beyond the scope of First Amendment protection.

Fanny Hill Case

Another element was added to the obscenity test in *A Book Named "John Cleland's Memoirs of a Woman of Pleasure" v. Massachusetts* (1966). It arose out of a Massachusetts court finding that the Cleland book — popularly known as *Fanny Hill* after its narrator and principal character — was obscene and not entitled to First Amendment protection. That state court had ruled *Fanny Hill* obscene, asserting that the fact that "this book has some minimal literary value does not mean it is of any social importance." "Social importance," in its view, did not mean that a book which met the requirements of prurient-interest appeal and patent offensiveness must be utterly worthless before it may be deemed obscene.

At the *Fanny Hill* conference, Justices Black and Douglas once again asserted their absolutist view of the First Amendment, urging that it protected obscene and nonobscene material alike. The majority, however, refused to repudiate the *Roth* holding that obscenity was beyond First Amendment protection. On the merits, nevertheless, the conference majority (Chief Justice Warren and Justices Clark, Harlan, Brennan, and White) voted to affirm. However, Justice Fortas expressed strong concern that an affirmance would give rise to a new wave of "book-burning." Justice Brennan then decided to write an opinion to reverse. His opinion found that *Fanny Hill* was not obscene, since, even on the view of the court below, it possessed "a modicum of social value." The decision was based on Brennan's three-prong definition of obscenity: "Under this definition . . . three elements must coalesce: it must be established that (a) the dominant theme of the material taken as a whole appeals to a prurient interest in sex; (b) the material is patently offensive because it affronts contemporary community standards relating to the description or representation of sexual matters; and (c) the material is utterly without redeeming social value."

To the *Roth* requirement of prurient-interest appeal and that of patent offensiveness, *Fanny Hill* added one of utter lack of redeeming social importance: "A book cannot be proscribed unless it is found to be *utterly* without redeeming social value. This is so even though the book is found to possess the requisite prurient appeal and to be patently offensive."

Chief Justice Warren and Justice Fortas joined the Brennan opinion soon after it was circulated. Justice Stewart had also said that he was prepared to join that part of Brennan's opinion stating the definition of obscenity because he thought it important to have a majority statement of the definition. However, Justice Clark circu-

lated a dissent that took issue with Brennan's three-pronged definition of obscenity, objecting that requiring a book to be "utterly
without redeeming social value" meant giving "the smut artist free
rein to carry on his dirty business." The Clark dissent contained a
description of the sexual episodes in *Fanny Hill*. This led to a
Memorandum to the Conference from Justice Douglas: "In view of
Brother Clark's passion for detail, why don't we all chip in and buy
him a copy of MY LIFE & LOVES, by FRANK HARRIS, published by
Grove Press, Inc."

After he read the Clark dissent, Justice Stewart withdrew his
agreement to join Justice Brennan. He had concurred in the Brennan
opinion only for the purpose of obtaining a majority statement of the
constitutional definition, and withdrew his concurrence now that it
was clear that it would no longer achieve that result. When Justice
Brennan delivered his opinion, it had only the concurrences of the
Chief Justice and Justice Fortas. Nevertheless, the plurality believed
that Brennan's obscenity definition would be the one followed by the
lower courts since Justices Black, Douglas, and Stewart indicated in
their separate concurrences that they would go at least that far in
delimiting the area of First Amendment protection.

Under the "social-importance" test stated by Justice Brennan,
the Supreme Court decision in *Fanny Hill* was plainly correct. The
detailed description of the many sexual episodes in the book contained in Justice Clark's dissent is, if anything, a pallid portrayal of
the original prose; Cleland's narration by a prostitute of the particulars of her trade has, indeed, been characterized as "the pornographic
best seller of all time" — a nonstop romp through incessant scenes of
all sorts and types of sexual debauchment. But the whole point is that
all of this becomes irrelevant if we adopt the social-importance test as
it is stated by the high bench.

Whatever we may think about the scatological aspects of the
Cleland work, it can scarcely be said that it is *"utterly* without social
value." At a minimum, *Fanny Hill* has at least a modicum of historical value, both as an account which, in the words of one critic, "gives
a lively, though no doubt, a somewhat highly colored picture of
certain aspects of contemporary English life" and as illustrative of a
stage in the development of the English novel.

In addition, it cannot be denied that *Fanny Hill* has definite
literary appeal. Its language is elegant throughout, and though its
story, such as it is, exists only to provide occasion for detailed
accounts of sexual adventures, even its priapean passages are not
besmirched by gross or unseemly language. Compared to the
pornography that passes for the "realistic, naturalistic" novel of our

day, Cleland's work reads like a masterpiece — though, to one familiar with eighteenth-century English literature, it really reads like the third-rate novel of the period that it is.

Yet, third-rate as literature or not, it cannot truthfully be said that *Fanny Hill* has no historical or literary value at all. That being the case, it plainly meets the social-importance test, since it cannot be found to be "*utterly* without redeeming social value."

A more difficult question is that of whether the social-importance test, as it was applied in the *Fanny Hill* case, is itself valid. If we would be realistic about it, we would recognize that the test makes it possible for virtually all materials to pass First Amendment muster. As it is put by Justice White, dissenting in *Fanny Hill*, "If 'social importance' is to be used as the prevailing opinion uses it today, obscene material, however far beyond customary limits of candor, is immune if it has any literary style, if it contains any historical references or language characteristic of a bygone day, or even if it is printed or bound in an interesting way. Well written, especially effective obscenity is protected; the poorly written is vulnerable. And why shouldn't the fact that some people buy and read such material prove its 'social value'?"

The approach just stated is not as far-fetched as it may, at first, appear — particularly if we bear in mind the practice adopted by publishers of offensive materials of inserting high-sounding "messages" in each work published to give it a putative "redeeming social value" and hence bring it within the Supreme Court test. One can make out a case for the social value of almost any literature — even for hard-core pornography. Justice Douglas asks in a 1966 opinion, "When the Court today speaks of 'social value,' does it mean a 'value' to the majority? Why is not a minority value cognizable? . . . if the communication is of value to the masochistic community or to others of the deviant community, how can it be said to be 'utterly without redeeming social importance'?"

In addition, in these cases, judges trained in the law normally find it all but impossible to determine, on their own judgment alone, whether a challenged work is utterly without social importance or has, on the contrary, a modicum of social value. The element of "social value," says Justice Black in the same 1966 case, is "as uncertain, if not even more uncertain, than is the unknown substance of the Milky Way. . . . Whether a particular treatment of a particular subject is with or without social value in this evolving, dynamic society of ours is a question upon which no uniform agreement could possibly be reached among politicians, statesmen, professors, philosophers, scientists, religious groups or any other type of group."

If a case-by-case assessment of social values is to be made by individual judges and jurors, they must be aided by others. "We are judges," plaintively proclaims Justice Douglas' *Fanny Hill* concurring opinion, "not literary experts or historians or philosophers." The result is that the courts are not only willing, but most desirous, to hear the views of expert witnesses on the matter. In consequence, obscenity trials involve a procession of expert witnesses, who testify in terms of erudite literary, psychological, philosophical, theological, and other arcane disciplines.

The difficulty in all this is that, in the present state of learned thought in the disciplines involved, it is possible to produce apparent experts who will find social value in practically all matters of any nature. The quality of expertise in the field of obscenity is shown by the *Fanny Hill* case itself. An expert there testified that the book had "literary merit." To illustrate his assertion, he pointed to the description of a prostitute, "who is 'red-faced, fat and in her early 50's, who waddles into a room.' She doesn't walk in, she waddles in." Well might Justice Clark's dissent declare, "Given this standard for 'skillful writing,' it is not surprising that he found the book to have merit." Even more extreme was the reliance by Justice Douglas on a minister's comparison (printed at length as an appendix to his *Fanny Hill* opinion) between Cleland's work and a popular religious book, to show that both "symbolize the human quest for what is moral" — a comparison which would strike the reader throughout as delicious satire, except that it is made in all seeming seriousness.

Analysis of the reported decisions leads to the conclusion that, no matter how much challenged material may appeal to prurient interest and regardless of how patently offensive it may be, it is still possible to produce experts who will testify that, from a literary, psychological, or other learned point of view, it is not "*utterly* without social value." This was true in the Supreme Court cases discussed and it has also been true in other cases involving even more offensive material. Such testimony has been available even in cases involving the graphic portrayal of acts of sexual intercourse and even when sexual deviations of the most loathsome kind are displayed. In a case decided by a federal court of appeals in 1966, the Swedish film *491* (which had even been denied a license by the notoriously liberal Swedish Board of Film Censors) involved deviate acts (including the homosexual debauching of a young boy, sexual orgies, and the forcing of a large dog to have sexual relations with a prostitute). Yet the film importer was still able to produce impressive experts to testify (apparently with a straight face) that the film had social importance and worth as a criticism of the Swedish welfare state and of welfare methods and workers and was of theological or religious importance (which latter conclusion was, weightily enough, based upon the fact that most of the immoral action took place in the home of a well-intentioned, though weak, man named Krister — which some of the experts said showed that he was somehow connected with Christ).

All of this would be laughable except for the fact that the social-importance test as applied in *Fanny Hill* requires the courts to receive and evaluate this type of expert evidence in obscenity cases. Not long after *Fanny Hill* was decided, I urged, in my *Commentary on the Constitution* (1968), "it would be better for all concerned if the high bench were to give up the social-importance test, as applied in the *Fanny Hill* case." That is exactly what the Court did in *Miller v. California* (1973) — now the leading obscenity case.

Obscenity Redefined

Miller v. California arose out of a conviction for mailing unsolicited sexually explicit material in violation of a state statute that incorporated the *Fanny Hill* obscenity test. The Court used the case as the occasion for stating a revised definition of obscenity. In the first place, said the Burger opinion of the Court, "we now confine the permissible scope of [obscenity] regulation to works which depict or describe sexual conduct." The Court thus specifically rejects the view still followed in the English cases that nonsexual matters which "tend to deprave and corrupt" can also be held obscene. Under *Miller*, there is no room for a pornography of violence, as well as of sex, which government may be permitted to reach.

The *Miller* opinion then stated what the "basic guidelines for the trier of fact must be: (a) whether 'the average person, applying contemporary community standards' would find that the work, taken as a whole, appeals to the prurient interest; (b) whether the work depicts or describes, in a patently offensive way, sexual conduct specifically defined by the applicable state law; and (c) whether the work, taken as whole, lacks serious literary, artistic, political, or scientific value."

Miller stated specifically that it did not adopt the "*utterly* without redeeming social value" test of *Fanny Hill*. The third element listed by *Miller* is, unlike the *Fanny Hill* test, stated in positive rather than negative terms (*Fanny Hill*, said *Miller*, had "called on the prosecution to prove a negative, *i.e.*, that the material was *utterly* without redeeming social value — a burden virtually impossible to discharge under our criminal standards of proof "). In addition, greater leeway may be given for a finding of obscenity in the *Miller* shift from "utterly" to "serious" and the replacement of "social value" with "literary, artistic, political, or scientific value."

The Court offered a few "plain examples" of the second element stated by *Miller*:

(a) Patently offensive representations or descriptions of ultimate sexual acts, normal or perverted, actual or simulated.

(b) Patently offensive representation or descriptions of masturbation, excretory functions, and lewd exhibition of the genitals.

Under the second *Miller* element, assured the Court, "no one will be subject to prosecution for the sale or exposure of obscene materials unless these materials depict or describe patently offensive 'hard core' sexual conduct specifically defined by the regulating state law." And, even then, not when the materials "have serious literary, artistic, political, or scientific value."

It has been said that *Miller's* most controversial aspect is its rejection of the national-standards approach to its first element. Under both *Roth* and *Miller*, obscenity is to be determined by "applying contemporary community standards." *Miller*, however, rejected the widely followed view that obscenity proceedings must be structured around evidence of a *national* "community standard." Instead, state, rather than national, standards are to be applied. The First Amendment, said the *Miller* opinion, cannot be "read . . . as requiring that the people of Maine or Mississippi accept public depiction of conduct found tolerable in Las Vegas, or New York City . . . . People in different States vary in their tastes and attitudes, and this diversity is not to be strangled by the absolutism of imposed uniformity."

Other Obscenity Aspects

Scienter. An important limitation upon obscenity prosecutions was imposed in *Smith v. California* (1959). Smith owned a bookstore in Los Angeles. He was convicted of violating an ordinance making it unlawful for any bookseller to have an obscene book in his possession. As interpreted by the California courts, the offense consisted solely of the possession of the book, without any requirement of scienter — i.e., knowledge of the obscene character of the book. At the conference on the case, Chief Justice Warren conceded that the book in question was probably obscene. "But," he said, "the ordinance is bad for failure to require the element of scienter." All agreed that the ordinance was bad, except Justice Harlan. Justice Brennan issued an opinion of the

Court reversing, as the Chief Justice had urged, on the scienter ground. This ordinance, said the opinion, would have a chilling effect on the sale of all books, "by penalizing booksellers even though they had not the slightest notice of the character of the books they sold." At the *Smith* conference, Justices Black and Douglas had urged that the scienter ground was too narrow. Black said, "If I thought books could be censored, I'd think this case hard to distinguish from narcotics. So I'd reverse on the ground the Constitution doesn't allow censorship of any book." Douglas commented, "I don't think this is obscene by my standard or Lady Chatterley's. So I can go for reversal on either ground."

Justice Douglas was referring to the Court's 1959 decision striking down New York's attempt to ban the film, *Lady Chatterley's Lover*, as obscene. That decision had led retired Justice Sherman Minton to write to Justice Frankfurter that he would have voted the other way in the case. "Adultery," the retired Justice asserted, "has been outlawed since Moses brought the tablets down from the Mountain . . . . To say that this policy cannot be carried out by N.Y. preventing the teaching of adultery as a way of life because the Constitution makes teaching adultery something protected by it seems ridiculous to me — I suppose a gangster school set up to teach crime would be protected."

Pandering. *Ginzburg v. United States* (1966) was decided at the same time as the *Fanny Hill* case. Ginzburg had been convicted of violating the federal obscenity statute by selling through the mails *Eros* (a hard-cover magazine with articles and photographs on "love, sex, and sexual relations"); *Liaison* (a newsletter on sex and sexual relations); and *The Housewife's Handbook on Selective Promiscuity* ("a sexual autobiography detailing with complete candor the author's sexual experiences from age 6 to 36").

The *Ginzburg* conference was sharply divided. The vote was four (Chief Justice Warren, and Justices Clark, Brennan, and White) to affirm, and four (Justices Black, Douglas, Harlan, and Stewart) to reverse. Justice Fortas divided his vote among the publications *Ginzburg* had sold. He found *Liaison* obscene, and *Housewife's Handbook* not obscene because he thought it had therapeutic value. He said that he would probably join an opinion to hold *Eros* obscene.

After the conference, Chief Justice Warren persuaded Justice Fortas to join an opinion affirming Ginzburg's conviction based on a pandering approach. Though Ginzburg's pandering had not been discussed at the conference, a decision based on it fitted in directly with Warren's approach to obscenity. In his concurring opinion in the 1957 *Roth* case, Warren had stressed that defendants "were engaged in the commercial exploitation of the morbid and shameful craving for materials with prurient effect." And, in another opinion, the Chief Justice had said, "It is the conduct of the individual that should be judged," not the quality of the books he sold.

To Warren, Ginzburg was marketing his materials with the representation that they were pornographic. They were mailed from Intercourse and Blue Ball, Pennsylvania, and Middlesex, New Jersey, and what the Court called the "leer of the sensualist" permeated Ginzburg's advertising. The Chief Justice's approach here accepted the oft-voiced claim of the advertising industry that the image of a product becomes a part of the product itself.

Warren's pandering approach was also accepted by Justice Brennan, to whom the opinion was assigned. When he circulated a *Ginzburg* draft based on it, the Chief Justice immediately indicated his willingness to join. Warren did suggest one modification. He did not want the doctrine limited to cases where the *sole* emphasis was on the sexually provocative aspect of the material. Justice Brennan, however, insisted that the restriction imported by the word "sole" was necessary to prevent abuse of the pandering doctrine by the lower courts. Warren gave way on the point and the *Ginzburg* opinion stressed, "Where the purveyor's *sole* emphasis is on the sexually provocative aspects of his publication, that fact may be decisive in the determination of obscenity."

Under *Ginzburg*, at least in close cases, evidence of pandering may be used to show the obscene nature of given material. That, of course, makes application of the *Roth-Miller* test even more difficult. While Justice Brennan was announcing the *Ginzburg* decision, Chief Justice Warren passed him the following note: "Because of the quizzical expression on the faces of some of the Sol. Gen's. staff I wonder how happy they are with *Ginzburg*, because you know it will cast quite a work burden on that office and on the US Attorneys."

Variable Obscenity. In both *Roth* and *Miller*, the Court stressed that the governing test turned upon whether the material at issue would be considered obscene by "the average person." In adopting the "average-person" standard, the Court was, in effect, following the approach of Judge Woolsey in the celebrated 1933 *Ulysses* case, where he said that challenged material must be tested by "its effect on a person with average sex instincts — what the French would call *l'homme moyen sensual* — who plays, in this branch of legal inquiry, the same role of hypothetical reagent as does the 'reasonable man' in the law of torts and 'the man learned in the art' on questions of invention in patent law."

As a general proposition, the adoption by the Supreme Court of the average-person standard marks a significant step forward. It avoids the danger of lowering the level of legally allowable material to a point beyond that really necessary to protect the morals of the community. The problem in this respect was once stated graphically by an English judge: "Are we to take our literary standards as something that is suitable for a fourteen year old schoolgirl?"

The question just asked was answered with a resounding negative in *Butler v. Michigan* (1957). Butler had been convicted of violating Michigan's obscene literature statute that made it a crime to sell or distribute a book or other reading matter containing materials "tending to the corruption of the morals of youth." The Court struck down the Michigan law on the "narrow ground" that, in making it an offense to make available to the general public a book having a potentially deleterious influence upon youth, Michigan was reducing its adult population to reading only what is fit for children: "Surely this is to burn the house to roast the pig."

Butler does not, however, prevent the enactment of laws especially designed to protect children. As Chief Justice Warren put it in a 1964 opinion, "A technical or legal treatise on pornography may well be inoffensive under most circumstances but, at the same time, 'obscene' in the extreme when sold or displayed to children."

The Court adopted this approach in *Ginsberg v. New York* (1968). Ginsberg, owner of a stationery store and lunch counter, had sold "girlie" magazines with nude photos to a sixteen-year-old boy. He was convicted of violating a state law prohibiting the sale to minors under seventeen of materials defined to be obscene on the basis of appeal to them, even though they might not be obscene for adults.

Justice Brennan's *Ginsberg* opinion of the Court was influenced by a letter from Justice White. "As I understand this skillful and subtle opinion," White wrote, "state infringement of First Amendment rights is justified by the overriding state interest in the welfare of children, expressed here by a not unreasonable assertion that the described material is harmful to the young." Justice Brennan's original draft had emphasized that the invasion of First Amendment rights was not a significant one, given the state's interest in preventing access by children to obscene materials.

Justice White's letter stated, "This is perhaps a less stringent burden on the State than we have insisted on when First Amendment rights are at stake. Am I right that this is a new rule, perhaps limited to the reading material of minors?" White preferred a different approach: "If you had taken the pure obscenity route, I suppose you would have pursued further the idea that obscenity is outside the area of First Amendment protection. Although these magazines were protected with respect to adults, they are not when sold to children because they appeal to prurient interest (as they do [not] with adults), because they are beyond community limits of candor for children (which they are not in the case of adults) and because they have no social value — indeed, they are harmful to children (which cannot be so rationally said with respect to adults)."

The White letter recognized that Justice Brennan might have chosen a combined approach. "Perhaps you ride both horses in this case, that is, this junk is outside the First Amendment, but if it is not, it still may be kept from children because there is a sufficient reason to do so which overrides both the minor's right to read and the right of the publisher to disseminate. This is admirable eclecticism if it gets four other guys."

Justice Brennan revised his *Ginsberg* draft to meet Justice White's preference. He reworked the obscenity test to provide for a doctrine of "variable obscenity," which would reach material aimed at children, though not obscene to adults. Such material could be ruled "outside" the First Amendment, as Justice White had suggested.

Ginsberg is based upon the principle that the average-person test is relevant only to materials distributed to the public at large. On the other hand, materials distributed to children are intended to and do reach a special audience that is not made up of average mature adults of the type contemplated by the *Roth-Miller* test. Hence, it is reasonable not to apply the average-person standard to such materials aimed at such special audience.

The same may be true of material aimed at other special audiences. Soon after *Roth*, the Supreme Court reversed rulings that *One — The Homosexual Magazine* and other magazines designed to appeal to homosexuals were obscene. The contents of these publications were characterized by one Justice as "designed solely as sex stimulants for homosexuals." At the same time, it is difficult to see how, under a literal application of the *Roth* test, they can be considered obscene, since they plainly do not appeal to the prurient interest of the average person. To a sexually normal audience, the contents of such publications would be, at best, of no interest and, at worst, evocative of some disgust.

But there can be no doubt that the materials involved in these cases do have as their dominant theme an appeal to the prurient interest of the homosexual audience at which they are aimed. To apply only the average-person standard is to miss the whole point and results in treating a magazine "designed so as to attract the male homosexual" as just another "Jack and Jill" type of publication.

In a more recent decision on the matter, the highest tribunal itself has come to recognize that the average-person standard may not be appropriate for judging the obscenity of materials aimed at a sexually deviant audience. In *Mishkin v. New York* (1966), the books at issue were described by the Court as ones which "depict such deviations as sado-masochism, fetishism, and homosexuality. Many have covers with drawings of scantily clad women being whipped, beaten, tortured, or abused." It was contended that these depictions of deviant sexual practices, such as flagellation, fetishism, and lesbianism, did not satisfy the prurient-interest appeal requirement of *Roth* because they did not appeal to a prurient interest of the "average person" in sex, that "instead of stimulating the erotic, they disgust and sicken." The Court rejected the argument, saying it was founded on an unrealistic interpretation of the prurient-interest appeal requirement.

As stated by the *Mishkin* opinion, the governing rule is that "Where the material is designed for and primarily disseminated to a clearly defined deviant sexual group, rather than the public at large, the prurient-appeal requirement of the *Roth* test is satisfied if the dominant theme of the material taken as a whole appeals to the prurient interest in sex of the members of that group." In other words, when materials are aimed at a deviant group the criterion is met when there is prurient appeal to members of that group, even if not to the average person.

Stirring the Pot

Macaulay tells us "that extreme relaxation is the natural effect of extreme restraint and that an age of hypocrisy is, in the regular course of things, followed by an age of impudence." The great historian was speaking of the moral reaction in Restoration England that followed the age of overrestraint during the Puritan ascendancy. His comment is, all the same, equally applicable to our own day and explains the changing moral climate as a pendulous response to the Comstockery that prevailed not too long ago.

All history teaches us, nevertheless, that extremes beget extremes and that a pendulum, by its very nature, rarely stops after the first swing. The Victorian era of excessive restraint, particularly in sexual matters (at least so far as public morality was concerned), has given way to a period of freedom and frankness with regard to sex and other moral matters that has been all but unique in our society. The changed moral climate is apparent to any observer with even limited experience in the field; on all sides he sees materials made available to the public which, not too long ago, would without a doubt have been deemed within the scope of statutes banning obscenity.

So far has the pendulum swung, indeed, that the view has been widely expressed (even by members of the highest bench) that the Constitution must be construed to prohibit all obscenity laws. In the 1966 words of Justice Black, "the First Amendment forbids any kind or type or nature of governmental censorship over views as distinguished from conduct." The same opinion has been expressed in even stronger terms by a publisher with personal experience in the area. "The sooner," he asserts, "the Supreme Court . . . declares all obscenity statutes unconstitutional, the sooner will America enjoy true free speech. And the sooner will our Constitution cease to be mocked."

More recently, Justice Brennan, himself the author of the *Roth* opinion, stated that he had become convinced that the *Roth* approach "cannot bring stability to this area of the law without jeopardizing fundamental First Amendment values." That was true because neither *Roth* nor any other formulation of the Court could adequately distinguish obscene material unprotected by the First Amendment from protected expression. The time had therefore come, Brennan urged, in a 1973 opinion, to make a significant departure from the approach initiated in *Roth*: "I would hold, therefore, that at least in the absence of distribution to juveniles or obtrusive exposure to unconsenting adults, the First and Fourteenth Amendments prohibit the State and Federal Governments from attempting wholly to suppress sexually oriented materials on the basis of their allegedly 'obscene' contents."

There is much to be said for the Brennan view. In his already-mentioned letter on Justice Brennan's *Ginsberg* draft opinion, Justice White concluded, with regard to obscenity cases, "the more one stirs, the more this pot boils." Certainly, the Court's obscenity decisions lead one to agree with the White inference that it might be best to "stir the pot" as little as possible. After all in the words of one court summarizing the decisions on obscene literature, "a comparison of judicial reactions to recent *causes célèbres* suggests that the judiciary in our tormented modern civilization are also lost in a wilderness."

To be sure, society does have a legitimate interest in the protection of public morals, which is recognized in all developed systems of law — an interest specifically recognized by the Court as "a substantial government interest in protecting . . . morality" as recently as 1991. It is significant that until *Roth* the public power to proscribe obscenity was never seriously questioned. Now we are, for the first time in the law, met with the notion that the exercise of that power is inconsistent with the First Amendment. Complete freedom of expression in sexual matters has, in truth, become a basic tenet of many molders of contemporary opinion — so much so, in fact, that any attempt to assert for legal prohibitions even a restrained role in the area of obscenity is met on all sides by the tarnishing tag of philistinism.

If the extreme view that the First Amendment forbids any governmental intrusion and hence outlaws all obscenity laws be accepted, it means the total absence of authority to protect the community even from that hardcore pornography that Justice Stewart knew when he saw it — which D.H. Lawrence once characterized as "the catastrophe of our civilization" — a consequence so extreme that it has never been compelled by an American court.

Yet, though the power to protect the public from obscenity is recognized by the Constitution, its exercise is subject to significant safeguards. Foremost among these is, of course, the very existence of judicial control, which ensures that the relevant officials do not have the last word. The question of what constitutes obscenity in a given case is ultimately a judicial question, to be decided, in the final analysis, by the highest court to which the case is appealed. The duty to decide does, to be sure, impose upon the courts the dreary chore — "tedious, time-consuming and unwelcome," one Justice has termed it — of personally reading or examining all challenged materials. The availability of the judicial determination is, all the same, the ultimate safeguard to ensure against improper exercises of the power to proscribe obscenity.

In addition, as already seen, under *Smith v. California*, though traffic in obscene literature may be outlawed, one may not be subjected to any criminal sanction unless he is chargeable with knowledge of the obscenity. Obscenity laws are also subject to the general requirement that all criminal statutes must meet — that the terms used must be sufficiently definite to provide reasonably ascertainable standards of guilt; otherwise, the statutes will be ruled void for vagueness. According to the Court, however, the term "obscenity" itself, used in a criminal statute prohibiting obscenity, is sufficiently precise to meet the constitutional requirement. This holding is based upon the fact that such a statutory term is construed to include the *Roth-Miller* definition of obscenity, as it has been applied in the cases. So construed, the statute gives adequate warning of the conduct proscribed and marks boundaries sufficiently distinct for judges and juries fairly to administer the law.

There are also important restrictions imposed upon public power to deal with obscenity which are procedural in nature. In a 1964 opinion, Chief Justice Warren summarized the situation in this respect: obscene material may be proscribed, "provided always that the proscription, whatever it may be, is imposed in accordance with constitutional standards. If the proceeding involved is criminal, there must be a right to a jury trial, a right to counsel, and all the other safeguards necessary to assure due process of law. If the proceeding is civil in nature, the constitutional requirements applicable in such a case must also be observed. There has been some tendency in dealing with this area of the law for enforcement agencies to do only that which is easy to do — for instance, to seize and destroy books with only a minimum of protection."

The tendency referred to by the Chief Justice is one that goes counter to the procedural protections demanded by the Constitution. The organic guarantees protecting free expression preclude the summary seizure and destruction of materials alleged to offend statutory proscriptions against obscenity. This means that allegedly obscene literature and other materials may not be seized, and certainly not destroyed, without a judicial hearing on the question of obscenity. Even though, in one sense, obscene books may be considered contraband, it is erroneous to assume that the standards governing searches and seizures of allegedly obscene books do not differ from those applied with respect to narcotics, gambling paraphernalia, and other contraband. The possessor of obscene material is entitled to a judicial hearing on the issue of obscenity before his material may be treated as contraband.

One can also ask whether printed words alone can meet today's interpretation of the *Roth-Miller* test. It is true that the Court held specifically in *Kaplan v. California* (1973) that books containing only words and no pictures may be obscene. As Chief Justice Burger put it, "words alone can be legally obscene in the sense of being unprotected by the First Amendment." Under the *Roth-Miller* test, "no distinction was made as to the medium of the expression." Obscenity can manifest itself in written descriptions as well as conduct or pictorial representation.

It is true that the Court has treated all forms of expression with indiscriminate equality under the *Roth-Miller* test: no differentiation is made between the printed word, pictures, and presentations in the flesh. Nor is there difference of treatment, with regard to literature, as between hard-cover books, paperbacks, periodicals, and newspapers or, with regard to visual representations, between the theater and other "live" performances, motion pictures, and broadcasting. All come equally within the same obscenity test under the Supreme Court decisions.

Reflection will, however, demonstrate that a definition of obscenity that does not differentiate at all between the forms of expression that may be involved is bound, at best, to be procrustean in nature. If the existence of obscenity depends primarily, as the *Roth-Miller* test indicates, upon the effect of particular material upon the audience involved, it is all but self-evident that such effect will vary with the form and medium of expression used. In this respect, the old saw about a picture being worth a thousand words is certainly valid. No matter how graphic a written description of a subject dealing with sexual matters may be, it can scarcely have the impact of a picture; nor can the still picture compare in effect with a moving visual presentation; nor can even the moving picture possibly make the impression produced by living persons.

Properly applied, perhaps, the *Roth-Miller* test will by itself make the necessary differentiations between different forms and media of expression. That is true since the criteria of prurient-interest appeal and patent offensiveness will be met differently in accordance with the form in which allegedly offending materials are presented to their audience. From this point of view, a written description of sexual conduct — however graphic — will scarcely meet the *Roth-Miller* criteria in the same way as a live performance.

To apply the obscenity prohibition to the printed word is to ignore the lessons of centuries of experience with censorship. The authority of the censor, all history cautions us, is peculiarly subject to Lord Acton's famous aphorism on the corrupting nature of power. At one time or another, virtually all the now-acknowledged classics have come within the censors' attempted ban. Even Shakespeare has not been exempt. According to an early nineteenth-century critic, "Barefaced obscenities, low vulgarities and nauseous vice so frequently figure and pollute his pages that we cannot but regret the luckless hour he became a writer." And it was not so long ago that Bowdler published his expurgated version of Shakespeare, "in which . . . those words and expressions are omitted which cannot with propriety be read aloud in a family." Even if we accept the *Roth-Miller* test as a valid criterion, the courts should hesitate before using it to strike down the written word alone.

6

Libel and Privacy

One morning in January 1986, writes Leonard Garment in the *New Yorker*, "I got a phone call from Richard Nixon. 'Did you see Tony Lewis's review of that book in Sunday's Times?' he asked. 'Why don't you check it out? Maybe we'll find out what really happened in that case.' "

"That case" was *Time, Inc., v. Hill,* a case that had been decided by the Supreme Court in 1967. "That book" was my new volume, *The Unpublished Opinions of the Warren Court.* It analyzed eleven important Warren Court cases, including *Time, Inc. v. Hill,* in the light of conference notes, draft opinions, and memoranda written by the Justices during their decision process. (These previously secret documents had been made available to me while I was doing research for my judicial biography of Chief Justice Warren.)

Nixon was interested in *Time, Inc. v. Hill* because it was the only case that he had argued in the Supreme Court. Moreover, it was a case that he had lost when he thought that he had the better of the argument. He learned from the *Unpublished Opinions* book how the Court had originally decided in his favor. The draft opinion of the Court by Justice Fortas was converted into a dissent when several of the Justices switched their votes.

When he learned of the decision from the Clerk of the Court, Garment telephoned Nixon at his apartment. "He listened, asked one or two questions about the authorship of the opinions, and then said, 'I always knew I wouldn't be permitted to win a big appeal against the press.' "

Nixon had not, however, lost the case because of the personal antagonism of the Justices. Indeed, the two members of the Court who personally detested Nixon the most — Chief Justice Warren and Justice Fortas — voted for his position throughout the decision process on the case.

Time, Inc. v. Hill is noteworthy, however, not only because of Nixon's connection with it. The Court's decision there was the first and still the most important one on the constitutional relationship between the law of libel and the right of privacy that has become of such significance in contemporary law. Nevertheless, before we can discuss the case, we must deal in some detail with the impact of the First Amendment upon the law of libel, particularly under the landmark decision in *New York Times Co. v. Sullivan.*

Libel and the First Amendment

The law of defamation constitutes an exception to the freedom of expression guaranteed by the First Amendment. To a First Amendment absolutist such as Justice Black, even that exception was unwarranted. Black was once asked whether he would make an exception in freedom of speech and press for the law of defamation. He answered that he had no doubt that the First Amendment "as written and adopted, intended that there should be no libel or defamation law in the United States . . . just absolutely none so far as I am concerned."

The view expressed by Justice Black is a logical consequence of his conception that the rights secured by the First Amendment are absolute in nature and, as such, admit of absolutely no governmental limitation, at least where words alone are involved. Nor is there any difference in application of the Black view as between criminal and civil cases. Even with regard to the latter the Justice asserted that the law of defamation is inconsistent with the First Amendment: "it was not intended to authorize damage suits for mere words as distinguished from conduct." As Justice Black saw it, "libel laws are abridgements of speech and press and therefore are barred in both federal and state courts by the First and Fourteenth Amendments."

Despite the Black view to the contrary, it cannot be doubted that, as the Court stated in *Near v. Minnesota* (discussed in Chapter 1), "the common-law rules that subject the libeler to responsibility . . . are not abolished by the protection extended in our Constitutions." There is, Justice Douglas pointed out in an opinion concurred in by Justice Black himself, "special historical evidence" that "the law of libel . . . was intended to be treated in a special manner by those who drafted the First Amendment." From the beginning the law has recognized that the First Amendment furnished no protection against the penalties imposed by the law for libel and slander. We may thus conclude, with Justice Douglas, that "The individual today has recourse to the Courts to recover damages for slander or libel. The First Amendment gives no license to defame the citizen."

The law of libel has presented the greatest difficulty for those who urge an absolutist conception of the First Amendment. The

Black view of the incompatibility of libel and the First Amendment notwithstanding, not even most exponents of the absolutist conception, such as Justice Douglas, have really questioned the power of the law to restrict defamatory speech — at least where civil actions have been concerned. And even Justice Black himself, when once asked how soon he expected the courts to accept his view on private suits for defamation, answered, "Never."

It is not difficult to justify the law's refusal to bring libelous speech within the protection of the constitutional guaranty. Freedom of expression cannot immunize an actionable tort merely because the instrumentality by which the tort is committed happens to be language. The law looks upon the loss of reputation as similar to the loss of an arm or leg, and requires the inflictor to make comparable reparation. Defamation tends toward the category of "action," rather than pure speech, for purposes of First Amendment protection. The legitimate state interest underlying the law of libel is compensation for the harm inflicted by defamatory falsehood.

Since libelous speech may be treated as "action" which of itself injures the person defamed, there is no need to consider whether there is a direct relationship between such speech and other overt action. There is consequently no need to employ the test developed for speech that incites to action in violation of the law discussed in Chapter 3 in order to determine when libelous speech may be controlled by government. If we treat such speech as falling within the concept of unprotected speech, permitting recourse to the Courts for damages in libel suits is not inconsistent with the First Amendment — and that is the case regardless of whether there is any "clear and present danger" that the particular libelous speech will lead to any substantive evil that government has the power to prevent.

The point just made was stated expressly by the Supreme Court in a 1952 case: "Libelous utterances not being within the area of constitutionally protected speech, it is unnecessary, either for us or for the State courts, to consider the issues behind the phrase 'clear and present danger.' Certainly no one would contend that obscene speech, for example, may be punished only upon a showing of such circumstances. Libel, as we have seen, is in the same class."

New York Times Co. v. Sullivan

The relationship between the law of libel and the First Amendment received a new point of departure in *New York Times Co.*

v. Sullivan (1964). The too-freely-used hyperbolical term, landmark decision, may truthfully be employed to describe the action of the Supreme Court in that case. For, in its *New York Times* decision, the Court ruled for the first time that the governmental power to fix the bounds of libelous speech is confined by the First Amendment.

According to one of the most celebrated of Justice Holmes's aphorisms, "Great cases like hard cases make bad law." From this point of view, the facts involved in *New York Times Co. v. Sullivan* certainly may be said to have presented the Supreme Court with a hard case, as well as a great case. The immediate fact pattern there exercised a kind of hydraulic pressure which made what was previously clear seem doubtful and before which even seemingly settled principles of law had to bend.

The case arose out of a libel action brought by the elected police commissioner of Montgomery, Alabama, against four individual defendants and the *New York Times*. The complaint alleged that Sullivan had been libeled by statements in a full-page advertisement in the *Times*. The advertisement was flamboyant in character and described alleged violations of black rights by the police in Montgomery. The text appeared over the names of sixty-four persons, many of whom were widely known, and then there appeared the names of the four defendants, as individual Southern clergymen. The advertisement was inserted and paid for by a civil rights organization. Because the advertisement was placed by a responsible person, was signed by so many well-known persons, and seemed accurate on its face, the *Times* published it without seeking to confirm its accuracy.

Even though nowhere in the advertisement was there any charge made against Sullivan by name, the Alabama court had ruled that the impersonal statements in the ad were libelous per se and had upheld a verdict in his favor of half a million dollars (the largest verdict awarded in any libel case in the state). According to a federal judge, "The Supreme Court of the United States was confronted by a somewhat baffling problem insofar as the facts of the case were concerned. The jury had rendered a grotesquely huge verdict for $500,000, although there was no contention that the plaintiff had suffered any pecuniary loss . . . . If the verdict had stood, it does not seem unreasonable to suggest that there would have been a miscarriage of justice."

At the oral argument, counsel for the *Times* based his argument for reversal on the broadest possible ground. He characterized the Alabama judgment as a "hazard to the freedom of the press in a dimension not confronted since the early days of the Republic."

When Justice Brennan asked him whether the First Amendment gave the published article absolute protection, he replied that it did. In effect, counsel for the *Times* was asserting the absolutist view of the First Amendment that had been urged for years by Justice Black — that all such libel suits were barred by the First Amendment.

At the conference on the case, the Chief Justice urged reversal, but not on the broad constitutional ground argued by counsel for the *Times*. Warren said he "would not go on the First Amendment giving complete immunity to the *Times*." Instead, he stressed that, "in this area of speech and press, where criticism is of official conduct, we ought to require a high degree of certainty that this involved the official. We must look more carefully to see if it was directed at the official or was in the area of fair comment."

Here, Chief Justice Warren indicated, the references to the police were really not libelous. Thus, the advertisement charged that the Montgomery police had "ringed" a black college campus. To the Chief Justice, " 'ringed' the place with police is not libelous. It's really synonymous with deployment, which actually occurred." Warren concluded that a "test of fair comment might be forged" and the case should be decided under it.

Most of the others agreed, with even Justice Douglas stating, "In the area of public affairs, the doctrine of fair comment is available to protect the *Times* and the other petitioners". Justice Black, however, strongly differed. "If libel laws are valid when the press criticizes official conduct," he declared, "I'd find it hard to set this aside." But of course Black rejected all libel actions in such cases, saying, "If there's anything clear to me it is that in public affairs it was intended to foreclose any kind of proceedings which would deter full and open discussion. At least in the area of public affairs, the First Amendment permits any type of discussion, including false."

The case against the Black position was stated by Justice Harlan. "The First Amendment," he maintained, "does not outlaw state libel laws in this field of public discussion." Instead, Harlan said, the competing interests at stake must be balanced against each other. "This case presents a classic illustration of a First Amendment problem where the public interest in discussion has to be accommodated with the private right not to be defamed."

Justice Harlan asserted that "we have to set down some constitutional standards to which state libel actions are subject." He urged adoption of two federal rules: "1) a high standard of proof across the board on all elements of the action; 2) while punitive damages are not constitutionally outlawed, they can't be assessed without proof of actual malice."

Justice Clark agreed that the Court should "separate in matter of proof private libels from public affairs and put a much heavier burden on what it takes to tie something to a public official." Justice Brennan summed up the basis on which the conference voted to reverse the verdict. This was that the First Amendment should be interpreted to require "clear and convincing evidence" of every element of a cause of action for libel brought by a public official against a critic of his official conduct. In this case, evidence meeting this standard was lacking on such key elements as the defamatory nature of the advertisement and the "connection" between it and Sullivan. "None of these charges," Brennan asserted to the conference, "amount to this and we could reverse just on the ground this wasn't defamation."

The *New York Times Co. v. Sullivan* decision process illustrates how one Justice can play a creative role in molding Supreme Court jurisprudence. The Chief Justice assigned the case to Justice Brennan. In preparing his opinion the Justice did not confine himself to the narrow ground voted by the conference. Instead, the Brennan opinion of the Court stated an entirely new rule to govern such suits by public officials. The starting point of the *New York Times* decision is what the Brennan opinion terms the "general proposition that freedom of expression upon public questions is secured by the First Amendment." The *Times* case must consequently be considered "against the background of a profound national commitment to the principle that debate on public issues should be uninhibited, robust, and wide-open, and that it may well include vehement, caustic, and sometimes unpleasantly sharp attacks on government and public officials."

The Brennan opinion then went on to bring the advertisement at issue, "as an expression of grievance and protest on one of the major public issues of our time," within the bounds of constitutional protection. However, "The question is whether it forfeits that protection by the falsity of some of its factual statements and by its alleged defamation of respondent."

Justice Brennan answered the question thus posed by asserting that "the First Amendment guarantees have consistently refused to recognize an exception for any test of truth." Erroneous statement, too, must be protected if debate on public issues is to be truly free, for "factual error affords no warrant for repressing speech that would otherwise be free."

Under the *New York Times* decision then, neither factual error nor defamatory content suffices to remove the constitutional shield from criticism of official conduct, and the combination of the two elements is no less inadequate. The First Amendment is held to require a "rule that prohibits a public official from recovering damages for a defamatory falsehood relating to his official conduct unless he proves that the statement was made with 'actual malice' — that is, with knowledge that it was false or with reckless disregard of whether it was false or not." And plaintiff has the burden of proving that there was "actual malice."

The result is to limit the power to award damages for libel in actions brought by public officials against critics of their official conduct. The role of "the citizen-critic of government" is deemed so important in the society — "It is as much his duty to criticize as it is the official's duty to administer" — that it is necessary to immunize him from the deterrent effect of libel suits unless malice on his part can actually be proved. Honest error on the critic's part is thus protected as much as wholly truthful criticism.

In a 1991 case, the Court pointed out that the *New York Times* requirement of "malice" does not use the term in its ordinary sense of an evil intent or a motive arising from spite or ill will. Rather, "We have used the term actual malice as a shorthand to describe the First Amendment protections for speech injurious to reputation." Yet, the Court went on, not using a word with its ordinary meaning "can confuse as well as enlighten. In this respect, the phrase may be an unfortunate one." Hence, the Court now tells us, "In place of the term actual malice, it is better practice [to] refer to publication of a statement with knowledge of falsity or reckless disregard as to truth or falsity."

Public Officials to Public Figures

Under *New York Times Co. v. Sullivan*, the First Amendment requires the law of libel to recognize a "privilege of criticism of official conduct" that extends to honest misstatements of fact. Mere negligence does not suffice. The plaintiff, the Court has recently confirmed, must demonstrate that the author entertained serious doubts as to the truth or acted with awareness of probable falsity.

The *New York Times* opinion did not, however, answer the question of "how far down into the lower ranks of government employees, the 'public official' designation would extend." That question was given a partial answer in *Rosenblatt v. Baer* (1966). That case arose out of a libel action by Baer, the appointed Supervisor of a New Hampshire County Recreation Area, a facility operated by the county. A column by Rosenblatt in a local paper discussed the operation of the Recreation Area, noted it was doing better that year despite worse weather conditions, and asked, "What happened to all the money last year? and every other year?" Baer alleged that this falsely charged him with mismanagement or dishonesty. The jury awarded damages, and the New Hampshire Supreme Court affirmed.

In a Memorandum to the Conference on the case, Justice Brennan noted that the crucial question was "whether respondent was a public official within the meaning of *Times-Garrison*" — referring both to *New York Times v. Sullivan* and *Garrison v. Louisiana,* the case discussed in Chapter 3. "My own view," Brennan informed the Justices, "is that the nature of the public interest in free discussion, rather than the precise categorization of the function of the person defamed, should be determinative. On this reasoning, the category of public officials should include at least those persons whose conduct is a matter of public interest in a political context."

To Justice Brennan, Baer was definitely a public official, within *Times-Garrison.* "Clearly the public had an interest in respondent's discharge of his official duties. Moreover, his position was a [responsible] one, since he handled large sums of money and was apparently directly responsible to the governing body of the county. A formulation which included him could clearly avoid deciding whether all civil servants are public officials under the *New York Times* rule."

In his opinion of the Court, Justice Brennan concluded that Baer came within the *New York Times* doctrine: "the 'public official' designation applies at the very least to those among the hierarchy of government employees who have, or appear to the public to have, substantial responsibility for or control over the conduct of governmental affairs."

Justice Brennan explained his opinion in a memorandum to Justice Douglas: "it was my intent, however, to leave the issue of the 'little man' open, and even to hint that he might not be reached. This is why I noted that the interests protected in *Times* included *both* free discussion of public issues *and* free discussion of persons in positions of responsibility for and influence on such issues; and that *both* were factors that would influence the 'public official' determination."

"The test," the memo to Douglas went on, "is meant to suggest a 'table of organization' hierarchy, which would focus on the expected functions of persons (including reputed powers behind the throne of the Col. House type), and not some special role they might suddenly be revealed to have by the very publication which is challenged as libellous. I would be surprised to see public discussion of the qualifications of candidates for janitorial, secretarial, or like positions. I would be not at all surprised to see discussion of the qualifications of a proposed Recreation Area manager, whether or not rumors of peculation were abroad. To me, this is a tenable, functional, important distinction."

Under *Rosenblatt v. Baer*, according to Justice Brennan's opinion, "the 'public official' designation applies at the very least to those among the hierarchy of government employees who have, or appear to the public to have, substantial responsibility for or control over the conduct of governmental affairs." This includes all officials except those at the bottom of the governmental hierarchy, such as the "little man" illustrations in the Brennan memo.

In *Curtis Publishing Co. v. Butts* and *Associated Press v. Walker* (1967), *New York Times v. Sullivan* was extended to libel suits by "public figures" who were not government officials. Butts was a leading football coach who sued to recover damages for a *Saturday Evening Post* article that accused him of conspiring to "fix" a game. The defense was that the article was true. The jury returned a large verdict for Butts.

The companion case involved a libel action by Walker, a retired general, against the Associated Press for a news dispatch on a riot at the University of Mississippi during efforts to enforce a decree ordering enrollment of a black student. The dispatch stated that Walker had encouraged the rioters to use violence and had led a charge against federal marshals. The jury awarded $500,000 in damages, and the award was affirmed by the highest state court, which held that the *New York Times* rule was inapplicable.

At the conference on the cases, all the justices voted to reverse in *Walker*, but there was little agreement on the grounds of decision. In *Butts*, the vote was four-to-four, with Justice Harlan passing. Chief Justice Warren and Justices Clark, Stewart, and Fortas voted to affirm the judgment for Butts. The joke in the Court was that the Chief Justice's *Butts* vote was based upon his love of sports and that, to him, football coaches had a special status under the First Amendment. Warren did, however, agree that *New York Times* should apply to public figures as well as public officials. But he would at first not go along with Justices Black, Douglas, Brennan, and White and hold that this required reversal in *Butts*. He insisted that the *Saturday Evening Post* had engaged in shoddy practices and that Butts ought to be vindicated.

Justice Harlan, who had been assigned the cases, wrote a draft opinion that applied the *New York Times* standard to punitive damages. But it stated a special test for compensatory damages substantially similar to that stated in Justice Harlan's published opinion. Under it, public figures who were not public officials could recover for libel on a showing less than that required by *New York Times*. They needed to show only "highly unreasonable conduct constituting an extreme departure from the standards . . . adhered to by responsible publishers."

The catalyst for decision in *Butts* and *Walker* was, however, a Brennan draft opinion advocating full application of *New York Times* to public figures. Justice Brennan's draft criticized what he called Harlan's "hodgepodge" standard for compensatory damages.

The Brennan draft led the Chief Justice to tell Justice Brennan that he, too, was dissatisfied with Harlan's "hodgepodge" standard, although he was dead set against a reversal in *Butts*. Warren's willingness to apply the *New York Times* standard now made it possible to secure a Court majority for that standard. The Chief Justice wrote a separate concurrence applying "the *New York Times* standard in the case of 'public figures' as well as 'public officials.' " Justices Brennan and White joined the Warren opinion on this holding and Justices Black and Douglas joined on the application of *New York Times* in order to make a majority on that point. This meant that there were now five for applying the *New York Times* standard to public figures. When Justice Harlan announced the judgments of the Court in *Butts* and *Walker* on June 12, he added a statement (which appears as a footnote in his published opinion) that a majority of the Court rested decision on grounds other than those stated in his opinion.

Public Interest

Justice Brennan was the crucial influence in the Warren Court decisions applying the First Amendment to libel law. Both the *New York Times* rule and its application to public figures were Brennan's handiwork. The Justice continued his efforts to expand the *New York Times* rule — this time to matters of "public interest" — and he was successful in the first case on the subject in the Burger Court: *Rosenbloom v. Metromedia* (1971).

Metromedia's radio station had broadcast news of Rosenbloom's arrest for possession of pornography. The report said the police believed that they had hit the supply of a main distributor of obscene material. Rosenbloom sued for libel. The jury awarded substantial damages, but the court of appeals reversed, holding that the *New York Times* standard applied even though "plaintiff was not a public figure" and that plaintiff's evidence did not meet that standard.

As in the other libel cases discussed, Justice Brennan was the key figure in *Rosenbloom*. He was determined to push *New York Times* even further, and he was given the opportunity when the conference voted five to three (Justice Douglas not participating) to affirm and he was assigned the opinion. The majority votes were cast by Chief Justice Burger and Justices Black, Brennan, White, and Blackmun. Since the votes of the Chief Justice and Justice Blackmun seemed to be based largely on their stated unwillingness to allow a "smut peddler" any libel award, and since Justice Black followed his consistent view that all libel statutes were unconstitutional, Justice Brennan doubted that an opinion could be written that would command five votes.

Despite his doubt, Justice Brennan decided to write an opinion discarding the focus of earlier cases on the plaintiff as a "public official" or "public figure" and applying the *New York Times* standard to all cases involving a subject of general or public interest. A draft to that effect was circulated. The draft was intended to ensure that within a sphere of public interest, the press's freedom to publish could not be abridged by libel judgments based on the uncertain line of a jury's determination of negligence. The main questions that the Justice had to decide in writing the draft were the wording of the "test" to be used to describe the extent of the constitutional protection — "legitimate public" or "general public" interest were the two main contenders — and whether the opinion should assert that "public figures and officials" also had areas of privacy. Justice Brennan settled on "legitimate public interest" and the flat assertion that certain areas of the lives of even the most public men would be outside the constitutional requirement imposed.

Chief Justice Burger wrote to Justice Brennan that he had "considerable trouble" with the draft, although he "agreed with the general proposition that participation in any activity that is affected with an important public interest draws the participants somewhere in the 'target zone' the Court has given public officials and public figures." Almost a month later, Justice Brennan received a Burger letter joining the Brennan opinion, without any comment.

Justice Blackmun sent Brennan a note stating that he also would join if two changes were made in the draft: 1) Eliminate a reference to Professor Meiklejohn's article, *The First Amendment Is an Absolute* (Blackmun had written, "I suspect I am not an absolutist

119

so far as the First Amendment is concerned."); and 2) Limit the holding to protection for "for a genuine segment" of the media. Justice Brennan dropped the cite to Meiklejohn and specified in the holding that the news medium involved was a "licensed radio station." The latter change was intended to avoid the implications of Blackmun's desire for an express limitation to "genuine" news media. Justice Blackmun then joined the Brennan opinion and Justice Black circulated his concurrence in the result.

Almost three months after Justice Brennan's circulation, the dissenting opinions of Justices Harlan and Marshall — the latter joined by Justice Stewart — were sent around. Justice Brennan feared that the strong dissents might persuade Chief Justice Burger and Justice Blackmun to change their votes, but the Chief Justice invited Brennan into his chambers and reaffirmed his support. Burger rejected the major argument of the Marshall-Harlan position — that the Brennan opinion required too much attention by the Court to evaluations of the record — in effect, constitutionalizing the fact-finding process. The Chief Justice said that he, like Brennan, thought that the Marshall-Harlan approach involved as much scrutiny of the record.

Justice White now circulated his concurrence, which took the more limited view that the *New York Times* rule had to apply to all reporting of "the official actions of public servants." Justice Brennan pointed out to him that his shift in focus from the person involved to the issue really put him in the Brennan camp. But Justice White remained firm on issuing his own opinion.

Justice Brennan did, however, make an important change in his opinion that was a response to Justice Marshall's criticism that the Brennan opinion placed courts in the position of saying what it was legitimate for the public to know. The final Brennan draft changed the formulation of the governing test from "legitimate public interest" to "of public or general interest," borrowing the phrase from Samuel Warren and Louis D. Brandeis's seminal 1890 law review article on *The Right to Privacy*. The change was intended to make clear the thrust of the test — to divide the public from the private, and allow the press full play in the former area.

Despite the fragmented nature of the *Rosenbloom* decision and the fact that Justice Brennan spoke for only a plurality of three, it was generally assumed, as Justice White specifically stated in his concurrence, that "at least five members of the Court would support [the rule that] if the publication . . . was in an area of legitimate public interest," the *New York Times* standard would apply.

Gertz v. Robert Welch, Inc.

The Brennan success in importing the public interest test into the Court's jurisprudence was to prove short-lived. Three years after *Rosenbloom*, a new majority rejected the Brennan view that *New York Times* "should extend to the defamatory falsehoods relating to private persons if the statements concerned matters of general or public interest."

The rejection came in *Gertz. v. Robert Welch, Inc.* (1974). A Chicago policeman named Nuccio was convicted of murder. The victim's family retained Gertz, "a reputable attorney," to represent them in civil litigation against Nuccio. An article appearing in the John Birch Society magazine alleged that Nuccio's murder trial was part of a Communist conspiracy to discredit the local police, and it falsely stated that Gertz had arranged Nuccio's "frame-up," implied that Gertz had a criminal record, and labeled him a "Communist-fronter." Gertz sued for libel. The jury returned a verdict for Gertz, but the lower courts decided that the *New York Times* standard should apply and set aside the verdict, relying on *Rosenbloom*.

At the *Gertz* conference, Justice Brennan, of course, spoke strongly in favor of following *Rosenbloom*. But this time he was fighting a losing battle. Two new Justices, Powell and Rehnquist, had been appointed and they both voted against the Brennan position (Justice Black, whom Powell had replaced, had concurred in *Rosenbloom*). In addition, Chief Justice Burger who had joined Brennan's *Rosenbloom* opinion, indicated that he would vote to reverse.

The Chief Justice began his conference discussion by noting that the key question was "whether *Times* applies." Burger concluded that it did not. "I reject the idea" he said, that "a lawyer becomes a public figure because his client is. And he seems to be just another lawyer. That's different from Rosenbloom, who was a target among the law breakers."

Justices Stewart, Marshall, Powell, and Rehnquist also rejected the *Rosenbloom* test. "I can't accept the 'public interest' standard," declared Justice Powell, who was to write the *Gertz* opinion, "because it leaves the power to the press to determine what is 'public interest.'" That left the pre-*Rosenbloom* "public figure" standard as the relevant one and the consensus agreed with Justice Stewart when he stated, "Gertz for me is not a public figure in the *Times* sense merely because he's a prominent and well-known lawyer. So I'd let him have a state remedy."

At the conference, Justice Blackmun was ambivalent. He noted that he had joined *Rosenbloom* and still agreed with its test, but indicated that he would reverse for a new trial. Ultimately, Justice Blackmun joined the Powell *Gertz* opinion rejecting the *Rosenbloom* test. Blackmun did so, he wrote, in order to ensure that there was a Court majority for Powell's opinion, since it was "of profound importance for the Court . . . to have a clearly defined majority position that eliminates the unsureness engendered by *Rosenbloom*'s diversity."

As it turned out, only the Brennan concurrence continued to adhere to the public interest standard in *Gertz*. The Powell opinion of the Court flatly refused to apply *New York Times* to private individuals, as contrasted with public officials and public figures. Gertz himself was treated as a private individual by the Court. To be a public figure, he would have had to achieve "pervasive fame or notoriety" or be one who "voluntarily injects himself . . . into a particular public controversy." Gertz's participation in community and professional affairs was not enough.

In this respect, *Gertz* withdrew to the boundary fixed by the pre-*Rosenbloom* cases. As long as they did not impose liability without fault, the states were permitted to define for themselves the appropriate standard of liability for defamatory falsehoods.

Gertz is certainly less favorable to the press than the test urged by Justice Brennan. Yet *Gertz* hardly is enough to justify the conclusion that the Burger Court was hostile to the press. In *Gertz* the Court did not repudiate the *New York Times* rule of press protection; it only refused to extend it beyond the public-official/ public-figure test recognized by the Warren Court.

Even with regard to defamation suits by private individuals, it should be noted, *Gertz* laid down important limits that are protective of the press. Thus, the Powell opinion held specifically that though the states may fix the liability standard in such suits, they may not impose strict liability for defamatory speech; nor may punitive damages be permitted unless a plaintiff proves the *New York Times* type of "malice" — that is, "a showing of knowledge of falsity or reckless disregard for the truth."

What these *Gertz* limitations mean was pointed out in a letter from Justice White to Justice Powell on the latter's draft *Gertz* opinion. Under the opinion, Justice White wrote, "you still require fault beyond the damaging circulation of falsehoods. This pretty well forces the States to revise their libel laws substantially. Likewise, requiring that the private plaintiff prove actual injury to reputation imposes a substantial federal limitation on state libel laws, and pretty well scuttles the ingrained idea that there are certain statements that are per se libellous." In Justice White's view, as stated in another letter, there was no "satisfactory evidence or basis for further restricting state court power to protect private persons against reputation-damaging falsehoods published by the press or others."

As Justice White shows in his *Gertz* dissent, the restrictions on absolute liability and punitive damages imposed by *Gertz* do constitute substantial protections for the press. They may, in fact, be even more meaningful in terms of damage awards than the public interest test urged by Justice Brennan. From this point of view, *Gertz* was as much a victory as a defeat for the press and the vindication of its First Amendment rights.

Privacy and the Press

We come back now to *Time, Inc. v. Hill* — the case that Richard Nixon argued, where he found out why he lost in the Supreme Court from my book. The case arose out of New York's so-called privacy statute, and a word must be said about it before the *Hill* case itself can be discussed.

The right of privacy guaranteed by the New York law has its legal starting point in the now-celebrated Samuel D. Warren-Louis D. Brandeis article, *The Right of Privacy*. That article did nothing less than add a chapter to the law — one in which the individual was to be given a legally enforceable right of privacy.

Privacy is a right that is closely connected with the development of modern techniques that permit privacy to be invaded to an extent that would have been inconceivable not too long ago. It is more than mere coincidence that the rise of sensational journalism in the United States is usually dated from the acquisition of the *New York World* by Joseph Pulitzer in 1883, while the right of privacy was first asserted as a legal right in the Warren-Brandeis article of less than a decade later. It is, in fact, probable that the Warren-Brandeis article itself was a direct result of an invasion of the private life of one of the coauthors by the "yellow journalism" of the day.

What Warren and Brandeis were advocating was an individual right of privacy that the law should protect as against infringement by other individuals — a right to be vindicated by the private law of torts. The private-law right thus advocated was soon put to the judicial test and found wanting by the highest court of New York in the 1902 case of *Roberson v. Rochester Folding Box Co.*

In the *Roberson* case, the defendant had used a photograph

of the plaintiff, a pulchritudinous young woman, without her consent, to advertise its brand of flour, along with the legend "The Flour of the Family." Dean Prosser, a leading authority on tort law, once said that "the feebleness of the pun might have been enough in itself to predispose the court in favor of recovery." But the New York court held otherwise and, rejecting the Warren-Brandeis approach, ruled flatly that the right of privacy did not exist as a legally protected right.

However right the *Roberson* decision may have been under the law as it then stood, the holding that plaintiff was entitled to no protection whatsoever against the unauthorized use of her likeness upon an advertisement gave rise to a storm of public disapproval. "There was," the New York court conceded in a later case, "a natural and widespread feeling that such use . . . in the absence of consent was indefensible in morals and ought to be prevented by law." The consequence was a law enacted by the very next session of the New York Legislature giving statutory protection to the right violated in the *Roberson* case. Entitled "Right of Privacy," the New York statute makes it an actionable tort to use the name, portrait, or picture of any person "for advertising purposes, or for the purposes of trade" without written consent. This statute was the basis for the action brought in *Time, Inc. v. Hill*.

The action itself arose out of a story in *Life* magazine about a Broadway play, *The Desperate Hours*, which had been inspired by the experience of James J. Hill and his family, who had been held hostage in their home by escaped convicts. The play was fictionalized and had added scenes of violence for dramatic effect. The *Life* article portrayed the play as a reenactment of the Hills' experience and it contained photographs of scenes acted in the home where the Hills had been held. Hill sued *Life's* publisher under the New York privacy statute. Hill alleged that the *Life* article falsely represented that the play mirrored the Hill family's experience. The New York courts awarded Hill $30,000.

To the press, of course, *Time Inc. v. Hill* was newsworthy primarily because it marked Richard M. Nixon's debut before the Justices. Nixon, appearing for Hill, later said (and Leonard Garment confirms) that he had prepared for the occasion by carefully reviewing every case under New York's privacy statute, as well as numerous books, articles, and other materials. His preparation did not, however, prevent him from slipping up on the law of his native state during the argument. Relying on a California case to support his position, Nixon referred to it as resting on the common law. Chief Justice Warren, himself a California lawyer, was quick to correct him, asking whether there was any common law in the state.

Embarrassed, Nixon hesitated, then corrected himself, conceding that it was under the California Code.

The Justices differed in their estimate of Nixon's presentation. Former Justice Fortas told me that his performance was "mediocre." But others disagree. One Justice says that he was "first-rate" during the original argument in April 1966. At lunch after the argument, the Justices expressed surprise at how good he was. On the other hand, according to the same Justice, Nixon did not really seem to have his mind on the case during the October 1966 reargument, when he had taken time off from stumping for Congressional candidates to appear before the Court.

Although Warren made no secret of his antipathy toward Nixon (Warren's son once said that Nixon was one of only two men whom the Chief Justice termed an "evil man" — the other was a right-wing oil magnate), he consistently voted for Nixon's position in the *Hill* case. In the first conference on the case, the Chief Justice declared, "It's a fictionalization of these people's experience and false and, in that circumstance, there's no First Amendment problem. In this limited application, I see no threat to a free press." Justice Black took the opposite position, saying "newspapers have the right to report and criticize plays. This is nothing but a statute prohibiting the press from publishing certain things." The conference agreed with Chief Justice Warren and voted six-to-three to affirm the New York judgment, with Justices Black, Douglas, and White voting for reversal.

Chief Justice Warren assigned the case to Justice Fortas, who circulated a sixteen-page draft opinion of the Court. The Fortas draft contained what one of the Justices said was an "invective" against the press — Leonard Garment wrote that its "language . . . verged on excoriation." After summarizing the case, Fortas declared, "The facts of this case are unavoidably distressing. Needless, heedless, wanton injury of the sort inflicted by *Life's* picture story is not an essential instrument of responsible journalism. Magazine writers and editors are not, by reason of their high office, relieved of the common obligation to avoid inflicting wanton and unnecessary injury. The prerogatives of the press — essential to our liberty — do not preclude reasonable care and thoughtfulness. They do not confer a license for pointless assault."

The Fortas draft rejected the claim that the *Life* article was privileged as a newsworthy article because it was "a fictionalized version of the Hill incident, deliberately or heedlessly distorted beyond semblance of reality." Fortas concluded that, as applied to such an article, the New York statute was not "in fatal collision with the freedom of the press. The deliberate, callous invasion of the Hill's right to be let alone — this appropriation of a family's right not to be molested or to have its name exploited and its quiet existence invaded — cannot be defended on the ground that it is within the purview of a constitutional guarantee designed to protect the free exchange of ideas and opinions. This is exploitation, undertaken to titillate and excite, for commercial purposes."

The Fortas draft concluded that the New York statute, as applied to this case, was not contrary to the First Amendment. Freedom of the press is not violated by imposition of liability on publications responsible for "misappropriation of [plaintiff's] identity for purposes which . . . are nothing more than the knowingly false attribution of events to a named person for the purpose of accentuating the dramatic or entertainment value of a publication."

The Fortas draft did not, however, come down as the opinion of the Court because of a dispute between Justices Fortas and White over the interpretation by the New York courts of the state's privacy statute. This led to an order setting the case for reargument in which counsel were requested to clarify the New York law on the matter.

Before the Court reconsidered the case, Justice Black circulated a sixteen-page printed memorandum on which, according to his wife's diary, he had worked all summer. The memo began with an acerbic attack on the "weighing process," under which "it is concluded . . .that, under the circumstance, it is more important to abridge than to permit the exercise of free speech." (The memorandum is more scathing in its condemnation of the "weighing process" than anything else ever published by Justice Black. What the Justice wrote on the matter in his ultimate *Time, Inc. v. Hill* concurrence was but a pale reflection of the polemic contained here.) Above all, the Black memorandum stressed the baneful effect that it asserted the tentative majority decision would have on First Amendment rights. Under the Fortas draft opinion, Justice Black asserted, the First Amendment prohibition against abridging freedom of speech and the press "has added to it . . . the language 'unless a majority of the United States Supreme Court in its sole, unreviewable wisdom decides that it would or might serve the public interest to curtail or penalize publication of certain matters.' "

The Fortas draft, according to the Black memo, had stated "the facts in such a way as to buttress its determination to deprive *Life* of its First Amendment rights." Justice Black was particularly biting in his comments on the language in Fortas' proposed *Times v. Hill* opinion. The result would be a chilling effect that would frighten the press so much that publishers would hesitate to report news as long as there was "doubt as to the complete accuracy of the newsworthy facts."

That result, Justice Black concluded, would hardly be consistent with the intent of the Framers "to guarantee the press a favored spot in our free society." Indeed, the Black memo went so far as to assert, "After mature refection I am unable to recall any prior case in this Court that offers a greater threat to freedom of speech and press than this one does, either in the tone and temper of the Courts' opinion or in its resulting holding and judgment."

The scathing Black memorandum had the effect its author intended. At the postreargument conference, the Court changed its decision and voted seven to two for reversal. Only Chief Justice Warren and Justice Fortas still voted for affirmance. Justice Black, as senior majority Justice, assigned the case to Justice Brennan.

The new Brennan opinion of the Court held that the *New York Times v. Sullivan* standard must be applied to actions under the New York privacy statute. In a case like *Time, Inc. v. Hill*, plaintiff must show not only "fictionalization," but also "knowledge of the falsity or that the article was prepared with reckless disregard of the truth." The case was remanded to give the New York courts an opportunity to apply the statute in the constitutionally prescribed manner.

The Black memorandum, in his wife's words in her diary, "got the Court on his *Time* Magazine Libel case." Justice Black's success in this respect had an important effect upon the law governing privacy and the press. Had the Fortas draft come down as the opinion of the Court in *Time, Inc. v. Hill* it would, in effect, have applied the pre-*New York Times v. Sullivan* libel rule (under which truth alone was a valid defense even in suits brought by government officials and public figures) to privacy suits. This would have made for a substantial difference between libel actions for defamation and actions for invasion of privacy, so far as the press was concerned.

More important, it might have made it possible for plaintiffs to avoid the *New York Times* limitations by framing their actions against the press in privacy, rather than defamation, terms. The result might have been a chilling effect that would have discouraged press ardor in vindicating First Amendment rights. As Justice Black put it in his memorandum criticizing the Fortas draft, "One does not have to be a prophet, I think, to foresee that judgments like the one in this case can frighten and punish the press so much that publishers will cease trying to report news in a lively and readable fashion as long as there is — and there always will be — doubt as to the complete accuracy of the newsworthy facts."

The Fortas draft had been based upon what Fred Rodell called its author's "tremendous respect" for the right of privacy — a right which, to Justice Fortas, outweighed even the First Amendment in a case such as *Time, Inc. v. Hill.* Fortas himself, according to Bruce A. Murphy, his leading biographer, "had what can only be termed a hatred of the press." To Justice Fortas, as he told a friend, reporters were "mongers," who were both "dirty" and "crooked" and "destroy[ed] people." Garment tells us that Fortas always maintained that the *Life* article that forced his resignation had been *Time, Inc.'s* punishment of him for his stand in the *Hill* case.

Justice Black's position was, of course, entirely different. His First Amendment absolutism was not affected by any abuses the press might have committed. Black's fundamentalist approach to the Constitution led him to place freedom of the press, specifically guaranteed, above a right such as privacy, which did not have any express constitutional foundation.

In addition, Justice Black's hostility toward the Fortas view in *Time, Inc. v. Hill* was undoubtedly influenced by his personal antipathy toward Justice Fortas. Soon after Fortas was appointed to the Court, he was met by Black's continuing hostility. It is not clear why the Alabaman displayed such distaste for his new colleague. In part, at least, it was caused by Justice Black's fear that Justice Fortas was reviving the constitutional approach of balancing competing interests that had been urged by Justice Frankfurter, for so many years Justice Black's principal antagonist on the Court.

At any rate, as Garment put it in his *New Yorker* article, one of the ironies of *Time, Inc. v. Hill* "is that after all the speculation about how the Court would respond to Richard Nixon, the personal animus that determined the course of the *Hill* case was not antagonism toward Nixon by any member of the Court." On the contrary, the two Justices who personally detested Nixon the most — Chief Justice Warren and Justice Fortas — fought for Nixon's position throughout the case. If personal hostility influenced the decision, it was that between Justices Black and Fortas.

In conclusion, however, it should be noted that *Time, Inc. v. Hill* itself was not the last word on the legal issue presented to the Justices. Cases decided by the Court since the retirement of Chief Justice Warren have narrowed the scope of both *Time, Inc. v. Hill* and the *New York Times v. Sullivan* doctrine upon which it was based.

As seen, *Time, Inc. v. Hill*, as finally decided, held that Hill's action under the New York privacy statute was governed by the *New York Times* doctrine — i.e., Hill had to prove not only that the *Life* account was fictionalized, but also that it was written "with 'actual malice' — that is, with knowledge that it was false or with reckless disregard of whether it was false or not." Hill himself was treated by the Court as a "public figure" to whose suit the *New York Times* standard was applicable. Under *Gertz v. Robert Welch, Inc.,* however, someone like Hill would no longer be treated as a "public figure" for purposes of the *New York Times* doctrine. As we saw, *Gertz* holds that, unless there is clear evidence of general fame or notoriety in the community and pervasive involvement in the affairs of society, an individual should not be deemed a public figure unless he voluntarily injects himself into a particular public controversy.

Under *Gertz*, someone in Hill's position would not be a "public figure" to whose libel suit the *New York Times* limitation would apply. The same should now logically be true of Hill's privacy action. This view is borne out by a statement in the *Cox Broadcasting* case (discussed in Chapter 4) by Justice Powell, who delivered the *Gertz* opinion. According to him, "The Court's abandonment [in *Gertz*] of the 'matter of general or public interest' standard as the determining factor for deciding whether to apply the *New York Times* malice standard to defamation litigation brought by private individuals . . . calls into question the conceptual basis of *Time, Inc. v. Hill."*

Since *Time, Inc. v. Hill* applies the *New York Times* standard to privacy suits, the *Gertz* modification of *New York Times* should also apply to such suits. This means that an action such as that brought by Hill, under what the *Cox Broadcasting* opinion calls "a false-light theory of invasion of privacy" (which alleges publication of false and misleading information as well as invasion of privacy), would now be governed by a more relaxed standard for liability for the publisher than that laid down in both *New York Times* and *Time, Inc. v. Hill.* This appears to bring the law on the matter back to where it would have been if *Time, Inc. v. Hill* had been decided in accordance with the original opinion of the Court drafted by Justice Fortas.

7

"Or of the Press"

The First Amendment guarantees both freedom of speech and freedom of the press. The freedom of speech guaranty is one of freedom of expression. To be sure, publishers are guaranteed freedom of expression by the amendment, but so are we all because of the free speech guaranty. As Justice Stewart put it in a noted 1974 addresp, "If the Free Press guarantee meant no more than freedom of expression, it would be a constitutional redundancy." When James Madison and his colleagues prohibited Congress from making any law "abridging the freedom of speech," they specifically added, *"or of the press."* Why were those words added if all that was intended was to guarantee publishers the freedom of expression which they were already entitled to under the Free Speech Clause? If the words are not redundant, what, if anything, do they add to the freedom of expression previously secured by the Free Speech Clause?

Press as Fourth Estate

There is no doubt that the First Amendment was intended to guarantee to the press full freedom of expression — in Leonard Levy's phrase, "a right to engage in rasping, corrosive, and offensive discussion on all topics of public interest." Yet, as seen, that right was already guaranteed to all Americans by the Free Speech Clause. There are suggestive indications that, in adding "or of the press" to the First Amendment, Madison and his colleagues meant the words to be more than a redundant appendage to the free speech guaranty. The language they used indicated an intention to provide a guaranty that is unique among those contained in the Bill of Rights. This difference was pointed out in Justice Stewart's 1974 speech: "Most of the other provisions in the Bill of Rights protect specific liberties or specific rights of individuals: freedom of speech, freedom of worship, the right to counsel, the privilege against compulsory self-incrimination, to name a few. In contrast, the Free Press Clause extends protection to an institution."

More specifically, said Stewart, " The primary purpose of the constitutional guarantee of a free press was to create a fourth institution outside the government as an additional check on the three official branches."

Thomas Carlyle tells us, in his *Heroes and Hero Worship*, "[Edmund] Burke said that there were three estates in Parliament; but in the Reporters' Gallery yonder, there sat a *Fourth Estate* more important far than them all." Carlyle went on, "It is not a figure of speech or a witty saying; it is a literal fact — very momentous to us in these times. Indeed," Carlyle noted, "in modern Society . . . the Press is to such a degree superseding the Pulpit, the Senate, the *Senatus Academicus* and much else."

The Fourth Estate aphorism does not appear in Burke's published speeches and other writings. Yet it is unlikely that Carlyle made up his attribution. If Burke did make the statement, it is most likely that it was known on this side of the Atlantic, since Burke's words were as widely known here as they were in England. What is clear, at any rate, is that, influenced by Burke or not, Americans did develop a concept of the press as a Fourth Estate Institution by the time the Bill of Rights was ratified.

Under the Burke notion, Justice Stewart tells us, "a free press was not just a neutral vehicle for the balanced discussion of diverse ideas. Instead, the free press meant organized, expert scrutiny of government." This was precisely the concept of the press that was stated in the First American document asserting a right to freedom of the press — the Address to the Inhabitants of Quebec of 1774, in which the Continental Congress presented its case to our northern neighbor. It contained an exposition of the fundamental rights of the colonists as they were understood by the representative assembly chosen from all the Colonies. For the first time in an American official document, freedom of the press was recognized as an essential right. The right was stated to be important not only because of its "advancement of truth, science, morality, and arts in general," but also because by the press's actions "oppressive officers are shamed or intimidated, into more honorable and just modes of conducting affairs."

There are further indications as well that, whether or not they were influenced by any Burke statement, the Americans of the day had a concept of the press similar to that attributed to Burke by Carlyle. Leonard Levy, in his *Emergence of a Free Press* (the leading history of freedom of the press in early America), concludes that, by the time of the First Amendment, American newspapers had achieved a "watchdog function as the Fourth Estate." Indeed, Levy tells us, "Freedom of the press . . . meant that the press had achieved a special status as an unofficial fourth branch of government, the Fourth Estate; whose function was to check the three official branches by exposing misdeeds and policies contrary to the public interest."

To support this conclusion Levy cites a 1790 statement by a Virginia paper that the press was the source from which the people "learn the circumstances of our country, its various interests, and relations. Here too public men and measures are scrutinized. Should any man or body of men dare to form a system against our interests, by this means it will be unfolded to the great body of the people, and the alarm instantly spread through every part of the continent. In this way only, can we know how far our public servants perform the duties of their respective stations."

A year earlier, John Adams, in a letter to Chief Justice William Cushing, had referred to "Our chief magistrates and Senators and Company" and asked, "How are their characters and conduct to be known to their constituents but by the press?" It was freedom of the press, said Philip Freneau, a leading Jeffersonian editor, that allowed newspapers to "estimate justly the wisdom of leading measures of administration."

To the Framers of the First Amendment, it can be argued, freedom of the press meant an institutional role for publishers and editors to criticize government and public officials to ensure that they would act properly in the exercise of their powers. From this point of view, the First Amendment was intended to confirm what the *Minneapolis Star* opinion, discussed in Chapter 4, called "the basic assumption of our political system that the press will often serve as an important restraint on government."

What is clear is that, starting with the 1776 Virginia Declaration of Rights, the first American Bill of Rights, American organic instruments provided separate protection for freedom of the press, in addition to constitutional guarantees protecting freedom of speech. When Madison drafted the amendments that became the Federal Bill of Rights, he followed the same approach, providing separate guarantees for both freedom of speech and of the press. in what became the First Amendment.

Indeed, in his proposed amendments, Madison went even further in providing specific protection for the press. The Madison proposals included a provision that "No State shall violate . . . the freedom of the press." Though Madison said that he "conceived this to be the most valuable amendment in the whole list," it was eliminated by the Senate and never became part of the Federal Bill of Rights.

Both his draft of the First Amendment and his rejected

amendment prohibiting the states from infringing upon freedom of the press indicate that Madison sought to provide specific protection for the press in addition to that secured under the freedom of speech guaranty. In so doing, he was following the constitutional practice that had prevailed in the drafting of the state Bills of Rights, starting with the 1776 Virginia Declaration of Rights.

The record is, of course, too obscure to enable us to speak with assurance, but it can be argued that the First Amendment was intended to give effect to the institutional Fourth Estate conception of the press. If that is true, freedom of the press is not limited to the freedom of expression otherwise guaranteed by the First Amendment. The press becomes a protected institution and the First Amendment becomes the instrument that enables the press to perform its institutional role.

If this was the intent behind the First Amendment, it has in large part been frustrated by the Supreme Court decisions. Except in one area — that of defamation — the Court has refused to treat the press differently from the public generally. The governing principle in the cases is that stated by Chief Justice Warren to his law clerk and discussed in Chapter 2: the "right of the news media . . . is merely the right of the public." Under the prevailing jurisprudence the press as an institution has no greater rights to enable it to fulfill a Fourth Estate function. Instead, whatever First Amendment rights the press possesses, it possesses (in Warren's words) "not because it is the press, but because it is part of the public."

No Press Privilege

The indication that the addition of press protection in the First Amendment was intended to raise the Fourth Estate institutional conception to the constitutional plane is, as already conceded, based upon a most sketchy record. On the other side, it can be said that there is a simple explanation for the specific additional guaranty of freedom of the press in the First Amendment. To us today, the amendment's Free Speech Clause is a broad guaranty of freedom of expression which protects all forms of expression including so-called symbolic speech — i.e. nonverbal expressive conduct such as the burning of the flag. This broadside concept of constitutionally protected expressive conduct has, however, been developed entirely during the present century. In Madison's day, it may be doubted that freedom of speech alone protected more than vocal expression.

The more limited meaning of *speech* two centuries ago is

confirmed by the one dictionary available at that time — that published by Samuel Johnson in 1755. All of his definitions of "speech" relate to vocal expression: "articulate utterance," "vocal words," "anything spoke[n]," "talk," and "oration." Only *press* in Johnson's lexicon has to do with printed matter, being defined as "The instrument by which books are printed."

Madison and his colleagues may thus have feared that, if freedom of speech alone was specifically guaranteed, it would not have included protection for expression in print. To ensure that that would not be the result, they added specific protection for the press, so that both vocal and print expression would come within the constitutional guaranty. If that is true, the addition of press freedom was intended not to provide institutional protection for a Fourth Estate check upon government, but only to make certain that the press was given the same freedom of expression that the Free Speech Clause gave to members of the public. Hence, the Warren equation of the right of the press with the right of the public is consistent with the intent behind the First Amendment.

Be that as it may, there is no doubt that the Supreme Court jurisprudence on the matter has rejected the Fourth Estate concept of the press with additional institutional rights and has instead accepted the Warren notion of the press vested only with the same rights as members of the public. In practice, this means that the press is, in the main given only the right guaranteed to everyone by the Free Speech Clause — full freedom of expression. From this point of view, the First Amendment did not give the press more rights than it would have if the Press Clause had never been added by Madison and his colleagues. The press has only the same rights as the public to enable it to perform its Fourth Estate function.

That this is the result under the Supreme Court jurisprudence may be seen from the cases on access to news discussed in Chapter 2. The Fourth Estate concept might have served as the basis for a broad press right of access to news. That would give the news media a right of access to public institutions and documents so that they can perform their function of informing the public and thus holding government to proper standards. As a federal court stated in a 1965 case enjoining enforcement of a state senate resolution barring a paper's reporters from its proceedings, "To sanction such a use of state power would be to take a dangerous step toward press control and censorship."

In his dissent in the *Houchins* case discussed in Chapter 2, Justice Stevens urged that the need for a press right of access "rested upon the special importance of allowing a democratic community access to knowledge about how its servants were [acting]." As we saw in Chapter 2, the Stevens opinion was originally prepared as the draft *Houchins* opinion of the Court, but a vote switch changed the decision and the opinion became the Stevens dissent. If the opinion had come down as the opinion of the Court, our law would have been on the way to confirming a press right of access to news. The final *Houchins* decision the other way meant that the new right was stillborn. Instead of the affirmation of the right of access to news that it would have been under the Stevens opinion, *Houchins* stands as the leading case denying that the right of access of the press is any greater than that of the public.

What is true of access to news has also been true of the other privileges claimed by the press to enable them to perform a Fourth Estate function. The claimed reporter's privilege not to disclose confidential sources was rejected in the *Branzburg* case discussed at the end of Chapter 2. Reporters are given only the same freedom of expression given to all of us by the Free Speech Clause. As Justice Stewart explained it in his 1974 address, "None of us — as individuals — has a right to refuse to tell a grand jury the identity of someone who has given us information relevant to the grand jury's legitimate inquiry. Only if a reporter is a representative of a protected institution does the question become a different one." Cases such as *Houchins* and *Branzburg* show that the Court has refused to accept the institutional notion of the press as an independent check on government upon which the Fourth Estate concept is based. If the First Amendment was intended to guarantee the institutional automony of the press, the cases in Chapter 2 go far to frustrate that intention.

Summing Up

According to Lucas Powe in a recent book on freedom of the press, "no legal issue so infuriates the press as does libel." Yet the area of defamation is one in which the law has definitely been tilted in favor of the press by *New York Times Co. v. Sullivan*, discussed in the previous chapter. Under it, defamation of a public official or public figure is constitutionally protected unless "malice" as defined by *New York Times* is proven. In practice, the *New York Times* rule is used by the press rather than the public, since it is the press which is responsible for the criticism of official conduct that *New York Times* was intended to shield.

The press has criticized the post-New York *Times* cases for unduly narrowing application of the *Times* rule, particularly in *Gertz v. Robert Welch, Inc.*, where, as seen in the previous chapter, the Court refused to extend *New York Times* to private individuals, even though they were involved in events of interest to the public. Despite the criticism, a strong case can be made that the right of privacy of such individuals is also deserving of protection in an age where the press is too often the prying tabloid with no consideration for the individual's right to be let alone — what Justice Brandeis called "the most comprehensive of rights and the right most valued by civilized men."

The truth is that the press itself is never satisfied with the current state of First Amendment law. As Anthony Lewis puts it in his book, *Make No Law*, "When the Supreme Court decides a case against a claimed press interest, editors and publishers too often act as if the Constitution were gone." In particular, the Burger and Rehnquist Court jurisprudence is condemned as depriving the constitutional guaranty of much of its force. Yet, even today in the midst of the Rehnquist Court's movement toward a more restrictive view of constitutional rights, the press in this country enjoys more freedom than the press in any other time or place. Let us summarize the different aspects of press freedom under the First Amendment as they have been discussed in the prior Chapters, to see how extensive they really are.

In the first place, of course, there are the core freedoms from licensing and prior restraints. What to Milton was the utopian vision of his *Areopagitica* has become the foundation of press law under the First Amendment. As far as the traditional press is concerned, the amendment categorically outlaws licensing, censorship, or restrictions upon publication, except in the extremely narrow circumstances mentioned in the *Pentagon Papers* case. "So far as the Constitution goes," says Justice Stewart in his 1974 address, "the autonomous press may publish what it knows, and may seek to learn what it can."

In addition, despite conflicting evidence on whether the Framers intended to go beyond the Blackstone conception of freedom of the press as embodying only freedom from prior restraint, the First Amendment today is interpreted as a broad shield against subsequent punishments for publication in the media. The law today agrees with Justice Holmes when he wrote to Zachariah Chafee concerning his earlier adherence to the Blackstone view in the *Patterson* case discussed in Chapter 3, "I simply was ignorant."

It is, however, more than the limited Blackstone view that the law rejects today. Chapter 3 has shown how, despite its persistence in our history — from the 1798 Sedition Act to the World War I Espionage Acts — the law of seditious libel must now be deemed inconsistent with the First Amendment. Criticism of government by the press, no matter how intemperate or mean-spirited, and even press advocacy of extreme governmental changes, may no longer by punished as seditious. Even press advocacy of violence or other unlawful action may not be punished unless it meets the strict requirements of the *Brandenburg* test discussed in Chapter 3 — it must "be directed to inciting or producing imminent lawless action and is likely to incite or produce such action." It is most probable, as we concluded in Chapter 3, that no press publication will ever be found to meet the *Brandenburg* requirement. We saw also that the Supreme Court has all but eliminated contempt by publication as a restriction upon the press.

It is true that the Supreme Court has not given the broadcast media full First Amendment protection. The physical nature of the medium may , to be sure, make is impossible for the core prohibition against licensing to be applied to broadcasters. One may wonder, however, whether that should mean that broadcasters should be subject to regulation that would violate the constitutional rights of the traditional press. If a right-to-reply law or a statutory require-ment of access to the medium would infringe upon the First Amend-ment rights of newspapers, the same should be true so far as broadcasters are concerned. The First Amendment ideal may be the Holmes concept of an open "market place" for ideas. But it is not for government to further that concept by imposing any enforced right of access to the press. That should be true for all the news media, not for the print press alone.

The argument, based on scarcity of broadcast frequencies, on which the Court relied in *Red Lion* and the other cases discussed in Chapter 4, does not really justify any governmental takeover of editorial judgment that would plainly be unconstitutional if imposed upon the printed media. The law should also take account of the changing picture with regard to media and media outlets. There are now some 13,000 broadcast stations, as compared with about 1,700 daily newspapers. What Justice Stewart at the *Miami Herald* conference called "the monopoly of newspapers, as opposed to the "spectrum of frequencies" which he asserted "is not limited as claimed," may now make the scarcity argument more applicable to newspapers than broadcasters. At any rate, the time may have come for the Court to require a greater equation between the newer media and the traditional press. A bifurcated First Amendment was after all the last thing that Madison and his colleagues had in mind.

As interpreted by the Court, freedom of the press gives the press the liberty to publish what it chooses; it does not give it the tools to enable it to perform its Fourth Estate function. The First Amendment ensures that government will not hobble the press in its efforts to publish what it knows. But the press must learn what it can unaided by a constitutional right of access to news and other information. "The press," as Justice Stewart tells us in his 1974 speech, "cannot expect from the Constitution any guarantee that it will succeed." The Constitution is, in Stewart's phrase, definitely not a Freedom of Information Act.

We thus end as we began in Chapter 2, with the basic principle stated by Chief Justice Warren to his law clerk: the rights of the press under the First Amendment are essentially the same as those of the public. In Warren's words, "the right of the news media . . . is merely the right of the public."

The cases discussed throughout this volume indicate that the Supreme Court has by and large followed the Warren approach in the matter. The press has the same freedom of expression guaranteed to all of us by the Free Speech Clause. Despite press complaints, the Court has interpreted that freedom most generously, so that the press in this country is the least restricted in history. The Court has refused to go beyond the Warren dictum and give the press institutional rights beyond those it has, in Warren's words, "not because it is the press, but because it is a part of the public."

This result may make the words "or of the press," in the First Amendment superfluous. If the Framers intended the Press Clause to vest additional institutional rights in the press to enable it to perform a Fourth Estate function, that intention has been frustrated by the case law. The public's right to know about its government is protected by the existence of a free press, but the protection is indirect, since it is based upon the broad right of expression under the Free Speech Clause, not on any greater rights to secure and report information vested in the press.

Appendixes

TABLE OF CONTENTS

Appendix A

NEW YORK TIMES CO. v. UNITED STATES

403 U.S. 713 (1971)

PER CURIAM*

We granted certiorari . . . in these cases in which the United States seeks to enjoin the New York Times and the Washington Post from publishing the contents of a classified study entitled "History of U.S. Decision-Making Process on Vietnam Policy."

"Any system of prior restraints of expression comes to this Court bearing a heavy presumption against its constitutional validity." *Bantam Books, Inc. v. Sullivan*, 372 U.S. 58, 70 (1963); see also *Near v. Minnesota ex rel. Olson*. The Government "thus carries a heavy burden of showing justification for the imposition of such a restraint." *Organization for a Better Austin v. Keefe*, 402 U.S. 415, 491 (1971). The District Court for the Southern District of New York in the *New York Times* case, 328 F. Supp. 324, and the District Court for the District of Columbia and the Court of Appeals for the District of Columbia Circuit, 446 F.2d 1327, in the *Washington Post* case held that the Government had not met that burden. We agree.

The judgment of the Court of Appeals for the District of Columbia Circuit is therefore affirmed. The order of the Court of Appeals for the Second Circuit is reversed, 444 F.2d 544, and the case is remanded with directions to enter a judgment affirming the judgment of the District Court for the Southern District of New York. The stays entered June 25, 1971, by the Court are vacated. The judgments shall issue forthwith.

JUSTICE BLACK, with whom JUSTICE DOUGLAS joins, concurring.

I adhere to the view that the Government's case against the Washington Post should have been dismissed and that the injunction against the New York Times should have been vacated without oral argument when the cases were first presented to this Court. I believe that every moment's continuance of the injunctions against these newspapers amounts to a flagrant, indefensible, and continuing violation of the First Amendment. Furthermore, after oral argu-

---

*Footnotes omitted

ment, I agree completely that we must affirm the judgment of the Court of Appeals for the Second Circuit for the reasons stated by my Brothers Douglas and Brennan. In my view it is unfortunate that some of my Brethren are apparently willing to hold that the publication of news may sometimes be enjoined. Such a holding would make a shambles of the First Amendment . . . .

[F]or the first time in the 182 years since the founding of the Republic, the federal courts are asked to hold that the First Amendment does not mean what it says, but rather means that the Government can halt the publication of current news of vital importance to the people of this country.

. . . When the Constitution was adopted, many people strongly opposed it because the document contained no Bill of Rights to safeguard certain basic freedoms. They especially feared that the new powers granted to a central government might be interpreted to permit the government to curtail freedom of religion, press, assembly, and speech. In response to an overwhelming public clamor, James Madison offered a series of amendments to satisfy citizens that these great liberties would remain safe and beyond the power of government to abridge. Madison proposed what later became the First Amendment in three parts, two of which are set out below, and one of which proclaimed: "The people shall not be deprived or abridged of their right to speak, to write, or to publish their sentiments; *and the freedom of the press, as one of the great bulwarks of liberty, shall be inviolable.*" The amendments were offered to curtail and restrict the general powers granted to the Executive, Legislative, and Judicial Branches two years before in the original Constitution. The Bill of Rights changed the original Constitution into a new charter under which no branch of government could abridge the people's freedoms of press, speech, religion, and assembly. . . . Both the history and language of the First Amendment support the view that the press must be left free to publish news, whatever the source, without censorship, injunctions, or prior restraints.

. . . The press was protected so that it could bare the secrets of government and inform the people. Only a free and unrestrained press can effectively expose deception in government. And paramount among the responsibilities of a free press is the duty to prevent any part of the government from deceiving the people and sending them off to distant lands to die of foreign fevers and foreign shot and shell. In my view, far from deserving condemnation for their courageous reporting, the New York Times, the Washington Post, and other newspapers should be commended for serving the purpose that the Founding Fathers saw so clearly. In revealing the workings of government that led to the Vietnam war, the newspapers nobly did precisely that which the Founders hoped and trusted they would do . . . .

[T]he Government argues in its brief that in spite of the First Amendment, "[t]he authority of the Executive Department to protect the nation against publication of information whose disclosure would endanger the national security stems from two interrelated sources: the constitutional power of the President over the conduct of foreign affairs and his authority as Commander-in-Chief."

In other words, we are asked to hold that despite the First Amendment's emphatic command, the Executive Branch, the Congress, and the Judiciary can make laws enjoining publication of current news and abridging freedom of the press in the name of "national security." The Government does not even attempt to rely on any act of Congress. Instead it makes the bold and dangerously far reaching contention that the courts should take it upon themselves to "make" a law abridging freedom of the press in the name of equity, presidential power and national security, even when the representatives of the people in Congress have adhered to the command of the First Amendment and refused to make such a law.

. . . To find that the President has "inherent power" to halt the publicaton of news by resort to the courts would wipe out the First Amendment and destroy the fundamental liberty and security of the very people the Government hopes to make "secure."

The word "security" is a broad, vague generality whose contours should not be invoked to abrogate the fundamental law embodied in the First Amendment. The guarding of military and diplomatic secrets at the expense of informed representative government provides no real security for our Republic. The Framers of the First Amendment, fully aware of both the need to defend a new nation and the abuses of the English and Colonial Governments, sought to give this new society strength and security by providing that freedom of speech, press, religion, and assembly should not be abridged. This thought was eloquently expressed in 1937 by Chief Justice Hughes — great man and great Chief Justice that he was — when the Court held a man could not be punished for attending a meeting run by Communists.

> The greater the importance of safeguarding the community from incitements to the overthrow of our institutions by force and violence, the more imperative is the need to preserve inviolate the constitutional rights of free speech, free press and free assembly in order to maintain the opportunity for free

political discussion, to the end that government may be responsive to the will of the people and that changes, if desired, may be obtained by peaceful means. Therein lies the security of the Republic, the very foundation of constitutional government.

JUSTICE DOUGLAS, with whom JUSTICE BLACK joins, concurring.

It should be noted at the outset that the First Amendment provides that "Congress shall make no law ... abridging the freedom of speech, or of the press." That leaves, in my view, no room for governmental restraint on the press.

There is, moreover, no statute barring the publication by the press of the material which the Times and the Post seek to use . . . .

So any power that the Government possesses must come from its "inherent power."

. . . The Constitution by Art. I, § 8, gives Congress, not the President, power "[t]o declare War." Nowhere are presidential wars authorized. We need not decide therefore what leveling effect the war power of Congress might have.

These disclosures may have a serious impact. But that is no basis for sanctioning a previous restraint on the press . . . .

The Government says that it has inherent powers to go into court and obtain an injunction to protect the national interest, which in this case is alleged to be national security.

Near v. Minnesota repudiated that expansive doctrine in no uncertain terms.

The dominant purpose of the First Amendment was to prohibit the widespread practice of governmental suppression of embarrassing information. It is common knowledge that the First Amendment was adopted against the widespread use of the common law of seditious libel to punish the dissemination of material that is embarrassing to the powers-that-be. . . . The present cases will, I think, go down in history as the most dramatic illustration of that principle. A debate of large proportions goes on in the Nation over our posture in Vietnam. That debate antedated the disclosure of the contents of the present documents. The latter are highly relevant to the debate in progress.

Secrecy in government is fundamentally anti-democratic, perpetuating bureaucratic errors. Open debate and discussion of public issues are vital to our national health. On public questions there should be "uninhibited, robust, and wide-open" debate. . . .

The stays in these cases that have been in effect for more than a week constitute a flouting of the priniciples of the First Amendment as interpreted in Near v. Minnesota.

JUSTICE BRENNAN, concurring.

. . . So far as I can determine, never before has the United States sought to enjoin a newspaper from publishing information in its possession.

The error that has pervaded these cases from the outset was the granting of any injunctive relief whatsoever, interim or otherwise. The entire thrust of the Government's claim throughout these cases has been that publicaton of the material sought to be enjoined "could," or "might," or "may" prejudice the national interest in various ways. But the First Amendment tolerates absolutely no prior judicial restraints of the press predicated upon surmise or conjecture that untoward consequences may result. Our cases, it is true, have indicated that there is a single, extremely narrow class of cases in which the First Amendment's ban on prior judicial restraint may be overridden. Our cases have thus far indicated that such cases may arise only when the Nation "is at war," *Schenck v. United States*, during which times "[n]o one would question but that a government might prevent actual obstruction to its recruiting service or the publication of the sailing dates of transports or the number and location of troops." *Near v. Minnesota ex rel. Olson*, 283 U.S. 697, 716. Even if the present world situation were assumed to be tantamount to a time of war, or if the power of presently available armaments would justify even in peacetime the suppression of information that would set in motion a nuclear holocaust, in neither of these actions has the Government presented or even alleged that publication of items from or based upon the material at issue would cause the happening of an event of that nature. . . . Thus, only governmental allegation and proof that publication must inevitably, directly, and immediately cause the occurrence of an event kindred to imperiling the safety of a transport already at sea can support even the issuance of an interim restraining order. In no event may mere conclusions be sufficient: for if the Executive Branch seeks judicial aid in preventing publication, it must inevitably submit the basis upon which that aid is sought to scrutiny by the judiciary. And therefore, every restraint issued in this case, whatever its form, has violated the First Amendment — and not less so because that restraint was justified as necessary to afford the courts an opportunity to examine the claim more thoroughly. Unless and until the Government has clearly made out its case, the First Amendment commands that no injunction may issue.

JUSTICE STEWART, with whom JUSTICE WHITE joins, concurring.

In the governmental structure created by our Constitution, the Executive is endowed with enormous power in the two related areas of national defense and international relations. This power, largely unchecked by the Legislative and Judicial branches, has been pressed to the very hilt since the advent of the nuclear missile age. For better or for worse, the simple fact is that a President of the United States posesses vastly greater constitutional independence in these two vital areas of power than does, say, a prime minister of a country with a parliamentary form of government.

In the absence of the governmental checks and balances present in other areas of our national life, the only effective restraint upon executive policy and power in the areas of national defense and international affairs may lie in an enlightened citizenry — in an informed and critical public opinion which alone can here protect the values of democratic government. For this reason, it is perhaps here that a press that is alert, aware, and free most vitally serves the basic purpose of the First Amendment. For without an informed and free press there cannot be an enlightened people.

Yet it is elementary that the successful conduct of internationl diplomacy and the maintenance of an effective national defense require both confidentiality and secrecy. Other nations can hardly deal with this Nation in an atmosphere of mutual trust unless they can be asssured that their confidences will be kept. And within our own executive departments, the development of considered and intelligent international policies would be impossible if those charged with their formulation could not communicate with each other freely, and in confidence. In the area of basic national defense the frequent need for absolute secrecy is, of course, self evident.

I think there can be but one answer to this dilemma, if dilemma it be. The responsibility must be where the power is. If the Constitution gives the Executive a large degree of unshared power in the conduct of foreign affairs and the maintenance of our national defense, then under the Constitution the Executive must have the largely unshared duty to determine and preserve the degree of internal security necessary to exercise that power successfully. It is an awesome responsiblity, requiring judgment and wisdom of a high order. . . . This is not to say that Congress and the courts have no role to play. Undoubtedly Congress has the power to enact specific and appropriate criminal laws to protect government property and preserve government secrets. Congress has passed such laws, and several of them are of very colorable relevance to the apparent circumstances of these cases. And if a criminal prosecution is instituted, it will be the responsiblity of the courts to decide the applicability of the criminal law under which the charge is brought. Morever, if Congress should pass a specific law authorizing civil proceedings in this field, the courts would likewise have the duty to decide the constitutionality of such a law as well as its applicability to the facts proved.

But in the cases before us we are asked neither to construe specific regulations nor to apply specific law. We are asked, instead, to perform a function that the Constitution gave to the Executive, not the Judiciary. We are asked, quite simply, to prevent the publication by two newspapers of material that the Executive Branch insists should not, in the national interest, be published. I am convinced that the Executive is correct with respect to some of the documents involved. But I cannot say that disclosure of any of them will surely result in direct, immediate, and irreparable damage to our Nation or its people. That being so, there can under the First Amendment be but one judicial resolution of the issues before us. I join the judgments of the Court.

JUSTICE WHITE, with whom JUSTICE STEWART joins, concurring.

I concur in today's judgments, but only because of the concededly extraordinary protection against prior restraints enjoyed by the press under our constitutional system. I do not say that in no circumstance would the First Amendment permit an injunction against publishing information about government plans or operations. Nor, after examining the materials the Government characterizes as the most sensitive and destructive, can I deny that revelation of these documents will do substantial damage to public interests. Indeed, I am confident that their disclosure will have that result. But I nevertheless agree that the United States has not satisfied the very heavy burden that it must meet to warrant an injunction against publication in these cases, at least in the absence of express and appropriately limited congressional authorization for prior restraints in circumstances such as these. . . .

At least in the absence of legislation by Congress, based on its own investigations and findings, I am quite unable to agree that the inherent powers of the Executive and the courts reach so far as to authorize remedies having such sweeping potential for inhibiting publications by the press. . . . To sustain the Government in these cases would start the courts down a long and hazardous road that I am not willing to travel, at least without congressional guidance and direction.

. . . Prior restraints require an unusually heavy justification under the First Amendment; but failure by the Government to justify prior restraints does not measure its constitutional entitlement to a conviction for criminal publication. That the Government mistakenly chose to proceed by injunction does not mean that it could not successfully proceed in another way. . . .

The Criminal Code contains numerous provisions potentially relevant to these cases. Section 797 makes it a crime to publish certain photographs or drawings of military installations. Section 798, also in precise language, proscribes knowing and willfull publication of any classified information concerning the cryptographic systems or communication intelligence activities of the United States as well as any information obtained from communication intelligence operations. If any of the material here at issue is of this nature, the newspapers are presumably now on full notice of the position of the United States and must face the consequences if they publish. I would have no difficulty in sustaining convictions under these sections on facts that would not justify the intervention of equity and the imposition of a prior restraint. . . .

It is thus clear that Congress has addressed itself to the problems of protecting the security of the country and the national defense from unauthorized disclosure of potentially damaging information. . . . It has not, however, authorized the injunctive remedy against threatened publication. It has apparently been satisfied to rely on criminal sanctions and their deterrent effect on the responsible as well as the irresponsible press. I am not, of course, saying that either of these newspapers has yet committed a crime or that either would commit a crime if it published all the material now in its possession. That matter must await resolution in the context of a criminal proceeding if one is instituted by the United States. In that event, the issue of guilt or innocence would be determined by procedures and standards quite different from those that have purported to govern these injunctive proceedings.

JUSTICE MARSHALL, concurring.

. . . I believe the ultimate issue in this case is . . . whether this Court or the Congress has the power to make law.

In these cases there is no problem concerning the President's power to classify information as "secret" or "top secret." Congress has specifically recognized Presidential authority, which has been formally exercised in Exec. Order 10501 (1953), to classify documents and information . . . . Nor is there any issue here regarding the President's power as Chief Executive and Commander in Chief to protect national security by disciplining employees who disclose information and by taking precautions to prevent leaks . . . .

It would, however, be utterly inconsistent with the concept of separation of powers for this Court to use its power of contempt to prevent behavior that Congress has specifically declined to prohibit . . . . The Constitution provides that Congress shall make laws, the President execute laws, and courts interpret laws. *Youngstown Sheet & Tube Co. v. Sawyer*, 374 U.S. 579 (1952). It did not provide for government by injunction in which the courts and the Executive Branch can "make law" without regard to the action of Congress. It may be more convenient for the Executive Branch if it need only convince a judge to prohibit conduct rather than ask the Congress to pass a law, and it may be more convenient to enforce a contempt order than to seek a criminal conviction in a jury trial. Morever, it may be considered politically wise to get a court to share the responsibility for arresting those who the Executive Branch has probable cause to believe are violating the law. But convenience and political considerations of the moment do not justify a basic departure from the principles of our system of government.

In these cases we are not faced with a situation where Congress has failed to provide the Executive with broad power to protect the Nation from disclosure of damaging state secrets. Congress has on several occasions given extensive consideration to the problem of protecting the military and strategic secrets of the United States. This consideration has resulted in the enactment of statutes making it a crime to receive, disclose, communicate, withhold, and publish certain documents, photographs, instruments, appliances, and information. . . .

Even if it is determined that the Government could not in good faith bring criminal prosecutions against the New York Times and the Washington Post, it is clear that Congress has specifically rejected passing legislation that would have clearly given the President the power he seeks here and made the current activity of the newspapers unlawful . . . .

It is not for this Court to fling itself into every breach perceived by some Government official nor is it for this Court to take on itself the burden of enacting law, especially a law that Congress refused to pass . . . .

JUSTICE HARLAN, with whom THE CHIEF JUSTICE and JUSTICE BLACKMUN join, dissenting.

In order to decide the merits of these cases properly, some or all of the following questions should have been faced:

1. Whether the Attorney General is authorized to bring these suits in the name of the United States . . . .
2. Whether the First Amendment permits the federal courts to enjoin publication of stories which would present a serious threat to national security. See *Near v. Minnesota.*
3. Whether the threat to publish highly secret documents is of itself a sufficient implication of national security to justify an injunction on the theory that regardless of the contents of the documents harm enough results simply from the demonstration of such a breach of secrecy.
4. Whether the unauthorized disclosure of any of these particular documents would seriously impair the national security.
5. What weight should be given to the opinion of high officers in the Executive Branch of the Government with respect to questions 3 and 4.
6. Whether the newspapers are entitled to retain and use the documents notwithstanding the seemingly uncontested facts that the documents, or the originals of which they are duplicates, were purloined from the Government's possession and that the newspapers received them with knowledge that they had been feloniously acquired . . . .
7. Whether the threatened harm to the national security of the Government's possessory interest in the documents justifies the issuance of an injunction against publication in light of —
   a. The strong First Amendment policy against prior restraints on publication.
   b. The doctrine against enjoining conduct in violation of criminal statutes; and
   c. The extent to which the materials at issue have apparently already been otherwise disseminated.

. . . It is plain to me that the scope of the judicial function in passing upon the activities of the Executive Branch of the Government in the field of foreign affairs is very narrowly restricted. This view is, I think, dictated by the concept of separation of powers upon which our constitutional system rests.

I agree that, in performance of its duty to protect the values of the First Amendment against political pressures, the judiciary must review the initial Executive determination to the point of satisfying itself that the subject matter of the dispute does lie within the proper compass of the President's foreign relations power. Constitutional considerations forbid "a complete abandonment of judicial control." *United States v. Reynolds*, 345 U.S. 1, 8. Moreover the judiciary may properly insist that the determination that disclosure of the subject matter would irreparably impair the national security be made by the head of the Executive Department concerned — here the Secretary of State — after actual personal consideration by that officer. This safeguard is required in the analogous area of executive claims of privilege for secrets of state . . . .

But in my judgment the judiciary may not properly go beyond these two inquiries and redetermine for itself the probable impact of disclosure on the national security . . . .

Even if there is some room for the judiciary to override the executive determination, it is plain that the scope of review must be exceedingly narrow. I can see no indication in the opinions of either the District Court or the Court of Appeals in the *Post* litigation that conclusions of the Executive were given even the deference owing to an administrative agency, much less that owing to a coequal branch of the Government operating within the field of its constitutional prerogative . . . .

Pending further hearings in each case conducted under the appropriate ground rules, I would continue the restraints on publication. I cannot believe that the doctrine prohibiting prior restraints reaches to the point of preventing courts from maintaining the *status quo* long enough to act responsibly in matters of such national importance as those involved here.

Appendix B

NEAR v. MINNESOTA

283 U.S. 697 (1931)

Mr. Chief Justice HUGHES delivered the opinion of the Court.

Chapter 285 of the Session Laws of Minnesota for the year 1925 provides for the abatement, as a public nuisance, of a "malicious, scandalous and defamatory newspaper, magazine or other periodical." . . .

Under this statute (section 1, clause (b), the county attorney of Hennepin county brought this action to enjoin the publication of what was described as a "malicious, scandalous and defamatory newspaper, magazine or other periodical," known as the Saturday Press, published by the defendants in the city of Minneapolis. The complaint alleged that the defendants, on September 24, 1927, and on eight subsequent dates in October and November, 1927, published and circulated editions of that periodical which were "largely devoted to malicious, scandalous and defamatory articles" concerning Charles G. Davis, Frank W. Brunskill, the Minneapolis Tribune, the Minneapolis Journal, Melvin C. Passolt, George E. Leach, the Jewish Race, the members of the grand jury of Hennepin county impaneled in November, 1927, and then holding office, and other persons, as more fully appeared in exhibits annexed to the complaint . . . .

Without attempting to summarize the contents of the voluminous exhibits attached to the complaint, we deem it sufficient to say that the articles charged, in subtance, that a Jewish ganster was in control of gambling, bootlegging, and racketeering in Minneapolis, and that law enforcing officers and agencies were not energetically performing their duties . . . .

. . . The plaintiff moved that the court direct the issue of a permanent injunction, and this was done.

The district court made findings of fact, which followed the allegations of the complaint and found in general terms that the editions in question were "chiefly devoted to malicious, scandalous and defamatory articles" concerning the individuals named. The court further found that the defendants through these publications "did engage in the business of regularly and customarily producing, publishing and circulating a malicious, scandalous and defamatory newspaper," and that "the said publication" "under said name of The Saturday Press, or any other name, constitutes a public nuisance under the laws of the State." Judgment was thereupon entered adjudging that "the newspaper, magazine and periodical known as The Saturday Press," as a public nuisance, "be and is hereby abated." The judgment perpetually enjoined the defendants "from producing, editing, publishing, circulating, having in their possession, selling or giving away any publication whatsoever which is a malicious, scandalous or defamatory newspaper, as defined by law," and also "from further conducting said nuisance under the name and title of said The Saturday Press or any other name or title."

The defendant Near appealed from this judgment to the Supreme Court of the State, again asserting his right under the Federal Constitution, and the judgment was affirmed. . . .

From the judgment as thus affirmed, the defendant Near appeals to this Court . . . .

The object of the statute is not punishment, in the ordinary sense, but suppression of the offending newspaper or periodical. The reason for the enactment, as the state court has said, is that prosecutions to enforce penal statutes for libel do not result in "efficient repression or suppression of the evils of scandal.". . .

If we cut through mere details of procedure, the operation and effect of the statute in substance is that public authorities may bring the owner or publisher of a newspaper or periodical before a judge upon a charge of conducting a business of publishing scandalous and defamatory matter — in particular that the matter consists of charges against public officers of official dereliction — and, unless the owner or publisher is able and disposed to bring competent evidence to satisfy the judge that the charges are true and are published with good motive and for justifiable ends, his newspaper or periodical is suppressed and further publication is made punishable as a contempt. This is of the essence of censorship.

The question is whether a statute authorizing such proceedings in restraint of publication is consistent with the conception of the liberty of the press as historically conceived and guaranteed. In determining the extent of the constitutional protection, it has been generally, if not universally, considered that it is the chief purpose of the guaranty to prevent previous restraints upon publication. The struggle in England, directed against the legislative power of the licenser, resulted in renunciation of the censorship of the press. The liberty deemed to be established was thus described by Blackstone:

"The liberty of the press is indeed essential to the nature of a free state; but this consists in laying no *previous* restraints upon publications, and not in freedom from censure for ciminial matter when published. Every freeman has an undoubted right to lay what sentiments he pleases before the public; to forbid this, is to destroy the freedom of the press; but if he publishes what is improper, mischievous or illegal, he must take the consequence of his own temerity." 4 Bl. Com. 151, 152. See Story on the Constitution, §§ 1884, 1889. The distinction was early pointed out between the extent of the freedom with respect to censorship under our constitutional system and that enjoyed in England. Here, as Madison said, "the great and essential rights of the people are secured against legislative as well as against executive ambition. They are secured, not by laws paramount to prerogative, but by constitutions paramount to laws. This security of the fredom of the press requires that it should be exempt not only from previous restraint by the Executive, as in Great Britain, but from legislative restraint also."

The objection has also been made that the principle as to immunity from previous restraint is stated too broadly, if every such restraint is deemed to be prohibited. That is undoubtedly true; the protection even as to previous restraint is not absolutely unlimited. But the limitation has been recognized only in exceptional cases. "When a nation is at war many things that might be said in time of peace are such a hindrance to its effort that their utterance will not be endured so long as men fight and that no Court could regard them as protected by any constitutional right." *Schenck v. United States*, 249 U.S. 47, 52, 39 S. Ct. 247, 249, 63 L. Ed. 470. No one would question but that a government might prevent actual obstruction to its recruiting service or the publication of the sailing dates of transports or the number and location of troops. On similar grounds, the primary requirements of decency may be enforced against obscene publications. The security of the community life may be protected against incitements to acts of violence and the overthrow by force of orderly government . . . . These limitations are not applicable here . . . .

The exceptional nature of its limitations places in a strong light the general conception that liberty of the press, historically considered and taken up by the Federal Constitution, has meant, principally although not exclusively, immunity from previous restraints or censorship . . . .

The fact that for approximately one hundred and fifty years there has been almost an entire absence of attempts to impose previous restraints upon publications relating to the malfeasance of public officers is significant of the deep-seated conviction that such restraints would violate constitutional right. Public officers, whose character and conduct remain open to debate and free discussion in the press, find their remedies for false accusations in actions under libel laws providing for redress and punishment, and not in proceedings to restrain the publication of newspapers and periodicals. . . .

The importance of this immunity has not lessened. While reckless assaults upon public men, and efforts to bring obloquy upon those who are endeavoring faithfully to discharge official duties, exert a baleful influence and deserve the severest condemnation in public opinion, it cannot be said that this abuse is greater, and it is believed to be less, than that which characterized the period in which our institutions took shape. Meanwhile, the administration of government has become more complex, the opportunities for malfeasance and corruption have multiplied, crime has grown to most serious proportions, and the danger of its protecton by unfaithful officials and of the impairment of the fundamental security of life and property by criminal alliances and official neglect, emphasizes the primary need of a vigilant and courageous press, especially in great cities. The fact that the liberty of the press may be abused by miscreant purveyors of scandal does not make any the less necessary the immunity of the press from previous restraint in dealing with official misconduct. Subsequent punishment for such abuses as may exist is the appropriate remedy, consistent with constitutional privilege . . . .

The statute in question cannot be justified by reason of the fact that the publisher is permitted to show, before injunction issues, that the matter published is true and is published with good motives and for justifiable ends. If such a statute, authorizing suppression and injunction on such a basis, is constitutionally valid, it would be equally permissible for the Legislature to provide that at any time the publisher of any newspaper could be brought before a court, or even an administrative officer (as the consitutional protection may not be regarded as resting on mere procedural details), and required to produce proof of the truth of his publication, or of what he intended to publish and of his motives, or stand enjoined. If this can be done, the Legislature may provide machinery for determining in the complete exercise of its discretion what are justifiable ends and restrain publication accordingly. And it would be but a step to a complete system of censorship. The recognition of authority to impose previous restraint upon publication in order to protect the community against the circulation of charges of misconduct, and especially of official misconduct, necessarily would carry with it the admission of the authority of the censor against which the constitutional barrier was erected . . . .

Equally unavailing is the insistence that the statute is designed to prevent the circulation of scandal which tends to disturb the public peace and to provoke assaults and the commission of crime. Charges of reprehensible conduct, and in particular of official malfeasance, unquestionably create a public scandal, but the theory of the constitutional guaranty is that even a more serious public evil would be caused by authority to prevent publication . . . .

For these reasons we hold the statute, so far as it authorized the proceedings in this action under clause (b) of section 1, to be an infringement of the liberty of the press guaranteed by the Fourteenth Amendment . . . .

Appendix C

NEBRASKA PRESS ASSOCIATION v. STUART

427 U.S. 539 (1976)

CHIEF JUSTICE BURGER delivered the opinion of the Court.*

The respondent State District Judge entered an order restraining the petitioners from publishing or broadcasting accounts of confession or admission made by the accused or facts "strongly implicative" of the accused in a widely reported murder of six persons . . . .

On the evening of October 18, 1975, local police found the six members of the Henry Kellie family murdered in their home in Sutherland, Neb., a town of about 850 people. Police released the description of a suspect, Erwin Charles Simants, to the reporters who had hastened to the scene of the crime. Simants was arrested and arraigned in Lincoln County Court the following morning, ending a tense night for this small rural community.

The crime immediately attracted widespread news coverage by local, regional, and national newspapers, radio and television stations. Three days after the crime, the County Attorney and Simants' attorney joined in asking the County Court to enter a restrictive order relating to "matters that may or may not be publicly reported or disclosed to the public," because of the "mass coverage by news media" and the "reasonable likelihood of prejudicial news which would make difficult, if not impossible, the impaneling of an impartial jury and tend to prevent a fair trial." The County Court . . . granted the prosecutor's motion for a restrictive order . . . .

Petitioners — several press and broadcast associations, publishers, and individual reporters — moved on October 23 for leave to intervene in the District Court [the trial Court] asking that the restrictive order imposed by the County Court be vacated. The District Court conducted a hearing, at which the County Judge testified and newspaper articles about the *Simants* case were admitted in evidence. The District Judge granted petitioners' motion to intervene and, on October 27, entered his own restrictive order. The judge found "because of the nature of the crimes charged in the

---

*Footnotes omitted

complaint that there is a clear and present danger that pretrial publicity *could* impinge upon the defendant's right to a fair trial." The order applied only until the jury was impaneled, and specifically prohibited petitioners from reporting five subjects: (1) the existence or contents of a confession Simants had made to law enforcement officers, which had been introduced in open court at arraignment; (2) the fact or nature of statements Simants had made to other persons; (3) the contents of a note he had written the night of the crime; (4) certain aspects of the medical testimony at the preliminary hearing; and (5) the identity of the victims of the alleged sexual assault and the nature of the assault. It also prohibited reporting the exact nature of the restrictive order itself . . . .

The Nebraska Supreme Court . . . modified the District Court's order to accommodate the defendant's right to a fair trial and the petitioners' interest in reporting pretrial events. The order as modified prohibited reporting of only three matters: (a) the existence and nature of any confessions or admissions made by the defendant to law enforcement officers, (b) any confessions or admissions made to any third parties, except members of the press, and (c) other facts "strongly implicative" of the accused. The Nebraska Supreme Court did not rely on the Nebraska Bar-Press Guidelines. After construing Nebraska law to permit closure in certain circumstances, the court remanded the case to the District Judge for reconsideration of the issue whether pretrial hearings should be closed to the press and public.

We granted certiorari . . . but we denied the motion to expedite review or to stay entirely the order of the State District Court pending Simants' trial . . . .

The Sixth Amendment in terms guarantees "trial, by an impartial jury . . ." in federal criminal prosecutions. Because "trial by jury in criminal cases is fundamental to the American scheme of justice," the Due Process Clause of the Fourteenth Amendment guarantees the same right in state criminal prosecutions . . . .

In the overwhelming majority of criminal trials, pretrial publicity presents few unmanageable threats to this important right. But when the case is a "sensational" one tensions develop between the right of the accused to trial by an impartial jury and the rights guaranteed others by the First Amendment . . . .

> Due process requires that the accused receive a trial by
> an impartial jury free from outside influences. Given the
> pervasiveness of modern communications and the diffi-
> culty of effacing prejudicial publicity from the minds of the
> jurors, the *trial courts must take strong measures to ensure*

that the balance is never weighed against the accused. . . .
Of course, there is nothing that proscribes the press from
reporting events that transpire in the courtroom. But
where there is a reasonable likelihood that prejudicial
news prior to trial will prevent a fair trial, the judge should
continue the case until the threat abates, *or transfer it to*
another county not so permeated with publicity. In addition, *sequestration of the jury* was something the judge
should have raised *sua sponte* with counsel. If publicity
during the proceedings threatens the fairness of the trial,
a new trial should be ordered. But we must remember that
reversals are but palliative; the cure lies in those remedial
measures that will prevent the prejudice at its inception.
The courts must take such steps by rule and regulation
that will protect their processes from prejudicial outside
interferences. Neither prosecutors, counsel for defense,
the accused, witnesses, court staff nor enforcement officers coming under the jurisdiction of the court should be
permitted to frustrate its function. Collaboration between
counsel and the press as to information affecting the
fairness of a criminal trial is not only subject to regulation,
but is highly censurable and worthy of disciplinary measures . . . .

[*Sheppard v. Maxwell*, 384 U.S. 333,] at 362-363 . . .

The thread running through all these [First Amendment]
cases is that prior restraints on speech and publication are the most
serious and the least tolerable infringement on First Amendment
rights. A criminal penalty or a judgment in a defamation case is
subject to the whole panoply of protections afforded by deferring the
impact of the judgment until all avenues of appellate review have
been exhausted . . .

A prior restraint, by contrast and by definition, has an
immediate and irreversible sanction. If it can be said that a threat of
criminal or civil sanctions after publication "chills" speech, prior
restraint "freezes" it at least for the time.

The damage can be particularly great when the prior restraint falls upon the communication of news and commentary on
current events. Truthful reports of public judicial proceedings have
been afforded special protection against subsequent punishment.
See *Cox Broadcasting Corp. v. Cohn*, 420 U.S. 469, 492-493. For the
same reasons the protection against prior restraint should have
particular force as applied to reporting of criminal proceedings,
whether the crime in question is a single isolated act or a pattern of
criminal conduct . . . . The extraordinary protections afforded by the
First Amendment carry with them something in the nature of a

fiduciary duty to exercise the protected rights responsibly — a duty widely acknowledged but not always observed by editors and publishers. It is not asking too much to suggest that those who exercise First Amendment rights in newspapers or broadcasting enterprises direct some effort to protect the rights of an accused to a fair trial by unbiased jurors.

Of course, the order at issue — like the order requested in *New York Times* — does not prohibit but only postpones publication. Some news can be delayed and most commentary can even more readily be delayed without serious injury, and there often is a self-imposed delay when responsible editors call for verification of information. But such delays are normally slight and they are self-imposed. Delays imposed by governmental authority are a different matter. . . .

The authors of the Bill of Rights did not undertake to assign priorities as between First Amendment and Sixth Amendment rights, ranking one as superior to the other. In this case, the petitioners would have us declare the right of an accused subordinate to the right to publish in all circumstances. But if the authors of these guarantees, fully aware of the potential conflicts between them, were unwilling or unable to resolve the issue by assigning to one priority over the other, it is not for us to rewrite the Constitution by undertaking what they declined to do. . . .

We turn now to the record in this case to determine whether, as Learned Hand put it, "the gravity of the 'evil,' discounted by its improbability, justifies such invasion of free speech as is necessary to avoid the danger." *United States v. Dennis*, 183 F.2d 201, 212 (CA2 1950), aff'd, 341 U.S. 494 (1951). To do so, we must examine the evidence before the trial judge when the order was entered to determine (a) the nature and extent of pretrial news coverage; (b) whether other measures would be likely to mitigate the effects of unrestrained pretrial publicity; and (c) how effectively a restraining order would operate to prevent the threatened danger. The precise terms of the restraining order are also important . . . .

Our review of the pretrial records persuades us that the trial judge was justified in concluding that there would be intense and pervasive pretrial publicity concerning this case. He could also reasonably conclude, based on common human experience, that publicity *could* impinge upon the defendant's right to a fair trial." (Emphasis added.) His conclusion as to the impact of such publicity on prospective jurors was of necessity speculative, dealing as he was with factors unknown and unknowable.

We find little in the record that goes to another aspect of our task, determining whether measures short of an order restraining all publicaton would have insured the defendant a fair trial. . . .

There is no finding that alternative measures would not have protected Simants' rights, and the Nebraska Supreme Court did no more than imply that such measures might not be adequate. Morever, the record is lacking in evidence to support such a finding.

We must also assess the probable efficacy of prior restraint on publication as a workable method of protecting Simants' right to a fair trial, and we cannot ignore the reality of the problems of managing and enforcing pretrial restraining orders. The territorial jurisdiction of the issuing court is limited by concepts of sovereignty. . . . The need for *in personam* jurisdiction also presents an obstacle to a restraining order that applies to publication at large as distinguished from restraining publication within a given jurisdiction. . . .

Finally, we note that the events disclosed by the record took place in a community of 850 people. It is reasonable to asume that, without any news accounts being printed or broadcast, rumors would travel swiftly by word of mouth. One can only speculate on the accuracy of such reports, given the generative propensities of rumors; they could well be more damaging than reasonably accurate news accounts. But plainly a whole community cannot be restrained from discussing a subject intimately affecting life within it . . . .

The record demonstrates, as the Nebraska courts held, that there was indeed a risk that pretrial news accounts, true or false, would have some adverse impact on the attitudes of those who might be called as jurors. But on the record now before us it is not clear that further publicity, unchecked, would so distort the views of potential jurors that 12 could not be found who would, under proper instructions, fulfill their sworn duty to render a just verdict exclusively on the evidence presented in open court. We cannot say on this record that alternatives to a prior restraint on petitioners would not have sufficiently mitigated the adverse effects of pretrial publicity so as to make prior restraint unnecessary. Nor can we conclude that the restraining order actually entered would serve its intended purpose. Reasonable minds can have few doubts about the gravity of the evil pretrial publicity can work, but the probability that it would do so here was not demonstrated with the degree of certainty our cases on prior restraint require.

Of necessity our holding is confined to the record before us. But our conclusion is not simply a result of assessing the adequacy of the showing made in this case; it results in part from the problems inherent in meeting the heavy burden of demonstrating, in advance of trial, that without prior restraint a fair trial will be denied. The practical problems of managing and enforcing restrictive orders will always be present. In this sense, the record now before us is illustrative rather than exceptional. . . . However difficult it may be, we need not rule out the possibility of showing the kind of threat to fair trial rights that would possess the requisite degree of certainty to justify restraint. This Court has frequently denied that First Amendment rights are absolute and has consistently rejected the proposition that a prior restraint can never be employed. . . .

We reaffirm that the guarantees of freedom of expression are not an absolute prohibition under all circumstances, but the barriers to prior restraint remain high and the presumption against its use continues intact. We hold that, with respect to the order entered in this case prohibiting reporting or commentary on judicial proceedings held in public, the barriers have not been overcome; to the extent that this order restrained publication of such material, it is clearly invalid. To the extent that it prohibited publication based on information gained from other sources, we conclude that the heavy burden imposed as a condition to securing a prior restraint was not met and the judgment of the Nebraska Supreme Court is therefore

Reversed.

Appendix D

EARL WARREN'S COMMENTS ON ESTES v. TEXAS, 381, U.S. 532 (1965)*

Memo to the Chief Justice

The following is a typed copy of my notes of your remarks to me concerning the *Estes* case.

Ever since we have had jury trial the endeavor has been to develop a system that would make the courtroom and court procedures dignified and objective, and uninfluenced as much as possible by outside pressures. Television in the courtroom turns the clock backwards and once again gives the courtroom the atmosphere of a public spectacle.

At English common law the jury was picked from members of the community who knew the facts; however, we have now come full circle to the point where people are supposed to have no knowledge of the case they are deciding or at least any knowledge they may have is not to affect their conduct as jurors. To give the defendant as fair a trial as possible we restrict the jury's contacts with the public while trial is going on and we attempt to keep the courtroom dignified and discreet — all for the purpose of keeping the trial completely objective.

In recent years through discovery and other pre-trial procedures we have endeavored to take out of the courtroom all elements of trickery, concealment, and surprise so that the objective pursuit of truth can come as close as possible to its goal. But now it is proposed that we turn back the clock and make everyone in the courtroom an actor before untold millions of people. We are asked again to make the determination of guilt or innocence a public spectacle and a source of entertainment for the idle and curious. This is not to say that all participants in the trial will distort it by deliberately playing up to the television audience, although some undoubtedly will. The evil of televised trials is that neither the judge, prosecutor, defense, jury, or witnesses will be able to go through the trial without considering the effect of their conduct on the viewing public. Whether they do so consciously or subconsciously, all will act differently because of the

Earl Warren Papers, Library of Congress

presence of the television camera. To the extent that television has such an inevitable impact it deprives the courtroom of the dignity and objectivity that is so essential for determining the guilt or innocence of persons whose life and liberty hinge on the outcome of the trial.

The American people were shocked and horrified when Premier Castro tried certain defendants in a stadium. Yet, if our courts must be opened to the pervasive influence of the television camera in order to accommodate the wishes of the news media, it is but a short step to holding court in a municipal auditorium, to accommodate them even more. As public interest increases in a particular trial, perhaps it will be moved from the courtroom to the municipal auditorium and from the auditorium to the baseball stadium. A courtroom is more than a location with seats for a judge, jury, defendant, prosecutor, defense counsel, and public observers. A courtroom is a courtroom because it has a certain dignity and objectivity which inspires all who enter and convinces them that the sole purpose of trial is to reach the truth.

The concept of public trial was not written into the Constitution for the benefit of the news media. It is a constitutional requirement for the benefit of the defendant, to assure him that he not be compelled to go through a Star Chamber proceeding. The press is entitled to be present at trials not because it is the press, but because it is a part of the public. Like any other segment of the public it has the right within the limits of the courtroom's facilities to be present, to speak publicly of what transpires, and to communicate courtroom events to the other members of the public. But there is no specific right of the news media to be present at trials, there is merely the right of the public to be present.

DMF

4/12/65
DW

Appendix E

1st DRAFT
SUPREME COURT OF
THE UNITED STATES

No. 76-1310

Thomas L. Houchins, Sheriff of the County of Alameda California, Petitioner	v.	KQED, Inc., et al., On Writ of Certiorari to the United States Court of Appeals for the Ninth Circuit

[March, 1978]

MR. JUSTICE STEVENS delivered the opinion of the Court.*

The question presented is whether a preliminary injunction requiring the Sheriff of Alameda County, Ca. to allow representatives of the news media access to the county jail is consistent with the holding in *Pell v. Procunier*, 417 U.S. 817,834, that "newsmen have no constitutional right of access to prisons or their inmates beyond that afforded the general public."

Respondent KQED, Inc., operates a public service television station in Oakland, Ca. It has televised a number of programs about prison conditions and prison inmates .... Petitioner is the Sheriff of Alameda County and has general supervision and control of the Santa Rita facility.

On March 31, 1975, KQED reported the suicide of a prisoner in the Greystone portion of the Santa Rita jail ....

KQED requested permission to visit and photograph the area of the jail where the suicide occurred. Petitioner refused, advising KQED that it was his policy not to permit any access to the jail by the news media. This policy was also invoked by petitioner to deny subsequent requests for access to the jail in order to cover news stories about conditions and alleged incidents within the facility.

---

*Footnotes omitted

Except for a carefully supervised tour in 1972, the news media were completely excluded from the inner portions of the Santa Rita jail until after this action was commenced.

Respondents KQED, and the Alamadea and Oakland branches of the National Association for the Advancement of Colored People, filed their complaint for equitable relief on June 17, 1975. The complaint alleged that petitioner had provided no "means by which the public may be informed of conditions prevailing in Greystone or by which prisoners' grievances may reach the public." It further alleged that petitioner's policy of "denying KQED and the public" access to the jail facility violated the First and Fourteenth Amendments to the Constitution and requested the court to enjoin petitioner "from excluding KQED news personnel from the Greystone cells and Santa Rita facilities and generally preventing full and accurate news coverage of the conditions prevailing therein . . . ."

On June 10, 1975, County Counsel stated that petitioner was contemplating monthly public tours for 25 persons, with the first tour tentatively scheduled for July 14. The tours, however, would not include the cell portions of Greystone and would not allow any use of cameras or communication with inmates. Respondents filed suit on June 17, 1975.

In a letter to the County Board of Supervisors dated June 19, 1975, petitioner outlined a pilot public tour program along the lines of that described to respondents' counsel. The Board approved six tours. Petitioner then filed his answer and supporting affidavit explaining why he had refused KQED access to the jail and identifying the recent changes in policy regarding access to the jail and communication between inmates and persons on the outside. Petitioner stated that if KQED's request had been granted, he would have felt obligated to honor similar requests from other representatives of the press and this could have disrupted mealtimes, exercise times, visiting times, and court appearances of inmates. . . .Petitioner also stated that KQED had been advised about the contemplated program of guided tours before the suit was filed and that the tours had since been approved and publicly announced. With respect to the scope of the proposed tours, petitioner explained that the use of cameras would be prohibited because it would not be possible to prevent 25 persons with cameras from photographing inmates and security operations. Moreover, communication with inmates would not be permitted because of excessive time consumption, "problems of control" with inmates and visitors, and a belief "that interviews would be excessively unwieldy."

An evidentiary hearing on the motion for a preliminary

injunction was held after the first four guided tours had taken place. The evidence revealed the inadequacy of the tours as a means of obtaining information about the inmates and their conditions of confinement for transmission to the public. The tours failed to enter certain areas of the jail. They afforded no opportunity to photograph conditions within the facility, and the photographs which the County offered for sale to tour visitors omitted certain jail characteristics, such as catwalks above the cells from which guards can observe the inmates. The tours provided no opportunity to question randomly encountered inmates about jail conditions. Indeed, to the extent possible inmates were kept out of sight during the tour, preventing the tour visitors from obtaining a realistic picture of the conditions of confinement within the jail. . . .

The District Court found that KQED had no acess to the jail and that the broad restraints on access were not required by legitimate penological interests.

The District Court thereafter issued a preliminary injunction, enjoining petitioner "from denying to KQED news personnel and responsible representatives of the news media access to the Santa Rita facilities, including Greystone, at reasonable times and hours," or from preventing such representatives "from utlizing photographic and sound equipment or from utilizing inmate interviews in providing full and accurate coverage of the Santa Rita facilities . . . ."

Petitioner took an interlocutory appeal to the United States Court of Appeals for the Ninth Circuit. The Court of Appeals affirmed . . . .

II

The preservation of a full and free flow of information to the general public has long been recognized as a core objective of the First Amendment to the Constitution. It is for this reason that the First Amendment protects not only the dissemination but also the receipt of information and ideas. See, *e.g., Virginia Pharmacy Board v. Virginia Consumer Council*, 425 U.S. 748, 756; *Procunier v. Martinez*, 416 U.S. 396, 408-409; *Kleindienst v. Mandel*, 408 U.S. 753, 762-63. Thus, in *Procunier v. Martinez, supra*, the Court invalidated prison regulations authorizing excessive censorship of outgoing inmate correspondence because such censorship abridged the rights of the intended recipients. See also *Morales v. Schmidt*, 489 F. 2d 1335, 13246, n. 8 (CA7 1973). So here, petitioner's prelitigation prohibition on mentioning the conduct of jail officers in outgoing correspondence must be considered an infringement on the noninmate correspondent's interest in receiving the intended communication.

In addition to safeguarding the right of one individual to receive what another elects to communicate, the First Amendment serves an essential societal function. Our system of self-government assumes the existence of an informed citizenry. As Madison wrote:

> A popular Government, without popular information or the means of acquiring it, is but a prologue to a farce or a tragedy; or perhaps both. Knowledge will forever govern ignorance. And a people who mean to be their own governors, must arm themselves with the power knowledge gives. (*Writings of James Madison,* 103, G. Hurst ed., 1910).

It is not sufficient, therefore, that the channels of communication be free of governmental restraints. Without some protection for the acquisition of information about the operation of public institutions such as prisons by the public at large, the process of self-governance contemplated by the Framers would be stripped of its substance.

For that reason information-gathering is entitled to some measure of constitutional protection. See, *e.g. Branzburg v. Hayes,* 408 U.S. 665, 681; *Pell v. Procunier,* 417 U.S., at 833; "a right to gather news, of some dimensions, must exist." As this Court's decisions clearly indicate, however, the protection is not for the private benefit of those who might qualify as representatives of the "press" but to insure that the citizens are fully informed regarding matters of public interest and importance.

In *Grosjean v. American Press Co.,* 297 U.S. 233, representatives of the "press" challenged a state tax on the advertising revenues of newspapers. In the Court's words, the issue raised by the tax went "to the heart of the natural right of the members of an organized society, united for their common good, to impart and acquire information about their common interests." *Id.,* at 243. The opinion described the long struggle in England against the stamp tax and tax on advertisements — the so-called "taxes on knowledge."

> [I]n the adoption of the . . . [taxes] the dominant and controlling aim was to prevent, or curtail the opportunity for the acquisition of knowledge by the people in respect of their governmental affairs. . . . The aim of the struggle [against those taxes] was . . . to establish and preserve the right of the English people to full information in respect of the doings or misdoings of their government. Upon the

correctness of this conclusion, the very characterizations of the exactions as 'taxes on knowledge' sheds a flood of corroborative light. In the ultimate, an informed and enlightened public opinion was the thing at stake. (*Id.*, at 247)

Noting the familiarity of the Framers with this struggle, the Court held:

[S]ince informed public opinion is the most potent of all restraints upon misgovernment, the suppression or abridgement of the publicity afforded by a free press cannot be regarded otherwise than with grave concern. The tax involved here is bad . . . because, in light of its history and its present setting, it is seen to be a deliberate and calculated device . . . to limit the circulation of information to which the public is entitled in virtue of the constitutional guarantees. (*Id.*, at 250)

A recognition that the "underlying right is the right of the public generally" is also implicit in the doctrine that "newsmen have no constitutional right of access to prisons or their inmates beyond that afforded the general public." *Pell v. Procunier*, 417 U.S., at 834. In *Pell* it was unnecessary to consider the extent of the public's right of access to information regarding the prison and its inmates in order to adjudicate the press claim to a particular form of access, since the record demonstrated that the flow of information to the public, both directly and through the press, was adequate to survive constitutional challenge; institutional considerations justified denying the single, additional mode of access sought by the press in that case.

Here, in contrast, the restrictions on access to the inner portions of the Santa Rita jail that existed on the date this litigation commenced concealed from the general public the conditions of confinement within the facility. The question is whether petitioner's policies, which cut off the flow of information at its source, abridged the public's right to be informed about those conditions.

The answer to that question does not depend upon the degree of public disclosure which should attend the operation of most governmental activity. Such matters involve questions of policy which generally must be resolved by the political branches of government. Moreover, there are unquestionably occasions when governmental activity may properly be carried on in complete secrecy. For example, the public and the press are commonly excluded from "grand jury proceedings, our own conferences, [and] the meetings of other official bodies gathering in executive session . . . ." *Branzburg v. Hayes*, 408 U.S. at 684; *Pell v. Procunier*, 417 U.S. at 834. In such situations the reasons for withholding information from the public are both apparent and legitimate.

In this case, however, "[r]espondents do not assert a right to force disclosure of confidential information or to invade in any way the decision-making process of governmental officials." They simply seek an end to petitioner's policy of concealing prison conditions from the public. Those conditions are wholly without claim to confidentiality. While prison officials have an interest in the time and manner of public acquisition of information about the institutions they administer, no one even suggests that there is any legitimate, penological justification for concealing from citizens the conditions in which their fellow citizens are being confined.

The reasons which militate in favor of providing special protection to the flow of information to the public about prisons relate to the unique function they perform in a democratic society. Not only are they public institutions, financed with public funds and administered by public servants; they are an integral component of the criminal justice system. The citizens confined therein are temporarily, and sometimes permanently, deprived of their liberty as a result of a trial which must conform to the dictates of the Constitution. By express command of the Sixth Amendment the proceeding must be a "public trial." It is important not only that the trial itself be fair, but also that the community at large have confidence in the integrity of the proceeding. That public interest survives the judgment of conviction and appropriately carries over to an interest in how the convicted person is treated during his period of punishment and hoped-for rehabilitation. While a ward of the State and subject to its stern discipline, he retains constitutional protections against cruel and unusual punishment, see *e.g.*, *Estelle v. Gambelle*, 429 U.S. 97, a protection which may derive more practical support from access to information about prisons by the public than by occasional litigation in a busy court.

Some inmates — in Santa Rita, a substantial number — are pretrial detainees. Though confined pending trial, they have not been convicted of an offense against society and are entitled to the presumption of innocence. Certain penological objectives, *i.e.*, punishment, deterrence and rehabilitation, which are legitimate in regard to convicted prisoners, are inapplicable to pretrial detainees. Society has a special interest in ensuring that unconvicted citizens are treated in accord with their status.

In this case, the record demonstrates that both the public and the press had been consistently denied any access to the inner portions of the Santa Rita jail, that there had been excessive censorship of inmate correspondence, and that there was no valid justification for these broad restraints on the flow of information. An affirmative answer to the question whether respondent established a likelihood of prevailing on the merits did not depend, in final analysis, on any right of the press to special treatment beyond that accorded the public at large. Rather, the probable existence of a constitutional violation rested upon the special importance of allowing a democratic community access to knowledge about how its servants were treating some of its members who have been committed to their custody. An official prison policy of concealing such knowledge from the public by arbitrarily cutting off the flow of information at its source abridges the freedom of speech and of the press protected by the First and Fourteenth Amendments to the Constitution.

III

The preliminary injunction entered by the District Court granted relief to KQED without providing any specific remedy for other members of the public. Moreover, it imposed duties on petitioner that may not be required by the Constitution itself. The injunction was not an abuse of discretion for either of these reasons.

If a litigant can prove that he has suffered specific harm from the application of an unconstitutional policy, it is entirely proper for a court to grant relief tailored to his needs without attempting to redress all the mischief that the policy may have worked on others. Though the public and the press have an equal right to receive information and ideas, different methods of remedying a violation of that right may sometimes be needed to accommodate the special concerns of the one or the other. Preliminary relief could therefore appropriately be awarded to KQED on the basis of its proof of how it was affected by the challenged policy without also granting specific relief to the general public. Indeed, since our adversary system contemplates the adjudication of specific controversies between specific litigants, it would have been improper for the District Court to attempt to provide a remedy to persons who have not requested separate relief. Accordingly, even though the Constitution provides the press with no greater right of access to information than that possessed by the public at large, a preliminary injunction is not invalid simply because it awards special relief to a successful litigant which is a representative of the press.

Nor is there anything novel about injunctive relief which goes beyond a mere prohibition against repetition of previous unlawful conduct. In situations which are both numerous and varied the chancellor has required a wrongdoer to take affirmative steps to eliminate the effects of a violation of law even though the law itself imposes no duty to take the remedial action decreed by the court. It follows that if prison regulations and policies have unconstitutionally suppressed information and interfered with communication in violation of the First Amendment, the District Court has the power to require, at least temporarily, that the channels of communication be opened more widely than the law would otherwise require in order to let relevant facts, which may have been concealed, come to light. . . .

The Court of Appeals found no reason to question the specific preliminary relief ordered by the District Court. Nor would it be appropriate for us to review the scope of the order. The order was preliminary in character, and is subject to revision in the light of experience and such evidence and argument as may be presented before the litigation is finally concluded.

The judgment of the Court of Appeals is

Affirmed.

Appendix F

RICHMOND NEWSPAPERS, INC. v. VIRGINIA

448 U.S. 555 (1980)

CHIEF JUSTICE BURGER announced the judgment of the Court and delivered an opinion in which JUSTICE WHITE and JUSTICE STEVENS joined.*

The narrow question presented in this case is whether the right of the public and press to attend criminal trials is guaranteed under the United States Constitution.

I

... Stevenson was ... convicted of second-degree murder in the Circuit Court of Hanover County, Va. The Virginia Supreme Court reversed the conviction in October 1977, holding that a bloodstained shirt purportedly belonging to Stevenson had been improperly admitted into evidence.

Stevenson was retried in the same court. This second trial ended in a mistrial on May 30, 1978 when a juror asked to be excused after trial had begun and no alternate was available.

A third trial ... also ended in a mistrial ... [which] may have been declared because a prospective juror had read about Stevenson's previous trials in a newspaper and had told other prospective jurors about the case before the retrial began.

... Before the [fourth] trial began, counsel for the defendant moved that it be closed to the public .... The prosecutor stated he had no objection and would leave it to the discretion of the court. Presumably referring to Virginia Code § 19.2-266, the trial judge then announced: "[T]he statute gives me that power specifically and the defendant has made the motion." He then ordered "that the Courtroom be kept clear of all parties except the witnesses when they testify." The record does not show that any objections to the closure order were made by anyone present at the time, including appellants Wheeler and McCarthy [reporters].

Later that same day, however, appellants sought a hearing

---

*Most footnotes omitted.

on a motion to vacate the closure order . . . . The court denied the motion to vacate and ordered the trial to continue the following morning "with the press and public excluded."

II

We begin consideration of this case by noting that the precise issue presented here has not previously been before this Court for decision. In *Gannett Co., Inc. v. DePasquale*, 443 U.S. 368 (1979), the Court was not required to decide whether a right of access *to trials*, as distinguished from hearings on pretrial motions, was constitutionally guaranteed. The Court held that the Sixth Amendment's guarantee to the accused of a public trial gave neither the public nor the press an enforceable right of access to a *pre*trial suppression hearing. . . .

. . . But here for the first time the Court is asked to decide whether a criminal trial may be closed to the public upon the unopposed request of a defendant, without any demonstraton that closure is required to protect the defendant's superior right to a fair trial, or that some other overriding consideration requires closure.

The origins of the proceeding which has become the modern criminal trial in Anglo-American justice can be traced back beyond reliable historical records. We need not here review all details of its development, but a summary of that history is instructive. What is significant for present purposes is that throughout its evolution, the trial has been open to all who cared to observe. . . .

We found nothing to suggest that the presumptive openness of the trial . . . was not also an attribute of the judicial systems of colonial America. In Virginia, for example, such records as there are of early criminal trials indicate that they were open, and nothing to the contrary has been cited. . . .

In some instances, the openness of trials was explicitly recognized as part of the fundamental law of the colony. The 1677 Concessions and Agreements of West New Jersey, for example, provided:

> That in all public courts of justice for trials of causes, civil or criminal, any person or persons, inhabitants of the said Province may freely come into, and attend the said courts, and hear and be present, at all or any such trials as shall be there had or passed, that justice may not be done in a corner nor in any covert manner. Reprinted in Sources of Our Liberties 188 (R. Perry ed. 1959). See also 1 B. Schwartz, The Bill of Rights: A Documentary History 129

(1971). The Pennsylvania Frame of Government of 1682 also provided "[t]hat all courts shall be open. . . .," Sources of Our Liberties, *supra* at 217; 1 B. Schwartz, *supra* at 140, and this declaration was reaffirmed in section 26 of the Constitution adopted by Pennsylvania in 1776. See 1 B. Schwartz, *supra* at 271. See also §§ 12 and 76 of the Massachusetts Body of Liberties, 1641, reprinted in 1 B. Schwartz, *supra*, at 73, 80.

. . . [T]he historical evidence demonstrates conclusively that at the time when our organic laws were adopted, criminal trials both here and in England had long been presumptively open. This is no quirk of history; rather, it has long been recognized as an indispensable attribute of an Anglo-American trial. . . . It gave assurance that the proceedings were conducted fairly to all concerned, and it discouraged perjury, the misconduct of participants, and decisions based on secret bias or partiality. . . .

. . . Even without such experts to frame the concept in words, people sensed from experience and observation that, especially in the administraton of criminal justice, the means used to achieve justice must have the support derived from public acceptance of both the process and its results.

When a shocking crime occurs, a community reaction of outrage and public protest often follows . . . .

Civilized societies withdraw both from the victim and the vigilante the enforcement of criminal laws, but they cannot erase from people's consciousness the fundamental, natural yearning to see justice done — or even the urge for retribution. The crucial prophylactic aspects of the administration of justice cannot function in the dark . . . .

People in an open society do not demand infallibility from their institutions, but it is difficult for them to accept what they are prohibited from observing. When a criminal trial is conducted in the open, there is at least an opportunity both for understanding the system in general and its workings in a particular case.

From this unbroken, uncontradicted history, supported by reasons as valid today as in centuries past, we are bound to conclude that a presumption of openness inheres in the very nature of a criminal trial under our system of justice. . . . And recently in *Gannett Co. v. DePasquale*, both the majority and dissenting opinions agreed that open trials were part of the common law tradition.

Despite the history of criminal trials being presumptively open since long before the Constitution, the State presses its contention that neither the Constitution nor the Bill of Rights contains any provision which by its terms guarantees to the public the right to attend criminal trials. . . .

III

[T]he First Amendment can be read as protecting the right of everyone to attend trials so as to give meaning to those explicit guarantees. . . . [T]he First Amendment guarantees of speech and press, standing alone, prohibit government from summarily closing courtroom doors which had long been open to the public at the time that amendment was adopted. . . .

It is not crucial whether we describe this right to attend criminal trials to hear, see, and communicate observations concerning them as a "right of access". . . or a "right to gather information," for we have recognized that "without some protection for seeking out the news, freedom of the press could be eviscerated." *Branzburg v. Hayes*, 408 U.S. 665 (1972). The explicit, guaranteed rights to speak and to publish concerning what takes place at a trial would lose much meaning if access to observe the trial could, as it was here, be foreclosed arbitrarily.

The right of access to places traditionally open to the public, as criminal trials have long been, may be seen as assured by the amalgam of the First Amendment guarantees of speech and press; and their affinity to the right of assembly is not without relevance. From the outset, the right of assembly was regarded not only as an independent right but also as a catalyst to augment the free exercise of the other First Amendment rights with which it was deliberately linked by the draftsmen. . . . A trial courtroom also is a public place where the people generally — and representatives of the media — have a right to be present, and where their presence historically has been thought to enhance the integrity and quality of what takes place.

The State argues that the Constitution nowhere spells out a guarantee for the right of the public to attend trials, and that accordingly no such right is protected. The possibility that such a contention could be made did not escape the notice of the Constitution's draftsmen: they were concerned that some important right might be thought disparaged because not specifically guaranteed. It was even argued that because of this danger no Bill of Rights should be adopted. See, *e.g.*, A. Hamilton, The Federalist no. 84. In a letter to Thomas Jefferson in October of 1788, James Madison explained why he, although "in favor of a bill of rights," had "not viewed it in an important light" up to that time: "I conceive that in a certain degree

. . . the rights in question are reserved by the manner in which the federal powers are granted." He went on to state "there is great reason to fear that a positive declaration of some of the most essential rights could not be obtained in the requisite latitude." Writings of James Madison 271 (Hunt ed. 1904).[15]

But arguments such as the State makes have not precluded recognition of important rights not enumerated. Notwithstanding the appropriate caution against reading into the Constitution rights not explicitly defined, the Court has acknowledged that certain unarticulated rights are implicit in enumerated guarantees. For example, the rights of association and privacy, the right to be presumed innocent and the right to be judged by a standard of proof beyond a reasonable doubt in a criminal trial, as well as the right to travel, appear nowhere in the Constitution or Bill of Rights. Yet these important but unarticulated rights have nonetheless been found to share constitutional protection in common with explicit guarantees. The concerns expressed by Madison and others have thus been resolved; fundamental rights, even though not expressly guaranteed, have been recognized by the Court as indispensable to the enjoyment of rights explicitly defined.

We hold that the right to attend criminal trials is implicit in the guarantees of the First Amendment; without the freedom to attend such trials, which people have exercised for centuries, important aspects of freedom of speech and "of the press could be eviscerated." *Branzburg, supra,* at 681.

Having concluded there was a guaranteed right of the public under the First and Fourteenth Amendments to attend the trial of Stevenson's case, we return to the closure order challenged by appellants. The Court in *Gannett, supra* made clear that although the Sixth Amendment guarantees the accused a right to a public trial, it does not give a right to a private trial. 443 U.S., at 382. Despite the fact that this was the fourth trial of the accused, the trial judge made no findings to support closure; no inquiry was made as to whether alternative solutions would have met the need to ensure fairness; there was no recognition of any right under the Constitution for the public or press to attend the trial. In contrast to the pretrial proceeding dealt with in *Gannett, supra,* there exist in the context of the trial itself various tested alternatives to satisfy the constitutional

---

[15] [Court's footnote 15] Madison's comments in Congress also reveal the perceived need for some sort of constitutional "saving clause," which, among other things, would serve to foreclose application to the Bill of Rights of the maxim that the affirmation of particular rights implies a negation of those not expressly defined. See 1 Annals of Congress 438-440 (1789). See also, *e.g.*, J. Story, Commentaries on the Constitution of the United States and 651 (5th ed. 1891). Madison's efforts, culminating in the Ninth Amendment, served to allay the fears of those who were concerned that expressing certain guarantees could be read as excluding others.

demands of fairness. See, *e.g., Nebraska Press Association v. Stuart, 427 U.S., at 563-565; Sheppard v. Maxwell,* 384 U.S., at 357-362. There was no suggestion that any problems with witnesses could not have been dealt with by their exclusion from the courtroom or their sequestration during the trial. Nor is there anything to indicate that sequestration of the jurors would not have guarded against their being subjected to any improper information. All of the alternatives admittedly present difficulties for trial courts, but none of the factors relied on here was beyond the realm of the manageable. Absent an overriding interest articulated in findings, the trial of a criminal case must be open to the public. Accordingly, the judgment under review is

Reversed.

Appendix G

ABRAMS v. UNITED STATES

250 U.S. 616 (1919)

JUSTICE HOLMES, joined by Justice Brandeis, filed the following dissent:

This indictment is founded wholly upon the publication of two leaflets which I shall describe in a moment. The first count charges a conspiracy pending the war with Germany to publish abusive language about the form of government of the United States, laying the preparation and publishing of the first leaflet as overt acts. The second count charges a conspiracy pending the war to publish language intended to bring the form of government into contempt, laying the preparation and publishing of the two leaflets as overt acts. The third count alleges a conspiracy to encourage resistance to the United States in the same war, and to attempt to effectuate the purpose by publishing the same leaflets. The fourth count lays a conspiracy to incite curtailment of production of things necessary to the prosecution of the war, and to attempt to accomplish it by publishing the second leaflet to which I have referred. . . .

[The opinion summarizes the two leaflets]

No argument seems to me necessary to show that these *pronunciamentos* in no way attack the form of government of the United States, or that they do not support either of the first two counts. What little I have to say about the third count may be postponed until I have considered the fourth. With regard to that it seems too plain to be denied that the suggestion to workers in the ammunition factories that they are producing bullets to murder their dearest, and the further advocacy of a general strike, both in the second leaflet, do urge curtailment of production of things necessary to the prosecution of the war within the meaning of the Act of May 16, 1918. . . . But to make the conduct criminal, that statute requires that it should be "with intent by such curtailment to cripple or hinder the United States in the prosecution of the war." It seems to me that no such intent is proved.

I am aware, of course, that the word "intent" as vaguely used in ordinary legal discussion means no more than knowledge at the time of the act that the consequences said to be intended will ensue. Even less than that will satisfy the general principle of civil and criminal liability. A man may have to pay damages, may be sent to prison, at common law might be hanged, if at the time of his act he knew facts from which common experience showed that the consequences would follow, whether he individually could foresee them or not. But, when words are used exactly, a deed is not done with intent to produce a consequence unless that consequence is the aim of the deed. It may be obvious, and obvious to the actor, that the consequence will follow, and he may be liable for it even if he regrets it, but he does not do the act with intent to produce it unless the aim to produce it is the proximate motive of the specific act, although there may be some deeper motive behind.

It seems to me that this statute must be taken to use its words in a strict and accurate sense. They would be absurd in any other. A patriot might think that we were wasting money on aeroplanes, or making more cannon of a certain kind than we needed, and might advocate curtailment with success; yet, even if it turned out that the curtailment hindered and was thought by other minds to have been obviously likely to hinder the United States in the prosecution of the war, no one would hold such conduct a crime. I admit that my illustration does not answer all that might be said, but it is enough to show what I think and to let me pass to a more important aspect of the case. I refer to the 1st Amendment to the Constitution that Congress shall make no law abridging the freedom of speech.

I never have seen any reason to doubt that the questions of law that alone were before this court in the cases of *Schenck, Frohwerk,* and *Debs,* were rightly decided. I do not doubt for a moment that by the same reasoning that would justify punishing persuasion to murder, the United States constitutionally may punish speech that produces or is intended to produce a clear and imminent danger that it will bring about forthwith certain substantive evils that the United States constitutionally may seek to prevent. The power undoubtedly is greater in time of war than in time of peace because war opens dangers that do not exist at other times.

But, as against dangers peculiar to war, as against others, the priniciple of the right to free speech is always the same. It is only the present danger of immediate evil or an intent to bring it about that warrants Congress in setting a limit to the expression of opinion where private rights are not concerned. Congress certainly cannot forbid all effort to change the mind of the country. Now nobody can suppose that the surreptitious publishing of a silly leaflet by an unknown man, without more, would present any immediate danger that its opinions would hinder the success of the government arms or have any appreciable tendency to do so. Publishing those opinions for the very purpose of obstructing, however, might indicate a greater danger, and at any rate would have the quality of an attempt. So I assume that the second leaflet, if published for the purposes alleged in the fourth count, might be punishable. But it seems pretty clear to me that nothing less that that would bring these papers within the scope of this law. An actual intent in the sense that I have explained is necessary to constitutute an attempt, where a further act of the same individual is required to complete the substantive crime, for reasons given in *Swift & Co. v. United States*, 196 U.S. 375, 396. It is necessary where the success of the attempt depends upon others, because if that intent is not present, the actor's aim may be accomplished without bringing about the evils sought to be checked. An intent to prevent interference with the revolution in Russia might have been satisfied without any hindrance to carrying on the war in which we were engaged.

I do not see how anyone can find the intent required by the statute in any of the defendants' words. The second leaflet is the only one that affords even a foundation for the charge, and there, without invoking the hatred of German militarism expressed in the former one, it is evident from the beginning to the end that the only object of the paper is to help Russia and stop American intervention there against the popular government — not to impede the United States in the war that it was carrying on. To say that two phrases, taken literally, might import a suggestion of conduct that would have interference with the war as an indirect and probably undesired effect, seems to me by no means enough to show an attempt to produce that effect.

I return for a moment to the third count. That charges an intent to provoke resistance to the United States in its war with Germany. Taking the clause in the statute that deals with that in connection with the other elaborate provisions of the act, I think that resistance to the United States means some forcible act of opposition to some proceeding of the United States in pursuance of the war. I think the intent must be the specific intent that I have described, and for the reasons that I have given I think that no such intent was proved or existed in fact. I also think that there is no hint at resistance to the United States, as I construe the phrase.

In this case sentences of twenty years' imprisonment have been imposed for the publishing of two leaflets that I believe the defendants had as much right to publish as the government has to publish the Constitution of the United States now vainly invoked by them. Even if I am technically wrong, and enough can be squeezed from these poor and puny anonymities to turn the color of legal litmus paper — I will add, even if what I think the necessary intent were shown — the most nominal punishment seems to me all that possibly could be inflicted, unless the defendants are to be made to suffer not for what the indictment alleges, but for the creed that they avow — a creed that I believe to be the creed of ignorance and immaturity when honestly held, as I see no reason to doubt that it was held here, but which, although made the subject of examination at the trial, no one has a right even to consider in dealing with the charges before the court.

Persecution for the expression of opinions seems to me perfectly logical. If you have no doubt of your premises or your power and want a certain result with all your heart you naturally express your wishes in law and sweep away all opposition. To allow opposition by speech seems to indicate that you think the speech impotent, as when a man says that he has squared the circle, or that you do not care whole-heartedly for the result, or that you doubt either your power or your premises. But when men have realized that time has upset many fighting faiths, they may come to believe even more than they believe the very foundations of their own conduct that the ultimate good desired is better reached by free trade in ideas — that the best test of truth is the power of the thought to get itself accepted in the competition of the market; and that truth is the only ground upon which their wishes safely can be carried out. That, at any rate, is the theory of our Constitution. It is an experiment, as all life is an experiment. Every year, if not every day, we have to water our salvation upon some prophecy based upon imperfect knowledge. While that experiment is part of our system I think that we should be eternally vigilant against attempts to check the expression of opinions that we loathe and believe to be fraught with death, unless they so imminently threaten immediate interference with the lawful and pressing purposes of the law that an immediate check is required to save the country. I wholly disagree with the argument of the government that the 1st Amendment left the common law as to seditious libel in force. History seems to me against the notion. I had conceived that the United States through many years had shown its repentance for the Sedition Act of July 14, 1798 by repaying fines that it imposed. Only the emergency that makes it immediately dangerous to leave the correction of evil counsels to time warrants making any exception to the sweeping command, "Congress shall make no law abridging the freedom of speech." Of course I am speaking only of expressions of opinion and exhortations, which were all that were uttered here; but I regret that I cannot put into more impressive words my belief that in their conviction upon this indictment the defendants were deprived of their rights under the Constitution of the United States.

Appendix H

BRANDENBURG v. OHIO

395 U.S. 44 (1969)

PER CURIAM.

The appellant, a leader of a Ku Klux Klan group, was convicted under the Ohio Criminal Syndicalism statute for "advocat[ing] . . . the duty, necessity, or propriety of crime, sabotage, violence, or unlawful methods of terrorism as a means of accomplishing industrial or political reform" and for "voluntarily assembl[ing] with any society, group, or assemblage of persons formed to teach or advocate the doctrines of criminal syndicalism." Ohio Rev. Code Ann. § 2923.13. He was fined $1,000 and sentenced to one to 10 years' imprisonment. The appellant challenged the constitutionality of the criminal syndicalism statute under the First and Fourteenth Amendments to the United States Constitution, but the intermediate appellate court of Ohio affirmed his conviction without opinion. The Supreme Court of Ohio dismissed his appeal, *sua sponte*, "for the reason that no substantial constitutional question exists herein." It did not file an opinion or explain its conclusions. Appeal was taken to this Court. . . . We reverse.

The record shows that a man, identified at trial as the appellant, telephoned an announcer-reporter on the staff of a Cincinnati television station and invited him to come to a Ku Klux Klan "rally" to be held at a farm in Hamilton County. With the cooperation of the organizers, the reporter and a cameraman attended the meeting and filmed the events. Portions of the films were later broadcast on the local station and on a national network.

The prosecution's case rested on the films and on testimony identifying the appellant as the person who communicated with the reporter and who spoke at the rally. The State also introduced into evidence several articles appearing in the film, including a pistol, a rifle, a shotgun, ammunition, a Bible, and a red hood worn by the speaker in the films.

One film showed 12 hooded figures, some of whom carried firearms. They were gathered around a large wooden cross, which they burned. No one was present other than the participants and the newsmen who made the film. Most of the words uttered during the scene were incomprehensible when the film was projected, but scattered phrases could be understood that were derogatory of Negroes and, in one instance, of Jews. Another scene on the same film showed the appellant, in Klan regalia, making a speech. The speech, in full, was as follows:

> This is an organizers' meeting. We have had quite a few members here today which are — we have hundred, hundreds of members throughout the State of Ohio. I can quote from a newspaper clipping from the Columbus, Ohio Dispatch, five weeks ago Sunday morning. The Klan has more members in the State of Ohio than does any other organization. We're not a revengent organization, but if our President, our Congress, our Supreme Court, continues to suppress the white, Caucasian race, it's possible that there might have to be some revengeance taken. We are marching on Congress July Fourth, four hundred thousand strong. From there we are dividing into two groups, one group to march on St. Augustine, Florida, the other group to march into Mississippi. Thank you.

The second film showed six hooded figures one of whom, later identified as the appellant, repeated a speech very similar to that recorded on the first film. The reference to the possibility of "revengeance" was omitted, and one sentence was added: "Personally, I believe the nigger should be returned to Africa, the Jew returned to Israel." Though some of the figures in the films carried weapons, the speaker did not.

The Ohio Criminal Syndicalism Statute was enacted in 1919. From 1917 to 1920, identical or quite similar laws were adopted by 20 States and two territories. E. Dowell, A History of Criminal Syndicalism Legislation in the United States 21 (1939). In 1927, this Court sustained the constitutionality of California's Criminal Syndicalism Act, the text of which is quite similar to that of the laws of Ohio. *Whitney v. California*. The Court upheld the statute on the ground that, without more, "advocating" violent means to effect political and economic change involves such danger to the security of the State that the State may outlaw it. Cf. *Fiske v. Kansas*, 274 U.S. 380 (1927). But Whitney has been thoroughly discredited by later decisions. See *Dennis v. United States*. These later decisions have fashioned the principle that the constitutional guarantees of free speech and free press do not permit a State to forbid or proscribe advocacy of the use of force or of law violation except where such advocacy is directed to inciting or producing imminent lawless action and is likely to incite or produce such action. As we said in *Noto v. United States*, 367 U.S. 290, 297-298 (1961), "the mere abstract teaching . . . of the moral propriety or even moral necessity for a resort to force and violence, is not the same as preparing a group for violent action and steeling it to such action.". . . A statute which fails to draw this distinction impermissibly intrudes upon the freedoms guaranteed by the First and Fourteenth Amendments. It sweeps within its condemnation speech which our Constitution has immunized from governmental control . . . .

Measured by this test, Ohio's Criminal Syndicalism Act cannot be sustained. The Act punishes persons who "advocate or teach the duty, necessity, or propriety" of violence "as a means of accomplishing industrial or political reform"; or who "justify" the commission of violent acts "with intent to exemplify, spread or advocate the propriety of the doctrines of criminal syndicalism." Neither the indictment nor the trial judge's instructions to the jury in any way refined the statute's bald definition of the crime in terms of mere advocacy not distinguished from incitement to imminent lawless action.

Accordingly, we are here confronted with a statute which, by its own words and as applied, purports to punish mere advocacy and to forbid, on pain of criminal punishment, assembly with others merely to advocate the described type of action. Such a statute falls within the condemnation of the First and Fourteenth Amendments. The contrary teaching of *Whitney v. California* cannot be supported, and that decision is therefore overruled.

Reversed.

Appendix I

RED LION BROADCASTING CO. v. F.C.C.

395 U.S. 367 (1969)

JUSTICE WHITE delivered the opinion of the Court.

The Federal Communications Commission has for many years imposed on radio and television broadcasters the requirement that discussion of public issues be presented on broadcast stations, and that each side of those issues must be given fair coverage. This is known as the fairness doctrine, which originated very early in the history of broadcasting and has maintained its present outlines for some time. It is an obligation whose content has been defined in a long series of FCC rulings in particular cases, and which is distinct from the statutory requirement of § 315 of the Communications Act that equal time be allotted all qualified candidates for public office. Two aspects of the fairness doctrine, relating to personal attacks in the context of controversial public issues and to political editorializing, were codified more precisely in the form of FCC regulations in 1967 . . . .

The Red Lion Broadcasting Company is licensed to operate a Pennsylvania radio station, WGCB. On November 27, 1964, WGCB carried a 15-minute broadcast by the Reverend Billy James Hargis as part of a "Christian Crusade" series. A book by Fred J. Cook entitled "Goldwater—Extremist on the Right" was discussed by Hargis, who said that Cook had been fired by a newspaper for making false charges against city officials; that Cook had then worked for a Communist-affiliated publication; that he had defended Alger Hiss and attacked J. Edgar Hoover and the Central Intelligence Agency; and that he had now written a "book to smear and destroy Barry Goldwater." When Cook heard of the broadcast he concluded that he had been personally attacked and demanded free reply time, which the station refused. After an exchange of letters among Cook, Red Lion, and the FCC, the FCC declared that the Hargis broadcast constituted a personal attack on Cook; that Red Lion had failed to meet its obligation under the fairness doctrine . . . to send a tape, transcript, or summary of the broadcast to Cook and offer him reply time; and that the station must provide reply time whether or not Cook would pay for it. On review in the Court of Appeals for the District of Columbia Circuit, the FCC's position was upheld as constitutional and otherwise proper . . . .

[The opinion explores the statutory authority for the fairness doctrine and concludes: "The history of the emergence of the fairness doctrine and of the related legislation shows that the Commission's action in the *Red Lion* case did not exceed its authority, and that in adopting the new regulations the Commission was implementing congressional policy rather than embarking on a frolic of its own."]

The broadcasters challenge the fairness doctrine and its specific manifestations in the personal attack and political editorial rules on conventional First Amendment grounds, alleging that the rules abridge their freedom of speech and press. Their contention is that the First Amendment protects their desire to use their allotted frequencies continuously to broadcast whatever they choose, and to exclude whomever they choose from ever using that frequency. No man may be prevented from saying or publishing what he thinks, or from refusing in his speech or other utterances to give equal weight to the views of his opponents. This right, they say, applies equally to broadcasters.

Although broadcasting is clearly a medium affected by a First Amendment interest . . . differences in the characteristics of new media justify differences in the First Amendment standards applied to them . . . .

Just as the Government may limit the use of sound-amplifying equipment potentially so noisy that it drowns out civilized private speech, so may the Government limit the use of broadcast equipment. The right of free speech of a broadcaster, the user of a sound truck, or any other individual does not embrace a right to snuff out the free speech of others . . . .

When two people converse face to face, both should not speak at once if either is to be clearly understood. But the range of the human voice is so limited that there could be meaningful communications if half the people in the United States were talking and the other half listening. Just as clearly, half the people might publish and the other half read. But the reach of radio signals is incomparably greater than the range of the human voice and the problem of interference is a massive reality. The lack of know-how and equipment may keep many from the air, but only a tiny fraction of those with resources and intelligence can hope to communicate by radio at the same time if intelligible communication is to be had, even if the entire radio spectrum is utilized in the present state of commercially acceptable technology.

It was this fact, and the chaos which ensued from permitting anyone to use any frequency at whatever power level he wished, which made necessary the enactment of the Radio Act of 1927 and the Communications Act of 1934 .... It was this reality which at the very least necessitated first the division of the radio spectrum into portions reserved respectively for public broadcasting and for other important radio uses such as amateur operation, aircraft, police, defense, and navigation; and then the subdivision of each portion, and assignment of specific frequencies to individual users or groups of users. Beyond this, however, because the frequencies reserved for public broadcasting were limited in number, it was essential for the Government to tell some applicants that they could not broadcast at all because there was room for only a few.

Where there are substantially more individuals who want to broadcast than there are frequencies to allocate, it is idle to posit an unbridgeable First Amendment right to broadcast comparable to the right of every individual to speak, write, or publish. If 100 persons want broadcast licenses but there are only 10 frequencies to allocate, all of them may have the same "right" to a license; but if there is to be any effective communication by radio, only a few can be licensed and the rest must be barred from the airwaves. It would be strange if the First Amendment, aimed at protecting and furthering communications, prevented the Government from making radio communication possible by requiring licenses to broadcast and by limiting the number of licenses so as not to overcrowd the spectrum.

This has been the consistent view of the Court. Congress unquestionably has the power to grant and deny licenses and to eliminate existing stations .... No one has a First Amendment right to a license or to monopolize a radio frequency; to deny a station license because "the public interest" requires it "is not a denial of free speech." *National Broadcasting Co. v. United States*, 319 U.S. 190, 227.

By the same token, as far as the First Amendment is concerned those who are licensed stand no better than those to whom licenses are refused. A license permits broadcasting, but the licensee has no constitutional right to be the one who holds the license or to monopolize a radio frequency to the exclusion of his fellow citizens. There is nothing in the First Amendment which prevents the Government from requiring a licensee to share his frequency with others and to conduct himself as a proxy or fiduciary with obligations to present those views and voices which are representative of his community and which would otherwise, by necessity, be barred from the airwaves . . . . It is the right of the viewers and listeners, not the right of the broadcasters, which is paramount . . . . It is the purpose of the First Amendment to preserve an uninhibited marketplace of ideas in which truth will ultimately prevail, rather than to countenance monopolization of that market, whether it be by the Government itself or a private licensee . . . . It is the right of the public to receive suitable access to social, political, aesthetic, moral, and other ideas and experiences which is crucial here. That right may not constitutionally be abridged either by Congress or by the FCC.

Rather than confer frequency monopolies on a relatively small number of licensees, in a Nation of 200,000,000, the Government could surely have decreed that each frequency should be shared among all or some of those who wish to use it, each being assigned a portion of the broadcast day or the broadcast week. The ruling and regulations at issue here do not go quite so far. They assert that under specified circumstances, a licensee must offer to make available a reasonable amount of broadcast time to those who have a view different from that which has already been expressed on his station. The expression of a political endorsement, or of a personal attack while dealing with a controversial public issue, simply triggers this time sharing. As we have said, the First Amendment confers no right on licensees to prevent others from broadcasting on "their" frequencies and no right to an unconditional monopoly of a scarce resource which the Government has denied others the right to use.

In terms of constitutional principle, and as enforced sharing of a scarce resource, the personal attack and political editorial rules are indistinguishable from the equal-time provision of § 315, a specific enactment of Congress requiring stations to set aside reply time under specified circumstances and to which the fairness doctrine and these constituent regulations are important complements. That provision, which has been part of the law since 1927, has been held valid by this Court as an obligation of the licensee relieving him of any power in any way to prevent or censor the broadcast, and thus insulating him from liability for defamation . . . .

Nor can we say that is inconsistent with the First Amendment goal of producing an informed public capable of conducting its own affairs to require a broadcaster to permit answers to personal attacks occurring in the course of discussing controversial issues, or to require that the political opponents of those endorsed by the station be given a chance to communicate with the public. Otherwise, station owners and a few networks would have unfettered power to make time available only to the highest bidders, to communicate only their own views on public issues, people and candidates, and to permit on the air only those with whom they agreed. There is no sanctuary in the First Amendment for unlimited private censorship operating in a medium not open to all . . . .

It is strenuously argued, however, that if political editorials or personal attacks will trigger an obligation in broadcasters to afford the opportunity for expression to speakers who need not pay for time and whose views are unpalatable to the licensees, then broadcasters will be irresistibly forced to self-censorship and their coverage of controversial public issues will be eliminated or at least rendered wholly ineffective. Such a result would indeed be a serious matter, for should licensees actually eliminate their coverage of controversial issues, the purposes of the doctrine would be stifled.

At this point, however, as the Federal Communications Commission has indicated, that possibility is at best speculative. The communications industry, and in particular the networks, have taken pains to present controversial issues in the past, and even now they do not assert that they intend to abandon their efforts in this regard. It would be better if the FCC's encouragement were never necessary to induce the broadcasters to meet their responsibility. And if experience with the administration of those doctrines indicates that they have the net effect of reducing rather than enhancing the volume and quality of coverage, there will be time enough to reconsider the constitutional implications. The fairness doctrine in the past has had no such overall effect. . . .

We need not and do not now ratify every past and future decision by the FCC with regard to programming. There is no question here of the Commission's refusal to permit the broadcaster to carry a particular program or to publish his own views; of a discriminatory refusal to require the licensee to broadcast certain views which have been denied access to the airwaves; of government censorship of a particular program contrary to § 326; or of the official government view dominating public broadcasting. Such questions would raise more serious First Amendment issues. But we do hold that the Congress and the Commission do not violate the First Amendment when they require a radio or television station to give reply time to answer personal attacks and political editorials.

It is argued that even if at one time the lack of available frequencies for all who wished to use them justified the Government's choice of those who would best serve the public interest by acting as proxy for those who would present differing views, or by giving the latter access directly to broadcast facilities, this condition no longer prevails so that continuing control is not justified. To this there are several answers.

Scarcity is not entirely a thing of the past. Advances in technology, such as microwave transmission, have led to more efficient utilization of the frequency spectrum, but uses for that spectrum have also grown apace. Portions of the spectrum must be reserved for vital uses unconnected with human communication, such as radio-navigational aids used by aircraft and vessels. Conflicts have even emerged between such vital functions as defense preparedness and experimentation in methods of averting midair collisions through radio warning devices. "Land mobile services" such as police, ambulances, fire department, public utility, and other communications systems have been occupying an increasingly crowded portion of the frequency spectrum and there are, apart from licensed amateur radio operators' equipment, 5,000,000 transmitters operated on the "citizens' band" which is also increasingly congested. Among the various uses for radio frequency space, including marine, aviation, amateur, military, and common carrier users, there are easily enough claimants to permit use of the whole with an even smaller allocation to broadcast radio and television uses than now exists.

Comparative hearings between competing applicants for broadcast spectrum space are by no means a thing of the past. The radio spectrum has become so congested that at times it has been necessary to suspend new applications. The very high frequency television spectrum is, in the country's major markets, almost entirely occupied, although space reserved for ultra high frequency television transmission, which is a relatively recent development as a commercially viable alternative, has not yet been completely filled . . . .

Even where there are gaps in spectrum utilization, the fact remains that existing broadcasters have often attained their present position because of their initial government selection in competition with others before new technological advances opened new opportunities for further uses. Long experience in broadcasting, confirmed habits of listeners and viewers, network affiliation, and other advantages in program procurement give existing broadcasters a substantial advantage over new entrants, even where new entry is technologically possible. These advantages are the fruit of a preferred position conferred by the Government. Some present possibility for new entry by competing stations is not enough, in itself, to render unconstitutional the Government's effort to assure that a broadcaster's programming ranges widely enough to serve the public interest.

In view of the scarcity of broadcast frequencies, the Government's role in allocating those frequencies, and the legitimate claims of those unable without governmental assistance to gain access to those frequencies for expression of their views, we hold the regulations and ruling at issue here are both authorized by statute and constitutional . . . .

Appendix J

COHEN v. COWLES MEDIA CO.

111 S. Ct. 2513 (1991)

Justice WHITE delivered the opinion of the Court.

The question before us is whether the First Amendment prohibits a plaintiff from recovering damages, under state promissory estoppel law, for a newspaper's breach of a promise of confidentiality given to the plaintiff in exchange for information. We hold that it does not.

During the closing days of the 1982 Minnesota gubernatorial race, Dan Cohen, an active Republican associated with Wheelock Whitney's Independent-Republican gubernatorial campaign, approached reporters from the St. Paul Pioneer Press Dispatch (Pioneer Press) and the Minneapolis Star and Tribune (Star Tribune) and offered to provide documents relating to a candidate in the upcoming election. Cohen made clear to the reporters that he would provide the information only if he was given a promise of confidentiality. Reporters from both papers promised to keep Cohen's identity anonymous and Cohen turned over copies of two public court records concerning Marlene Johnson, the Democratic-Farmer-Labor candidate for Lieutenant Governor. The first record indicated that Johnson had been charged in 1969 with three counts of unlawful assembly, and the second that she had been convicted in 1970 of petit theft. . . .

After consultation and debate, the editorial staffs of the two newspapers independently decided to publish Cohen's name as part of their stories concerning Johnson. In their stories, both papers identified Cohen as the source of the court records . . . . The same day the stories appeared, Cohen was fired by his employer.

Cohen sued respondents, the publishers of the Pioneer Press and Star Tribune, in Minnesota state court, alleging fraudulent misrepresentation and breach of contract. The trial court rejected respondents' argument that the First Amendment barred Cohen's lawsuit. A jury returned a verdict in Cohen's favor, awarding him $200,000 in compensatory damages . . . .

A divided Minnesota Supreme Court reversed the compensatory damages award. 457 N.W.2d 199 (Minn. 1990). After affirming the Court of Appeals' determination that Cohen had not established a claim for fraudulent misrepresentation, the court considered his breach of contract claim and concluded that "a contract cause of action is inappropriate for these particular circumstances." *Id.*, at 203. The court then went on to address the question whether Cohen could establish a cause of action under Minnesota law on a promissory estoppel theory . . . .

After a brief discussion, the court concluded that "in this case enforcement of the promise of confidentiality under a promissory estoppel theory would violate defendants' First Amendment Rights."

We granted certiorari to consider the First Amendment implications of this case . . . .

Respondents rely on the proposition that "if a newspaper lawfully obtains truthful information about a matter of public significance then state officials may not constitutionally punish publication of the information, absent a need to further a state interest of the highest order." *Smith v. Daily Mail Publishing Co.*, 443 U.S. 97 (1979). That proposition is unexceptionable, and it has been applied in various cases that have found insufficient the asserted state interest in preventing publication of truthful, lawfully obtained information . . . .

This case however, is not controlled by this line of cases but rather by the equally well-established line of decisions holding that generally applicable laws do not offend the First Amendment simply because their enforcement against the press has incidental effects on its ability to gather and report the news. As the cases relied on by respondents recognize, the truthful information sought to be published must have been lawfully acquired. The press may not with impunity break and enter an office or dwelling to gather news. Neither does the First Amendment relieve a newspaper reporter of the obligation shared by all citizens to respond to a grand jury subpoena and answer questions relevant to a criminal investigation, even though the reporter might be required to reveal a confidential source. *Branzburg v. Hayes*, 408 U.S. 665 (1972). The press, like others interested in publishing, may not publish copyrighted material without obeying the copyright laws. See *Zacchini v. Scripps-Howard Broadcasting Co.*, 433 U.S. 562, 576-579 (1977). Similarly, the media must obey the National Labor Relations Act, *Associated Press v. NLRB*, 301 U.S. 103 (1937), and the Fair Labor Standards Act, *Oklahoma Press Publishing Co. v. Walling*, 327 U.S. 176, 192-193 (1946); may not restrain trade in violation of the antitrust laws, *Associated Press v. United States*, 326 U.S. 1 (1945); *Citizen Publish-*

ing Co. v. United States, 394 U.S. 131, 139 (1969); and must pay non-discriminatory taxes. *Murdock v. Pennsylvania*, 319 U.S. 105, 112, *Minneapolis Star and Tribune Co. v. Minnesota Commissioner of Revenue*, 460 U.S. 575, 581-583 (1983). *Cf. University of Pennsylvania v. EEOC*, 493 U.S. 182, 201-202 (1990). It is therefore beyond dispute that "[t]he publisher of a newspaper has no special immunity from the application of general laws. He has no special privilege to invade the rights and liberties of others." *Associated Press v. NLRB, supra,* 301 U.S., at 132-133. Accordingly, enforcement of such general laws against the press is not subject to stricter scrutiny than would be applied to enforcement against other persons or organizations.

There can be little doubt that the Minnesota doctrine of promissory estoppel is a law of general applicability. It does not target or single out the press. Rather, in so far as we are advised, the doctrine is generally applicable to the daily transactions of all the citizens of Minnesota. The First Amendment does not forbid its application to the press.

Justice BLACKMUN suggests [in his dissent] that applying Minnesota promissory estoppel doctrine in this case will "punish" Respondents for publishing truthful information that was lawfully obtained. This is not strictly accurate because compensatory damages are not a form of punishment, as were the criminal sanctions at issue in *Smith*. If the contract between the parties in this case had contained a liquidated damages provision, it would be perfectly clear that the payment to petitioner would represent a cost of acquiring newsworthy material to be published at a profit, rather than a punishment imposed by the State. The payment of compensatory damages in this case is constitutionally indistinguishable from a generous bonus paid to a confidential news source. In any event, as indicated above, the characterization of the payment makes no difference for First Amendment purposes when the law being applied is a general law and does not single out the press. Moreover, Justice BLACKMUN'S reliance on cases like *The Florida Star* and *Smith v. Daily Mail* is misplaced. In those cases, the State itself defined the content of publications that would trigger liability. Here, by contrast, Minnesota law simply requires those making promises to keep them. The parties themselves, as in this case, determine the scope of their legal obligations and any restrictions which may be placed on the pubication of truthful information are self-imposed.

Also, it is not at all clear that Respondents obtained Cohen's name "lawfully" in this case, at least for purposes of publishing it. Unlike the situation in *The Florida Star*, where the rape victim's name was obtained through lawful access to a police report, Respondents obtained Cohen's name only by making a promise which they did not honor. The dissenting opinions suggest that the press should not be subject to any law, including copyright law for example, which in any fashion or to any degree limits or restricts the press' right to report truthful information. The First Amendment does not grant the press such limitless protection . . . .

Respondents and *amici* argue that permitting Cohen to maintain a cause of action for promissory estoppel will inhibit truthful reporting because news organizations will have legal incentives not to disclose a confidential source's identity even when the person's identity is itself newsworthy . . . . But if this is the case, it is no more than the incidental, and constitutionally insignificant, consequence of applying to the press a generally applicable law that requires those who make certain kinds of promises to keep them. Although we conclude that the First Amendment does not confer on the press a constitutional right to disregard promises that would otherwise be enforced under state law, we reject Cohen's request that in reversing the Minnesota Supreme Court's judgment we reinstate the jury verdict awarding him $200,000 in compensatory damages. The Minnesota Supreme Court's incorrect conclusion that the First Amendment barred Cohen's claim may well have truncated its consideration of whether a promissory estoppel claim had otherwise been established under Minnesota law and whether Cohen's jury verdict could be upheld on a promissory estoppel basis. Or perhaps the State Constitution may be construed to shield the press from a promissory estoppel cause of action such as this one. These are matters for the Minnesota Supreme Court to address and resolve in the first instance on remand. Accordingly, the judgment of the Minnesota Supreme Court is reversed, and the case is remanded for further proceedings not inconsistent with this opinion.

So ordered.

Appendix K
(Roth v. United States, 1957)

MEMORANDUM BY THE CHIEF JUSTICE
[Original in Earl Warren's Handwriting, June 17, 1957]

No. 582 Roth v. United States
No. 61 Alberts v. State of Calif.

I agree with the result reached by the Court, but because we are operating in the field of expression and because broad language used here will eventually be applied to the arts and sciences and freedom of expression generally, I would limit our writing to the facts before us and to the validity of the statute in question as applied. This can be done without difficulty as the issue is clear.

The petitioner Albert[s] was charged with lewdly and knowingly selling obscene literature, and at the trial obscenity was defined as a portrayal of sex in such manner as to cause the publication as a whole to appeal to the prurient interest. He was accorded all the protections of a criminal trial. His contention here is that the word "obscene" is too vague to support a criminal conviction and that his right of free expression is being abridged in violation of the First Amendment of the Constitution of the United States, as incorporated in the Fourteenth.

The word "obscene" is neither a new word nor one that is without meaning for the average person. It has been used, understood, and forbidden in all ages. It is a term that comes to us distilled by centuries of use. Like other words, such as negligence, it is capable of little further distillation, except as applied to specific situations. It was punishable in England before Jamestown was founded three hundred and fifty years ago. It was punishable throughout the colonial period, and is now punishable in all but one of the States of the Union. There are among those who have studied the subject with an eye to seeing that the term will not be used in a manner to constrict free expression a belief that a more self-containing definition can be devised, but none of the States have seen fit to adopt any such proposal. The California statute as interpreted conforms to the general concept.

The known history and meaning of the term "obscienity" [sic], at the time of the adoption of our Bill of Rights, together with the uninterrupted action of all but one of the States as they came into the Union, convinces me that it was considered by the American people then as now to be an abuse of freedom of expression rather than a protected right.

Essential as it is that the term be not expanded so as to abridge free expression either in the discussion of public affairs, the freedom of the press or in the arts and sciences, we should not deprive the States of the right to protect their people from this form of depravity.

I would affirm the federal case of *Roth v. United States*, No. 582, on the same principle, adding only that the Congress has the additional responsibility of protecting the United States mails under Art. I, Sec. d of the Constitution.

Appendix L

MILLER v. CALIFORNIA

413 U.S. 15 (1973)

CHIEF JUSTICE BURGER delivered the opinion of the Court.*

This is one of a group of "obscenity-pornography" cases being reviewed by the Court in a re-examination of standards enunciated in earlier cases involving what Justice Harlan called "the intractable obscenity problem." *Interstate Circuit, Inc. v. Dallas*, 390 U.S. 676, 704 (1968) (concurring and dissenting).

Appellant conducted a mass mailing campaign to advertise the sale of illustrated books, euphemistically called "adult" material. After a jury trial, he was convicted of violating California Penal Code § 311.2 (a), a misdemeanor, by knowingly distributing obscene matter, and the Appellate Department, Superior Court of California, County of Orange, summarily affirmed the judgment without opinion. Appellant's conviction was specifically based on his conduct in causing five unsolicited advertising brochures to be sent through the mail in an envelope addressed to a restaurant in Newport Beach, California. The envelope was opened by the manager of the restaurant and his mother. They had not requested the brochures; they complained to the police.

The brochures advertise four books entitled "Intercourse," "Man-Woman," "Sex Orgies Illustrated," and "An Illustrated History of Pornography," and a film entitled "Marital Intercourse." While the brochures contain some descriptive printed material, primarily they consist of pictures and drawings very explicitly depicting men and women in groups of two or more engaging in a variety of sexual activities, with genitals often prominently displayed.

I

This case involves the application of a State's criminal obscenity statute to a situation in which sexually explicit materials have been thrust by aggressive sales action upon unwilling recipients who had in no way indicated any desire to receive such materials.

---

*Footnotes omitted

This Court has recognized that the States have a legitimate interest in prohibiting dissemination or exhibition of obscene material when the mode of dissemination carries with it a significant danger of offending the sensibilities of unwilling recipients or of exposure to juveniles. It is in this context that we are called on to define the standards which must be used to identify obscene material that a State may regulate without infringing on the First Amendment as applicable to the States through the Fourteenth Amendment . . . .

[I]t is useful for us to focus on two of the landmark cases in the somewhat tortured history of the Court's obscenity decisions. In *Roth v. United States*, 354 U.S. 476 (1957), the Court sustained a conviction under a federal statute punishing the mailing of "obscene, lewd, lascivious or filthy . . ." materials. The key to that holding was the Court's rejection of the claim that obscene materials were protected by the First Amendment. Five Justices joined in the opinion stating:

> All ideas having even the slightest redeeming social importance — unorthodox ideas, controversial ideas, even ideas hateful to the prevailing climate of opinion — have the full protection of the [First Amendment] guarantees, unless excludable because they encroach upon the limited area of more important interests.But implicit in the history of the First Amendment is the rejection of obscenity as utterly without redeeming social importance. . . . This is the same judgment expressed by this Court in *Chaplinsky v. New Hampshire*, 315 U.S. 568,571-572.
>
> ". . . There are certain well-defined and narrowly limited classes of speech, the prevention and punishment of which have never been thought to raise any Constitutional problem. *These include the lewd and obscene . . . . It has been well observed that such utterances are no essential part of any exposition of ideas, and are of such slight social value as a step to truth that any benefit that may be derived from them is clearly outweighed by the social interest in order and morality . . ."* [Emphasis by Court in *Roth* opinion.]
>
> We hold that obscenity is not within the areas of constitutionally protected speech or press. 354 U.S., at 484-485.

Nine years later, in *Memoirs v. Massachusetts*, 383 U.S. 413 (1966), the Court veered sharply away from the *Roth* concept and, with only three Justices in the plurality opinion, articulated a new test of obscenity. The plurality held that under the *Roth* definition as elaborated in subsequent cases, three elements must coalesce; it must be established that (a) the dominant theme of the material taken as a whole appeals to a prurient interest in sex; (b) the material is patently offensive because it affronts contemporary community standards relating to the description or representation of sexual matters; and (c) the material is utterly without redeeming social value. *Id.*, at 418.

The sharpness of the break with *Roth*, represented by the third element of the *Memoirs* test and emphasized by Justice White's dissent, *id.*, at 460-462, was further underscored when the *Memoirs* plurality went on to state:

> The Supreme Judicial Court erred in holding that a book need not be "unqualifiedly worthless before it can be deemed obscene." A book cannot be proscribed unless it is found to be *utterly* without redeeming social value. *Id.*, at 419. (emphasis in original).

While *Roth* presumed "obscenity" to be "*utterly* without redeeming social importance," the *Memoirs* plurality produced a drastically altered test that called on the prosecution to prove a negative, *i.e.*, that the material was "*utterly* without redeeming social value" — a burden virtually impossible to discharge under our criminal standards of proof. Such considerations caused Justice Harlan to wonder if the "*utterly* without redeeming social value" test had any meaning at all. See *Memoirs v. Massachusetts, id.*, at 459 (Harlan, J., dissenting).

Apart from the initial formulation in the *Roth* case, no majority of the Court has at any given time been able to agree on a standard to determine what constitutes obscene, pornographic material subject to regulation under the States' police power . . . "This is not remarkable, for in the area of freedom of speech and press the courts must always remain sensitive to any infringement on genuinely serious literary, artistic, political, or scientific expression. This is an area in which there are few eternal verities."

The case we now review was tried on the theory that the California Penal Code § 311 approximately incorporates the three-stage *Memoirs* test, *supra*. But now the *Memoirs* test has been abandoned as unworkable by its author, and no Member of the Court today supports the *Memoirs* formulation.

II

. . . We acknowledge . . . the inherent dangers of undertaking to regulate any form of expression. State statutes designed to regulate obscene materials must be carefully limited . . . . As a result, we now confine the permissible scope of such regulation to works which depict or describe sexual conduct. That conduct must be specifically defined by the applicable state law, as written or authoritatively construed. A state offense must also be limited to works which, taken as a whole, appeal to prurient interest in sex, which portray sexual conduct in a patently offensive way, and which, taken as a whole, do not have serious literary, artistic, political, or scientific value.

The basic guidelines for the trier of fact must be: (a) whether "the average person, applying contemporary community standards" would find that the work, taken as a whole, appeals to the prurient interest, *Roth v. United States*, 354 U.S., at 489; (b) whether the work depicts or describes, in a patently offensive way, sexual conduct specifically defined by the applicable state law; and (c) whether the work, taken as a whole, lacks serious literary, artistic, political or scientific value. We do not adopt as a constitutional standard the "utterly without redeeming social value" test of *Memoirs v. Massachusetts*, 383 U.S., at 419; that concept has never commanded the adherence of more than three Justices at one time. If a state law that regulates obscene material is thus limited, as written or construed, the First Amendment values applicable to the States through the Fourteenth Amendment are adequately protected by the ultimate power of appellate courts to conduct an independent review of constitutional claims when necessary.

We emphasize that it is not our function to propose regulatory schemes for the States. That must await their concrete legislative efforts. It is possible, however, to give a few plain examples of what a state statute could define for regulation under part (b) of the standard announced in this opinion, *supra*:

(a) Patently offensive representations or descriptions of ultimate sexual acts, normal or perverted, actual or simulated.

(b) Patently offensive representation or descriptions of masturbation, excretory functions, and lewd exhibition of genitals.

Sex and nudity may not be exploited without limit by films or pictures exhibited or sold in places of public accommodation any more than live sex and nudity can be exhibited or sold without limit in such public places. At a minimum, prurient, patently offensive depiction or description of sexual conduct must have serious literary, artistic, political or scientific value to merit First Amendment protection. For example, medical books for the education of physicians and related personnel necessarily use graphic illustrations and descriptions of human anatomy. In resolving the inevitably sensitive questions of fact and law, we must continue to rely on the jury system, accompanied by the safeguards that judges, rules of evidence, presumption of innocence, and other protective features provide, as we do with rape, murder, and a host of other offenses against society and its individual members.

Justice Brennan . . . has abandoned his former position and now maintains that no formulation of the Court, the Congress, or the States can adequately distinguish obscene material unprotected by the First Amendment from protected expression, *Paris Adult Theatre I v. Slaton.* Paradoxically, Justice Brennan indicates that suppression of unprotected obscene material is permissible to avoid exposure to unconsenting adults, as in this case, and to juveniles, although he gives no indication of how the division between protected and nonprotected materials may be drawn with greater precision for these purposes than for regulation of commercial exposure to consenting adults only. Nor does he indicate where in the Constitution he finds the authority to distinguish between a willing "adult" one month past the state law age of majority and a willing "juvenile" one month younger.

Under the holdings announced today, no one will be subject to prosecution for the sale or exposure of obscene materials unless these materials depict or describe patently offensive "hard core" sexual conduct specifically defined by the regulating state law, as written or construed. We are satisfied that these specific prerequisites will provide fair notice to a dealer in such materials that his public and commercial activities may bring prosecution. . . .

III

Under a National Constitution, fundamental First Amendment limitations on the powers of the State do not vary from community to community, but this does not mean that there are, or should or can be, fixed, uniform national standards of precisely what appeals to the "prurient interest" or is "patently offensive." These are essentially questions of fact, and our Nation is simply too big and too diverse for this Court to reasonably expect that such standards could be articulated for all 50 States in a single formulation, even assuming the prerequisite consensus exists. When triers of fact are asked to decide whether "the average person, applying contemporary community standards" would consider certain materials "prurient," it would be unrealistic to require that the answer be based on some abstract formulation. The adversary system, with lay jurors as the usual ultimate fact finders in criminal prosecutions, has historically permitted triers of fact to draw on the standards of their community, guided always by limiting instructions on the law. To require a State to structure obscenity proceedings around evidence of a *national* "community standard" would be an exercise in futility.

As noted before, this case was tried on the theory that the California obscenity statute sought to incorporate the tripartite test of *Memoirs*. This, a "national" standard of First Amendment protection enumerated by a plurality of this Court, was correctly regarded at the time of trial as limiting state prosecution under the controlling case law. The jury, however, was explicitly instructed that, in determining whether the "dominant theme of the material as a whole... appeals to the prurient interest and in determining whether the material 'goes substantially beyond customary limits of candor and affronts contemporary community standards of decency,' it was to apply contemporary community standards of the State of California."

During the trial, both the prosecution and the defense assumed that the relevant "community standards" in making the factual determination of obscenity were those of the State of California, not some hypothetical standard of the entire United States of America. Defense counsel at trial never objected to the testimony of the State's expert on community standards or to the instructions of the trial judge on "statewide" standards. On appeal to the Appellate Department, Superior Court of California, County of Orange, appellant for the first time contended that application of state, rather than national, standards violated the First and Fourteenth Amendments.

We conclude that neither the State's alleged failure to offer evidence of "national standards," nor the trial court's charge that the jury consider state community standards, were constitutional errors. Nothing in the First Amendment requires that a jury must consider hypothetical and unascertainable "national standards" when attempting to determine whether certain materials are obscene as a matter of fact . . . .

It is neither realistic nor constitutionally sound to read the First Amendment as requiring that the people of Maine or Mississippi accept public depiction of conduct found tolerable in Las Vegas, or New York City. People in different States vary in their tastes and attitudes, and this diversity is not to be strangled by the absolutism of imposed uniformity . . . . We hold that the requirement that the jury evaluate the materials with reference to "contemporary standards of the State of California" serves this protective purpose and is constitutionally adequate.

IV

The dissenting Justices sound the alarm of repression. But, in our view, to equate the free and robust exchange of ideas and political debate with commercial exploitation of obscene material demeans the grand conception of the First Amendment and its high purposes in the historic struggle for freedom. . . .

There is no evidence, empirical or historical, that the stern 19th century American censorship of public distribution and display of material relating to sex in any way limited or affected expression of serious literary, artistic, political, or scientific ideas. On the contrary, it is beyond any question that the era following Thomas Jefferson to Theodore Roosevelt was an "extraordinarily vigorous period," not just in economics and politics, but in *belles lettres* and in "the outlying fields of social and political philosophies." We do not see the harsh hand of censorship of ideas — good or bad, sound or unsound — and "repression" of political liberty lurking in every state regulation of commercial exploitation of human interest in sex . . . .

In sum, we (a) affirm the *Roth* holding that obscene material is not protected by the First Amendment; (b) hold that such material can be regulated by the States, subject to the specific safeguards enunciated above, without a showing that the material is *"utterly* without redeeming social value'" and (c) hold that obscenity is to be determined by applying "contemporary community standards," not "national standards." The judgment of the Appellate Department of the Superior Court, Orange County, California, is vacated and the case remanded to that court for further proceedings not inconsistent with the First Amendment standards established by this opinion.

Appendix M

NEW YORK TIMES COMPANY v. SULLIVAN

376 U.S. 254 (1964)

JUSTICE BRENNAN delivered the opinion of the Court.*

We are required in this case to determine for the first time the extent to which the constitutional protections for speech and press limit a State's power to award damages in a libel action brought by a public official against critics of his official conduct.

Respondent L. B. Sullivan is one of the three elected Commissioners of the City of Montgomery, Alabama. He testified that he was "Commissioner of Public Affairs and the duties are supervision of the Police Department, Fire Department, Department of Cemetery and Department of Scales." He brought this civil libel action against the four individual petitioners, who are Negroes and Alabama clergymen, and against petitioner the New York Times Company, a New York corporation which publishes the New York Times, a daily newspaper. A jury in the Circuit Court of Montgomery County awarded him damages of $500,000, the full amount claimed, against all petitioners, and the Supreme Court of Alabama affirmed . . . . Respondent's complaint alleged that he had been libeled by statements in a full-page advertisement that was carried in the New York Times on March 29, 1960. Entitled "Heed Their Rising Voices," the advertisement began by stating that "As the whole world knows by now, thousands of Southern Negro students are engaged in widespread non-violent demonstrations in positive affirmation of the right to live in human dignity as guaranteed by the U.S. Constitution and the Bill of Rights." It went on to charge that "in their efforts to uphold these guarantees, they are being met by an unprecedented wave of terror by those who would deny and negate that document which the whole world looks upon as setting the pattern for modern freedom . . . ." Succeeding paragraphs purported to illustrate the "wave of terror" by describing certain alleged events. The text concluded with an appeal for funds for three purposes: support of the student movement, "the struggle for the right-to-vote," and the legal defense of Dr. Martin Luther King, Jr., leader of the movement,

---

*Footnotes omitted

against a perjury indictment then pending in Montgomery.

The text appeared over the names of 65 persons, many widely known for their activities in public affairs, religion, trade unions, and the performing arts. Below these names, and under a line reading "We in the south who are struggling daily for dignity and freedom warmly endorse this appeal," appeared the names of the four individual petitioners and of 16 other persons, all but two of whom were identified as clergymen in various Southern cities. The advertisement was signed at the bottom of the page by the "Committee to Defend Martin Luther King and the Struggle for Freedom in the South," and the officers of the Committee were listed.

Of the 10 paragraphs of text in the advertisement, the third and a portion of the sixth were the basis of respondent's claim of libel. They read as follows:

Third Paragraph:

In Montgomery, Alabama, after students sang "My Country, 'Tis of Thee" on the State Capitol steps, their leaders were expelled from school, and truckloads of police armed with shotguns and tear-gas ringed the Alabama State College Campus. When the entire student body protested to state authorities by refusing to re-register, their dining hall was padlocked in an attempt to starve them into submission.

Sixth paragraph:

Again and again the Southern violators have answered Dr. King's peaceful protests with intimidation and violence. They have bombed his home almost killing his wife and child. They have assaulted his person. They have arrested him seven times — for "speeding," "loitering," and similar "offenses." And now they have charged him with "perjury" — a *felony* under which they could imprison him for *ten years* . . . .

Although neither of these statements mentions respondent by name, he contended that the word "police" in the third paragraph referred to him as the Montgomery Commissioner who supervised the Police Department, so that he was being accused of "ringing" the campus with police. He further claimed that the paragraph would be read as imputing to the police, and hence to him, the padlocking of the dining hall in order to starve students into submission. As to the sixth paragraph, he contended that since arrests are ordinarily made by the police, the statement "They have arrested [Dr. King] seven times" would be read as referring to him; he further contended that the "They" who did the arresting would be equated with the "They" who

committed the other described acts and with the "Southern violators." Thus, he argued, the paragraph would be read as accusing the
Montgomery police, and hence him, of answering Dr. King's protests
with "intimidation and violence," bombing his home, assaulting his
person, and charging him with perjury. Respondent and six other
Montgomery residents testified that they read some or all of the
statements as referring to him in his capacity as Commissioner.

It is uncontroverted that some of the statements contained in
the two paragraphs were not accurate descriptions of events which
occurred in Montgomery. Although Negro students staged a demonstration on the State Capital steps, they sang the National Anthem
and not "My Country, 'Tis of Thee." Although nine students were
expelled by the State Board of Education, this was not for leading the
demonstration at the Capitol, but for demanding service at a lunch
counter in the Montgomery County Courthouse on another day. Not
the entire student body, but most of it, had protested the expulsion,
not by refusing to register, but by boycotting classes on a single day;
virtually all the students did register for the ensuing semester. The
campus dining hall was not padlocked on any occasion, and the only
students who may have been barred from eating there were the few
who had neither signed a preregistration application nor requested
temporary meal tickets. Although the police were deployed near the
campus in large numbers on three occasions, they did not at any time
"ring" the campus, and they were not called to the campus in
connection with the demonstration on the State Capitol steps, as the
third paragraph implied. Dr. King had not been arrested seven
times, but only four; and although he claimed to have been assaulted
some years earlier in connection with his arrest for loitering outside
a courtroom, one of the officers who made the arrest denied that there
was such an assault.

On the premise that the charges in the sixth paragraph could
be read as referring to him, respondent was allowed to prove that he
had not participated in the events described. Although Dr. King's
home had in fact been bombed twice when his wife and child were
there, both of these occasions antedated respondent's tenure as
Commissioner, and the police were not only not implicated in the
bombing, but had made every effort to apprehend those who were.
Three of Dr. King's four arrests took place before respondent became
Commissioner. Although Dr. King had in fact been indicted (he was
subsequently acquitted) on two counts of perjury, each of which
carried a possible five-year sentence, respondent had nothing to do
with procuring the indictment. . . .

The cost of the advertisement was approximately $4800, and

it was published by the Times upon an order from a New York advertising agency acting for the signatory Committee. The agency submitted the advertisement with a letter from A. Philip Randolph, Chairman of the Committee, certifying that the persons whose names appeared on the advertisement had given their permission . . . . There was testimony that the copy of the advertisement which accompanied the letter listed only the 64 names appearing under the text, and that the statement, "We in the south . . . warmly endorse this appeal," and the list of names thereunder, which included those of the individual petitioners, were subsequently added when the first proof of the advertisement was received. Each of the individual petitioners testified that he had not authorized the use of his name, and that he had been unaware of its use until receipt of respondent's demand for a retraction. The manager of the Advertising Acceptability Department testified that he had approved the advertisement for publication because he knew nothing to cause him to believe that anything in it was false, and because it bore the endorsement of "a number of people who are well known and whose reputation" he "had no reason to question." Neither he nor anyone else at the Times made an effort to confirm the accuracy of the advertisement, either by checking it against recent Times news stories relating to some of the described events or by any other means . . . .

The jury was instructed that, because the statements were libelous *per se*, "the law . . . implies legal injury from the bare fact of publication itself," "falsity and malice are presumed," "general damages need not be alleged or proved but are presumed," and "punitive damages may be awarded by the jury even though the amount of actual damages is neither found nor shown." An award of punitive damages — as distinguished from "general" damages, which are compensatory in nature — apparently requires proof of actual negligence under Alabama law, and the judge charged that "mere carelessness is not evidence of actual malice or malice in fact, and does not justify an award of exemplary or punitive damages.". . .

In affirming the judgment, the Supreme Court of Alabama sustained the trial judge's ruling and instructions in all respects . . .

II

Under Alabama law as applied in this case, a publication is "libelous per se" if the words "tend to injure a person . . . in his reputation" or to "injure him in his public office, or impute misconduct to him in his office, or want of official integrity, or want of fidelity to a public trust . . . ." The jury must find the words were published "of and concerning" the plaintiff, but where the plaintiff is a public official his place in the governmental hierarchy is sufficient evidence to support a finding that his reputation has been affected by statements that reflect upon the agency of which he is in charge. Once "libel per se" has been established, the defendant has no defense as to stated facts unless he can persuade the jury that they were true in all their particulars . . . . His privilege of "fair comment" for expressions of opinion depends on the truth of the facts upon which the comment is based. Unless he can discharge the burden of proving truth, general damages are presumed, and may be awarded without proof of pecuniary injury. A showing of actual malice is apparently a prerequisite to recovery of punitive damages, and the defendant may in any event forestall a punitive award by a retraction meeting the statutory requirements. Good motives and belief in truth do not negate an inference of malice, but are relevant only in mitigation of punitive damages if the jury chooses to accord them weight . . . .

Respondent relies heavily, as did the Alabama courts, on statements of this Court to the effect that the Constitution does not protect libelous publications. These statements do not foreclose our inquiry here. None of the cases sustained the use of libel laws to impose sanctions upon expression critical of the official conduct of public officials . . . . In deciding the question now, we are compelled by neither precedent nor policy to give any more weight to the epithet "libel" than we have to other "mere labels" of state law . . . . Like insurrection, contempt, advocacy of unlawful acts, breach of the peace, obscenity, solicitation of legal business, and the various other formulae for the repression of expression that have been challenged in this Court, libel can claim no talismanic immunity from constitutional limitations. It must be measured by standards that satisfy the First Amendment . . . .

Thus we consider this case against the background of a profound national commitment to the principle that debate on public issues should be uninhibited, robust, and wide-open, and that it may well include vehement, caustic, and sometimes unpleasantly sharp attacks on government and public officials . . . . The present advertisement, as an expression of grievance and protest on one of the major public issues of our time, would seem clearly to qualify for the constitutional protection. The question is whether it forfeits that protection by the falsity of some of its factual statements and by its alleged defamation of respondent . . . .

Injury to official reputation error affords no more warrant for repressing speech that would otherwise be free than does factual error. Where judicial officers are involved, this Court has held that concern for the dignity and reputation of the courts does not justify the punishment as criminal contempt or criticism of the judge or his decision. *Bridges v. California*, 314 U.S. 252 . . . . Such repression can be justified, if at all, only by a clear and present danger of the obstruction of justice . . . . If judges are to be treated as "men of fortitude, able to thrive in a hardy climate," *Craig v. Harney, supra*, 331 U.S., at 376, surely the same must be true of other government officials, such as elected city commissioners. Criticism of their official conduct does not lose its constitutional protection merely because it is effective criticism and hence diminished their official reputations.

If neither factual error nor defamatory content suffices to remove the constitutional shield from criticism of official conduct, the combination of the two elements is no less inadequate. This is the lesson to be drawn from the great controversy over the Sedition Act of 1798, 1 Stat. 596, which first crystallized a national awareness of the central meaning of the First Amendment . . . . That statute made it a crime, punishable by a $5,000 fine and five years in prison, "if any person shall write, print, utter or publish . . . any false, scandalous and malicious writing or writings against the government of the United States, or either house of the Congress . . . or the President . . . with intent to defame . . . or to bring them, or either or any of them, into contempt or disrepute; or to excite against them, or either or any of them, the hatred of the good people of the United States." The Act allowed the defendant the defense of truth, and provided that the jury were to be judges both of the law and of the facts. Despite these qualifications, the Act was vigorously condemned as unconstitutional in an attack joined in by Jefferson and Madison . . . .

Although the Sedition Act was never tested in this Court, the attack upon its validity has carried the day in the court of history. Fines levied in its prosecution were repaid by Act of Congress on the ground that it was unconstitutional . . . . Jefferson, as President, pardoned those who had been convicted and sentenced under the Act and remitted their fines, stating: "I discharged every person under punishment or prosecution under the sedition law, because I considered, and now consider, that law to be a nullity, as absolute and as palpable as if Congress had ordered us to fall down and worship a golden image." Letter to Mrs. Adams, July 22, 1804, 4 Jefferson's Works (Washington ed.), pp. 555, 556 . . . .

What a State may not constitutionally bring about by means of a criminal statute is likewise beyond the reach of its civil law of libel. The fear of damage awards under a rule such as that invoked by the Alabama courts here may be markedly more inhibiting than the fear of prosecution under a criminal statute . . . . The judgment awarded in this case — without the need for any proof of actual pecuniary loss — was one thousand times greater than the maximum fine provided by the Alabama criminal statute, and one hundred times greater than that provided by the Sedition Act . . . . Whether or not a newspaper can survive a succession of such judgments, the pall of fear and timidity imposed upon those who would give voice to public criticism is an atmosphere in which the First Amendment freedoms cannot survive. . . .

The state rule of law is not saved by its allowance of the defense of truth. . . . Under such a rule, would-be critics of official conduct may be deterred from voicing their criticism, even though it is believed to be true and even though it is in fact true, because of doubt whether it can be proved in court or fear of the expense of having to do so. They tend to make only statements which "steer far wider of the unlawful zone. . . ."

The constitutional guarantees require, we think, a federal rule that prohibits a public official from recovering damages for a defamatory falsehood relating to his official conduct unless he proves that the statement was made with "actual malice" — that is, with knowledge that it was false or with reckless disregard of whether it was false or not. . . .

Such a privilege for criticism of official conduct is appropriately analogous to the protection accorded a public official when *he* is sued for libel by a private citizen. In *Barr v. Matteo, supra*, 360 U.S., at 571. Analagous considerations support the privilege for the citizen-critic of government. It is as much his duty to criticize as it is the official's duty to administer . . . . As Madison said, "the censorial power is in the people over the Government, and not in the Government over the people." It would give public servants an unjustified preference over the public they serve, if critics of official conduct did not have a fair equivalent of the immunity granted to the officials themselves.

We conclude that such a privilege is required by the First and Fourteenth Amendments.

III

We hold today that the Constitution delimits a State's power to award damages for libel in actions brought by public officials against critics of their official conduct. Since this is such an action, the rule requiring proof of actual malice is applicable. While Alabama law apparently requires proof of actual malice for an award of punitive damages, where general damages are concerned malice is "presumed." Such a presumption is inconsistent with the federal rule. . . . Since the trial judge did not instruct the jury to differentiate between general and punitive damages, it may be that the verdict was wholly an award of one or the other. But it is impossible to know, in view of the general verdict returned. Because of this uncertainty, the judgment must be reversed and the case remanded. . . .

Since respondent may seek a new trial, we deem that considerations of effective judicial administration require us to review the evidence in the present record to determine whether it could constitutionally support a judgment for respondent. This Court's duty is not limited to the elaboration of constitutional principles; we must also in proper cases review the evidence to make certain that those principles have been constitutionally applied. This is such a case . . . . We must "make an independent examination of the whole record," *Edwards v. South Carolina,* 372 U.S. 229, 235, so as to assure ourselves that the judgment does not constitute a forbidden intrusion on the field of free expression.

Applying these standards, we consider that the proof presented to show actual malice lacks the convincing clarity which the constitutional standard demands, and hence that it would not constitutionally sustain the judgment for respondent under the proper rule of law. The case of the individual petitioners requires little discussion. Even assuming that they could constitutionally be found to have authorized the use of their names on the advertisement, there was no evidence whatever that they were aware of any erroneous statements or were in any way reckless in that regard. The judgment against them is thus without constitutional support.

As to the Times, we similarly conclude that the facts do not support a finding of actual malice. The statement by the Times' Secretary that, apart from the padlocking allegation, he thought the advertisement was "substantially correct," affords no constitutional warrant for the Alabama Supreme Court's conclusion that it was a "cavalier ignoring of the falsity of the advertisement [from which] the jury could not have but been impressed with the bad faith of the Times, and its maliciousness inferable therefrom." The statement does not indicate malice at the time of the publication; even if the advertisement was not "substantially correct" — although respondent's own proofs tend to show that it was — that opinion was at least a reasonable one, and there was no evidence to impeach the witness' good faith in holding it . . . .

Finally, there is evidence that the Times published the

advertisement without checking its accuracy against the news stories in the Times' own files. The mere presence of the stories in the files does not, of course, establish that the Times "knew" the advertisement to be false, since the state of mind required for actual malice would have to be brought home to the persons in the Times' organization having responsibility for the publication of the advertisement. With respect to the failure of those persons to make the check, the record shows that they relied upon their knowledge of the good reputation of many of those whose names were listed as sponsors of the advertisement, and upon the letter from A. Philip Randolph, known to them as a responsible individual, certifying that the use of the names was authorized. . . . We think the evidence against the Times supports at most a finding of negligence in failing to discover the misstatements, and is constitutionally insufficient to show the recklessness that is required for a finding of actual malice. . . .

Reversed and remanded.

Appendix N

(Time, Inc. v. Hill, 1966)

SUPREME COURT OF THE UNITED STATES

No. 562 — October Term, 1965

Time, Inc., Appellant

v.

James J. Hill.

On Appeal to the Court of Appeals
of the State of New York.

[June, 1966]

MR. JUSTICE FORTAS delivered the opinion of the Court.*

This case presents for decision appellant's challenge to the constitutionality of the New York "right of privacy" statute (Civil Rights Law §§ 50-51). Since this case involves a claimed conflict between the statute and the fundamental guarantees of the First Amendment, a clear understanding of the facts is essential.

I

On September 9, 1952, three convicts escaped from the federal prison at Lewisburg. They stole an automobile, shotguns and ammunition, and money. Police and federal agents were in hot pursuit of the dangerous fugitives. On September 11, they entered the home of James J. Hill, in the quiet, prosperous Whitemarsh suburb of Philadelphia. They remained there for 19 hours, resting and eating. Hill, his wife, their daughters aged 11, 15 and 17, and twin sons aged 4, were, in effect, captives. They were treated courteously by the fugitives, but were warned not to call the police until after the men had left. Except for the general restraint of the family, the convicts were "gentlemanly" towards the family.

After the bandits departed, Hill advised the police of the incident. The family lived in fear of the fugitives and in the discomfort and embarrassment of public attention. Not the least of their discomfort was caused by inquiry as to whether the teen-age daugh-

---

*Footnotes omitted

ters and Mrs. Hill "had been violated.". . .

In April and May 1953, Joseph Hayes wrote a novel entitled "Desperate Hours." He thereafter adapted it as a play and a motion picture. "The Desperate Hours" was a dramatic narration of a fugitive-hostage incident. In 1946 he had written and published a short story involving the hostage theme. In 1947 he began collecting newspaper accounts of such incidents. In 1952 and 1953 Hayes read newspaper reports of fugitive-hostage incidents, similar to the Hill occurrence, in California, New York, and Detroit. He was aware of the Hill incident. He steadfastly denied, however, that the Hill incident inspired his novel. . . .

In the autumn of 1954 Hayes' play went into production. Pre-Broadway tryouts were scheduled in New Haven and Philadelphia. The director of the play suggested to Life that the production be covered by it. Life's Entertainment Editor, Prideaux, was interested, particularly because of a novel stage setting which was to be used. Shortly thereafter a free-lance photographer sometimes employed by Life told Prideaux that he was a neighbor of Hayes and that the play had a "substantial connection" with a true-life incident in Philadelphia. . . .

Prideaux and other members of Life's staff then began to create the picture story about the play which gave rise to the lawsuit. Prideaux located the former Hill home outside of Philadelphia. He arranged for actors and the cast of the play to stage scenes in the house. These were photographed . . . .

Prideaux's first draft reflected recognition that the play was not an account of the Hill family's experience . . . . But a senior editor thought the draft of the article was not "newsy enough." So he rewrote it in critical respects. Caution and restraint were discarded. In his hands, the play became a reenactment of the "desperate ordeal" of the "James Hill family." . . . The article, as published in Life, accompanied photographs of scenes from the play taken at the Hills' former home. Two of the photographs were headlined "Brutish Convict" and "Daring Daughter." The "Brutish Convict" is shown violently shaking the young son. A picture of a revolver in the hand of another convict is in the foreground. The "Daring Daughter" is shown biting the hand of a convict to make him drop his gun. The total effect is of violence in which the son and daughter were involved . . . .

The effect on the Hill family was serious . . . . Mr. Hill felt that the publication had "wiped out in just one minute" everything we had done, that "we were going to be subjected from that time on to continued, added insinuations, insults and so on." He testified that "we certainly couldn't understand how Life Magazine could publish an article such as this without . . . at least picking up a telephone to find out whether this was the truth or how we felt about it. It was just like we didn't exist, like we were dirt, like they didn't care." Mrs. Hill became seriously ill. The record contains the testimony of psychiatrists to the effect that the Life article was "the direct precipitating cause of her condition."

Mr. Hill resisted his impulse to resort to the direct remedy of a simpler age — physical violence upon those whom he considered had perpetrated an outrage on his family. He consulted an attorney and this lawsuit resulted. It was brought under the New York right-of-privacy statute, §§ 50-51, of the New York Civil Rights Law. Ultimately, a judgment in favor of Mr. Hill for $30,000 as compensatory damages was entered against appellant in the New York Supreme Court. Punitive or exemplary damages were not included. The appellate division (18 App. Div. 2d 485, 240 N.Y.S. 2d 286) and Court of Appeals affirmed (15 N.Y. 2d 986, 207 N.E. 2d 604). On appeal, we noted probable jurisdiction. 382 U.S. 936.

II

The facts of this case are unavoidably distressing. Needless, heedless, wanton and deliberate injury of the sort inflicted by Life's picture story is not an essential instrument of responsible journalism. Magazine writers and editors are not, by reason of their high office, relieved of the common obligation to avoid deliberately inflicting wanton and unnecessary injury. The prerogatives of the press — essential to our liberty — do not preclude reasonable care and avoidance of causal infliction of injury to others totally unexplainable by any purpose or circumstances related to its function of reporting or discussing the news or publishing matters of interest to its readers. They do not confer a license for pointless assault.

But this does not resolve the problem. We are dealing with a problem of law, and not merely a question of civilized standards. Our problem is whether the picture story here involved, regardless of its offensiveness, is entitled to immunity because of the First Amendment. This Nation and this Court are committed to the immunity which the Amendment extends to the press. We are committed to its broad and generous application. This Nation is prepared to pay a heavy price for the immunity of the press in terms of national discomfort and danger and in the tolerance of a measure of individual assault. See *New York Times Co. v. Sullivan*, 376 U.S. 254.

The New York right-of-privacy statute was enacted in 1903, following a decision of the New York Court of Appeals which held that New York's common law did not vindicate the right of privacy. The case involved use of a private person's portrait, without her consent, to advertise a commercial product. *Roberson v. Rochester Folding Box Co.*, 171 N.Y. 538, 64 N. E. 422 (1902). The statute, designed to overrule *Roberson*, forbids use "of the name or likeness of any living person without that person's consent for advertising purposes, or for the purposes of trade" (§ 50). Such use is a misdemeanor, and the aggrieved person may obtain injunctive relief and may also recover compensatory and exemplary damages (§§ 50-51).

The substance of the New York statute is narrow and particularized. It is not subject to attack on the ground that the public and private tort which it defines is so broad as to constitute a chilling threat to freedom.... The New York statute relates to only a segment of the basic right — the right of privacy.... A distinct right of privacy is now recognized, either as a "common-law" right or by statute, in at least 35 States. Its exact scope varies in the respective jurisdictions.

There is, however, no doubt that a fundamental right of privacy exists, and that it is of constitutional stature. It is not just the right to a remedy against false accusations provided, within limits, by the law of defamation; it is not only the right to be secure in one's person, house, papers and effects, except as permitted by law; it embraces the right to be free from coercion to incriminate oneself, however subtle; it is different from, but akin to the right to select and freely practice one's religion and the right to freedom of speech; it is more than the specific right to be secure against the Peeping Tom or the intrusion of electronic espionage devices and wiretapping. All of these are aspects of the right to privacy; but the right of privacy reaches beyond any of its specifics. It is, simply stated, the right to be let alone; to live one's life as one chooses, free from assault, intrusion or invasion except as they can be justified by the clear needs of community living under a government of law. As Brandeis said in his famous dissent in *Olmstead v. United States*, 277 U.S. 438, 478, the right of privacy is "the most comprehensive of rights and the right most valued by civilized men."

This Court has repeatedly recognized this principle....

In *Griswold v. Connecticut*, 381 U.S. 479, decided at the last Term of Court, the Court held unconstitutional a state law under which petitioners were prosecuted for giving married persons information and medical advice on the use of contraceptives. The holding was squarely based upon the right of privacy which the Court derived by implication from the specific guarantees of the Bill of Rights. Citing a number of prior cases, the Court (per Douglas, J.) held that "These cases bear witness that the right of privacy which presses for recognition here is a legitimate one." 381 U.S., at 485. As stated in the concurring opinion of Mr. Justice Goldberg, with whom THE CHIEF JUSTICE and MR. JUSTICE BRENNAN joined: "the right of privacy is a fundamental personal right, emanating 'from the totality of the constitutional scheme under which we live.' " 381 U.S. at 494.

If, then, privacy is a basic right, whether one considers it derived from the First, Fourth, Fifth or Ninth Amendments, or otherwise, it follows that the States may, by appropriate legislation and within proper bounds, enact laws to vindicate that right. . . . Difficulty presents itself because the application of such state legislation may impinge upon conflicting rights of those accused of invading the privacy of others. But this is not automatically a fatal objection. In the present case, the claimed conflict is with the First Amendment. . . .

We cannot say that the First Amendment prohibits a State from enacting a statue so confined. We cannot say that the First Amendment forbids a State from enacting a statute which in effect merely prohibits the deliberate appropriation of a person's identity — not as an incident of news or comment, but for the purposes of intensifying the appeal of a work of fiction (whether represented as fiction or not) — which merely requires that a person's consent be obtained before his name or portrait may be deliberately used so as to identify him with a knowingly false and fictionalized narrative.... Freedom of the press does not require that the State withhold its aid from persons threatened with misappropriation of their identity for purposes which have no relation to public information and which are nothing more than the knowingly false attribution of events to a named person for the purpose of accentuating the dramatic or entertainment value of a publication.

We do not believe that such a statute, so construed and applied, can or will inhibit the freedom of the press. It does not penalize mere error. It places no restraint upon comment and discussion. It is not an overhanging danger. It cannot ensnare the unwary or even the negligent. It reaches only those who deliberately circulate an account which is pervasively fictionalized and is falsely and deliberately attributed to a living person . . . .

Appellant argues that the article was a report on a newsworthy item — the exhibition of the play. So it was, and if the account published in Life had been essentially a report concerning the play, we do not understand that the New York courts would regard it as within the scope of the statute, even if plaintiff's name had been used . . . . But the jury was amply justified in evaluating the account not as a news report of the play, but as essentially a fictionalized version of the Hill incident, deliberately distorted beyond semblance of reality by its explicit, insistent and knowingly false identification with the play. . . .

Reports of news or newsworthy events and comments upon public figures are not deprived of immunity merely because of the purpose of the publication. They cannot be subjected to the sanctions of the law if a true account is given . . . . As we understand New York law, there must be deliberate, intentional, pervasive fictionalization. . . .

On this basis, we affirm the decision below. Our conclusion follows from *New York Times v. Sullivan*, 376 U.S. 254. *New York Times* did not provide blanket immunity to publications relating to "public figures." Consistently with this Court's solicitude for broadly protecting the freedom of the press and public debate, it held that a public official could not maintain an action for an allegedly libelous criticism unless he showed that the statements were made with " 'actual malice,' that is, with knowledge it was false or with reckless disregard of whether it was false or not." 376 U.S., at 272 . . . . The requirements for liability under the New York right-of-privacy statute as applied in this case are well within this test.

The deliberate, callous invasion of the Hills' right to be let alone — this appropriation of a family's right not to be molested or to have its name exploited and its quiet existence invaded — cannot be defended on the ground that it is within the purview of a constitutional guarantee designed to protect the free exchange of ideas and opinions. This is exploitation, undertaken to titillate and excite, for commercial purposes. It was not a retelling of a newsworthy incident or of an event relating to a public figure. It was not such an account. It was not so designed. It was fiction: an invention, distorted and put to the uses of the promotion of Life magazine and of a play. Many difficult problems may arise under the right-to-privacy statute, but we conclude that the present case, on its facts and on the New York law as construed by the courts of that State, does not permit the appellant to claim immunity from liability because of the First Amendment.

Accordingly, the judgment is *Affirmed*.

Index